Praise for Paul Edward and *Moving Forward*

"I assume that people interested in life-coaching books have tried Dr. Phil and Tony Robbins. So why are they still looking? My guess is that the approach of modifying behavior by being conscious of the results of our actions only goes so far. Paul Edward provides a psychological model that is deeper ... So read this book, not only because the material is well presented and makes you think, but also because it will enrich important aspects of your life, and, yes, allow you to 'move forward.'"
— *J. Lehman, Bookreview.com*

"This is the book for you if you want an objective approach to improving your life. As someone that has gone through numerous corporate and privately sponsored events on self-improvement, I can safely say "ditch the rest" and read this book first."
—*M. Cope, Corporate Executive*

"I would recommend this book to anyone who wants to move from simply dreaming about the life he or she wants to actually creating it. If you want to move from dreaming about your ideal life to actually living it, this book has the power to change your life."
—*S. Murray, National Certified Counselor*

"Move over Dr. Phil and Tony Robbins, Coach Paul has come to town! This book goes beyond self-help and gives the reader all the tools one needs to make real progress in life. A must read!"
—*S. Haskin, author of Safety First: A Stronger, Safer, You*

To Lynette:

Thank you for your
great service!

Best-

Pal

MOVING FORWARD

Thank you for your great service!

Best-

[signature]

MOVING FORWARD

**Turning Good Intentions Into Great Results
by Discovering Yourself, Your Place, & Your Path**

Paul Edward

Life-Changing Coaching®
PO Box 1899
Claremont, CA 91711
www.lifechangingcoaching.com
Phone: 1-909-457-8280

First published by Life-Changing Coaching 1/1/09

ISBN: 978-0-9814-9392-3 (sc)
ISBN: 978-0-9814-9393-0 (e)

Printed in the United States of America
Claremont, California

This book is printed on acid-free paper.

Cover design by Ruth Bury.
Cover photo by Sonja Stump.

this book is dedicated to all those who reached out to me over the course of my lifetime to help me MOVE FORWARD and become the man that i am today: God, mom, dad, aunts charlie and thelma, grandmothers, dr frietag, bishop blake, baxter duke, beverly wardlaw, ron ford, bud meador, joe and pam holt, john and kay reynolds, ralph and wilma porter, bob white, larry alb, jim stodola, bob and karen gaudi, mike vorst, guy williams, bob diemer, frank russell, and linda berens— thank you very much...without all of your involvement in my life, there is the great possibility that i would have become just another south-central los angeles statistic.

Contents

Introduction i

Part I—Deciphering Your Life Code xv
  1 Knowing Yourself 1
  2 Understanding the Masks We Wear 21
  3 How Do You Reenergize? 41
  4 What Kind of Information Do You Need? 69
  5 How Do You Evaluate Information? 97
  6 What Is Your Decision Drive? 119
  7 How Do You Communicate? 141
  8 Your Place in This World 165

Part II—Executing Your Life Plan 207
  9 Building a Vision 209
  10 Running to Win 245
  11 Surrounding Yourself With Support 273
  12 Getting Connected to the Community 303
  13 Making a Positive Impression 329
  14 Pursuing Your Passion 351
  15 Honoring Your Beginnings 379
  16 Giving Back 401

Conclusion 411

Appendix A Groups and Organizations 419
Appendix B Activities and Hobbies 421
Appendix C Volunteer Activities 423
Glossary 425
Index 431

Acknowledgements

I imagine that writing a book is as close as a man will ever come to having a baby. Therefore, I would like to thank these "literary midwives" for helping me bring my firstborn into the world: Stuart, for giving me the motivation; my family, for giving me the time and putting up with my periods of "focused effort;" Michael, for giving me honest and helpful feedback; and Suzanne, for helping me find my voice. I also want to thank God, for giving me all the gifts and talents that I possess.

Disclaimers

Although I have provided examples of people solving their problems in this book, I have modified the names of clients and their specific situation details to preserve confidentiality.

All copyrighted material that appears in this book, appears with the permission of the copyright owners.

Introduction

This book can change your life. Whether you find yourself struggling to achieve goals you've set or wrestling with how to create a fulfilling and meaningful life, this book will help you discover who you are and where you belong in this world.

Although most of us appear to be in motion—working on degrees, commuting to jobs, running errands, driving kids to school, and so on—many of us are actually stuck. We identify deeply with the words from Michael W. Smith's song, "Place in this World."

The wind is moving
But I am standing still
A life of pages
Waiting to be filled
A heart that's hopeful
A head that's full of dreams
But this becoming
Is harder than it seems
Feels like I'm
Looking for a reason
Roaming through the night to find
My place in this world.

As in Smith's song, many of us see movement all around us, but we are stuck in one place. Our bodies are probably moving, but it still feels like we're "standing still." Why? Because most of us are on the wrong paths in life. Instead of taking the roads that lead toward fulfillment of our life visions, most of us are on plain old hamster wheels—going around and around in circles, but never getting anywhere.

Was there a time when you had big dreams for your life, but today you find yourself wondering why none of them have come true? Or maybe you're just starting your journey, and you have all these ideas on how you want your life to be, but you don't know how to get there from here. Perhaps you slog to work every morning and you're tired of going through the motions at a job that holds no personal meaning.

Or maybe your career is on track, even soaring, but your personal life is a train wreck—you haven't met the life partner whom you've been hoping for, your marriage is a shambles, you don't have enough time for your children or friends or hobbies, or you have time to pursue your interests, but you just aren't motivated to do anything.

All of these situations are signs of being *stuck*—feeling like you're trapped and unable to move forward in life. Maybe it's the same old pit you've always been stuck in—the really deep one, filled with sticky mud—that you can never seem to climb out of. Maybe it's that all too familiar rut that you tend to drift back into at certain points in your life. Or maybe you just snagged your foot on a root while walking along on life's journey. The point is, *something*—whether new or familiar—is holding you back from achieving the kind of life you should *and could* be living.

If you are stuck in your life, you're not alone. All of us get that way sometimes, and some of us feel that way all the time. But you don't have to stay stuck. As a professional life coach, I help my clients get unstuck and move forward in their lives. No matter how frustrated or disillusioned or disbelieving you might be feeling right now, I promise you that it *is* possible for you to build a life in which you feel useful, fulfilled, content—a life where you are moving forward. I have witnessed this progression in my clients, and I know that with the right tools—the tools I offer you in this book—you can experience this same positive transformation in your life as well.

Strategies for Moving Forward

In this book, I am going to share with you the process that I use to help my influential clients (celebrities, dignitaries, and executives) solve their toughest problems, get unstuck, and move forward in their lives. No matter what challenge you are struggling with right now, this process will help you move past that difficulty and create a meaningful and fulfilling life that you can be proud of.

After working as a U.S. Marine officer, an organizational leader, a university professor, and a life coach, and after years

ii

of studying the teachings of the wisest people in the world, I have discovered that there are five requirements for moving forward in life:

1. You need to know yourself well.
2. You need to recognize when to live in-sync with who you are (which is most of the time).
3. You need to incorporate other people into your life—both giving to and receiving from others.
4. You need to have a life plan.
5. You need to recognize when to stretch beyond your natural self so you can accomplish your goals (which is some of the time).

If you can master these five *foundations*, then you will know who you are and where you belong in this world. You will have a picture of how you'd like your life to look, you will know how to design your life to accomplish that vision, and you will have people around you to help you achieve your goals. In short, you will be in a better position to lead the life of your dreams. This book will help you master the five principles for moving your life forward.

What This Book Is About

The goal of this book is to help you move forward when you get stuck in life by giving you the tools you need to live the life that you were meant to live—a life that achieves all of your goals; a life that is meaningful, fulfilling, and reflective of you as a person.

Moving forward means different things for different people. For some, it means advancing in their jobs. For others it means finding a partner to spend their lives with. Still others hope to let go of pains associated with their childhoods so they can find joy in their adult lives; while others who have been struggling with their identities seek ways to discover their true selves. You can use this book to learn how to move forward in any or all of these domains, plus several more, depending on your particular goals. The strategies I present focus on making you a more knowledgeable and much wiser person, which will give you the foundation needed to move forward in whatever area of your life needs attention.

One of the biggest goals I have for this book is to present you with straightforward strategies—small steps, really—that you can take at your own pace. In some ways, our lives are like large ocean freighters that take time to alter course. We have bad habits, old patterns of thinking, fears that hold us back, and people in our lives who don't support us. We can't change all of these in a single day, month, or even year. But if we break down these negative elements—one by one, over time—and replace them with healthy practices, constructive beliefs, and supportive people, we will eventually, bit by bit, be able to change our direction and head toward the realization of our dreams.

Learning About Yourself and Others

This book is divided into two parts. The first part, *Deciphering Your Life Code*, contains tools for discovering who you are. In this section, you are going to learn about the elements of your whole person—what makes you tick. You are going to learn about the parts of you that you were born with (your personality) and the parts of you that you've developed over time (your identity), and how these two things interact with each other and the world through which you move.

You are also going to learn about the three major areas of your life that affect your ability to achieve your goals: how you maintain your personal energy supply, how you make decisions, and how you communicate. You are going to learn to look at these three areas from the perspective of what I call your *five core personality preferences*. Preferences are your natural inclinations for acting and being in the world.

Finally, *Deciphering Your Life Code* also provides you with the information you need to understand the kind of relationships you have with others (mutual, receiving, and giving), since, as you will discover, others are essential to your ability to achieve your goals.

Pursuing Your Life Vision

The second part of this book, entitled *Executing Your Life Plan*, focuses on the actions that you will need to take to begin living the life you were meant to live. In this part, we will sketch out exactly what your unique life vision looks like, so you are clear on where you belong in this world and the best way to achieve your goals. I will also encourage you to get proactive about bringing supportive people into your life. These invaluable individuals are the ones who will ultimately help you succeed.

We'll also spend some time assessing whether now is the right time in your life for you to start making changes. There's nothing magical about achieving your life vision; it mostly revolves around hard work. The only way you're going to achieve your goals is if you are ready to commit to putting forth some effort.

Executing Your Life Plan will also give you some coaching on how to make a positive impression (which isn't always as obvious as it seems), and I will challenge you to start pursuing an avocation that you feel passionate about—within your paid job or outside of it. You will also learn how to deal with the people in your past who may be on a different course from you now and, finally, how to find or increase your sense of significance in the world by becoming an active member of a community.

When you have a clear understanding of who you are, when you are conscious of what contribution you are meant to make, when you have a plan for achieving your life vision, and when you are surrounded by supportive people, you will become more aware of the opportunities around you that can move you closer to realizing your dreams. As you read, process, and engage in the lessons of this book, you will become more and more prepared to respond to these life opportunities in positive ways.

Although the chapters in this book progress in a logical fashion, you don't have to read every chapter in the book to benefit from it and you don't have to read the chapters in the order that I present them to you. Every chapter has something valuable in it, but if you are dealing with a particular issue right now, feel free to turn to a specific chapter that jumps out at you. For example, if you are experiencing challenges with toxic friends and family, you may want to read chapters 8, 11, and 15. If you are longing to feel passionate about what you do for a living, consider reading chapter 14. And if you are feeling disconnected from your community, you may want to look at chapters 8, 12, and 16.

When you have time, you can read the book from start to finish since each chapter works together to help you develop a full toolset for getting unstuck and moving forward. And you may find yourself revisiting certain chapters when you reach a new stage in your life or when you find yourself bogged down. The road of life winds its way through mountains, hills, and valleys, and sometimes we find ourselves on the downhill slope. I hope that this book can be a trusted companion to you in such times—lowering you a rope or extending you a hand to help you reach your destination.

Getting the Most out of This Book

This book is designed to be a hands-on book. Although you can get a lot from just reading and reflecting on what you read in this book, you will be able to benefit even more if you are willing to roll up your sleeves and complete the hands-on exercises offered in most of the chapters. Some of the exercises will be simple ones that you can complete rather quickly, while others will require more time and thought. All of the exercises provide you with a method for processing the material I present in each chapter and for applying it to your unique life situation. The exercises are set up to be completed in a written fashion, but if you prefer to talk things through when completing the exercises, rather than writing things out, see if you can find a willing friend to do the exercises alongside of you so you can discuss them together. If you are working with a life coach or therapist, you can complete the exercises directly with your helping professional.

I recommend that you buy a journal, spiral notebook, or

loose-leaf binder to provide you with ample space to complete the exercises in this book and so that you will have a place to keep all of the exercises organized. Another option is to buy the *Coaching Experience Workbook*, which contains all of the exercises in this book in a workbook format.

When reading through this book, you will also want to keep your scheduling system handy—paper calendar, Day-Timer, Microsoft Outlook calendar, PDA, etc.—since some of the book's exercises will involve scheduling time to do certain activities. If you don't already have a scheduling system in place, I recommend that you pick one that you will use while reading this book. If you choose to use the *Coaching Experience Workbook*, it has a set of blank calendar pages to help you schedule the activities you'll be doing to move forward.

For those of you who like scheduling things, using a calendar will probably be an enjoyable process. For those of you who resist scheduling, you may feel reluctant to start using a calendar. I recommend that you acknowledge this reluctance, but try to move beyond your comfort zone and commit to using a calendar, or at least a brief to-do list, when completing the exercises in this book. When it comes to doing the kind of new activities that I recommend in this book, it can be very helpful, and sometimes essential, to make a schedule for completing activities.

Finally, throughout the course of this book, I will mention times that you may want to process certain material or work through particular issues by talking with a life coach or other helping professional. While engaging a helping professional is not a requirement for benefiting from this book, it is something you may want to consider, especially if you find that you are not able to work through a challenge simply by reading a chapter, completing the exercises in it, and reaching out to your social network for support. Remember, as the five requirements for moving forward in your life indicate, *you need to incorporate other people into your life if you want to move forward*. Sometimes, this means working with a paid professional, whether that be a a life coach, career counselor, a personal trainer, a financial planner, or a psychotherapist.

I use the term "helping professional" to refer to those professionals trained to help you achieve your life goals, address life challenges, or deal with mental health issues. Such professionals can include life coaches, counselors, social workers, psychologist, and psychiatrists. The kind of professional best suited to work with you will depend on your life situation and your needs. If you are a high-functioning individual who wants to make changes in your life and achieve particular goals, a life coach will probably be best suited to help you. By high-functioning, I mean that you are able to go to work every day, meet most of your life responsibilities, and interact with others in a conventional social manner. You may have life stresses, areas for self-improvement, and goals left to reach, but you are able to meet your adult responsibilities and may even appear quite successful to other people.

On the other hand, a counselor, social worker, or psychologist who specializes in psychotherapy or mental health might be better suited to support you if you struggle to function at a high level in your daily life, for example, if you are unable to meet some or many of your life responsibilities—like showing up to work on time and completing work tasks, adequately caring for your family, or maintaining a healthy household (clean, well-fed, financially stable). Such issues could signal that you will currently gain the most benefit from working with a psychotherapist. It's possible that emotional challenges from your past (for example, physical or sexual abuse, unsupportive parenting, severe teasing or bullying at school) or mental health issues that have a basis in your biology (for example, panic attacks, chronic depression, addiction, or bipolar disorder) are what's causing you to have trouble meeting your life responsibilities and functioning at a high level. Psychotherapists who are licensed and trained (and who you feel comfortable talking to after a first meeting) are in a wonderful position to help you work through such issues. Psychiatrists who engage in talk therapy can also function in this same role; in addition, and more commonly, psychiatrists are available to help you alleviate, reduce, and manage mental health issues through the use of certain kinds of medicines, with the goal of helping you to function at your best. Throughout the book, I refer to mental health professionals who engage in talk therapy as *therapists*.

> *Note*: Sometimes, people who function at high levels still have mental health issues that can be addressed well by working with therapists and/or psychiatrists. These people are able to meet most of their life responsibilities and project successful images to those around them but still contend with deeper issues that can be processed best in counseling rather than coaching settings. Signs of issues best processed in psychotherapy or with a psychiatrist can include the following in a continual or chronic form: sleeplessness, muscle tension, edginess or irritability, sadness, lack of motivation, hopelessness, feelings of worthlessness or guilt, difficulty concentrating, social withdrawal, and/or trouble making decisions.

If in doubt about what kind of a professional to engage, start with whichever kind of professional seems most appropriate for you, see how the relationship feels, and move on if necessary. You can also ask the professional during your initial phone call or at your first meeting to help you determine whether his or her support services correspond well with your current needs and life situation.

Why I Wrote This Book

I have written this book for three main reasons: because I care about helping people, because these strategies work, and because there are more people who could benefit from my coaching than I have time to personally coach.

I Really Care

I once heard a saying at an investment seminar, which has stuck with me ever since: "If you keep on doing what you've always done, you'll always get what you always got!" How true this is. In other words, the biggest reason that we remain stuck is because we keep trying to solve our same problems with the same tools that haven't worked in the past. We keep doing what we've always done, and guess what? We keep getting what we've always gotten.

What we need is for *someone to help us* by giving us *new* tools and showing us how to use them effectively. By picking up this book, you have brought a professional life coach (me!) into your world who can provide you with just these tools. And while providing you with these tools, I will be encouraging you to bring even more people into your life who can continue to help you move forward.

The old adage that "Two heads are better than one" really applies when we get stuck. Often, we are only able to solve problems and make breakthroughs when we work with other people. The truth is that despite what you may have heard at the latest success seminar or read in the most recent self-help book, we are not always capable of doing what we need to do *by ourselves. Most times we need help.* This is why self-help systems don't work consistently for everybody. This is why your shelves and CD cases are full of motivational books and recordings that have only served to highlight your *inability* to do what you know you need to do to be more "successful" in your life: because they do not integrate the idea of community into their prescriptions for solving life's problems. This book does.

Moving Forward is not a self-help book; *it is an others-help book.* I became a coach because I wanted to be one of those others that help people. I remain a coach because there is nothing more satisfying in life than helping other people find what they have been searching for.

These Strategies Really Work

I wrote *Moving Forward* for all of those people out there who have tried everything else, failed, and are on the verge of giving up on their hopes and dreams. This book is about rekindling your hope and helping you dream big again.

These strategies are based on the reality of our imperfect human condition. I don't expect you to get out of a slump all on your own—you can't, so there's no need to waste any more of your time (or money) on that approach. I also know there will be times when you will fall back into old habits and when you will allow fear to stop you dead in your tracks— that's normal, and I will give you some tools to help you get back onto the right path and overcome your fears.

I have seen the moving forward strategies transform the lives of my clients and students. I have watched my clients and students use these tools, get unstuck, and start moving forward. I have witnessed people finally realize the dreams that they had deferred for so long. Now it's your opportunity to do the same.

There's Only One of Me

This book was actually born out of frustration. It never fails that after I present these strategies at a conference or teach these strategies in a seminar, several people come up to me and ask if they could hire me to become their coach. And because I care about helping people, I want to say yes. But because my practice has been so successful, most times, I don't have the capacity to start working with new clients. So, I usually have to tell them that I am sorry but I can't be their coach, and I try my best to help them find another great coach to work with.

After experiencing this frustration for the past few years, my coach (yes, I have a coach too) recommended that I write a book that I could give to people. Although a book can never fully replace a live coach, it can give people a starting place to begin their journeys. My hope is that this book will be just such a starting place for you.

My Background

Back in 1986, long before the life-coaching profession got its name and before I even had a name for what I was doing, I was supporting and sometimes even coaching my friends, family, colleagues, and employees in discovering how to lead meaningful and fulfilling lives. I'm no Doctor Phil or Tony Robbins, but I do care about helping others solve their problems and realize their dreams, and I have spent a lot of my life learning how people, myself included, can best do that.

This personal interest in helping others—along with my experiences as a U.S. Marine officer, corporate executive, university professor, and professional life coach—has given me a living "lab" to study human nature and identify the toolset that we all need to successfully solve our problems and achieve our goals.

For example, one of the key things I learned as a Marine was the critical nature of teamwork when attempting to accomplish any mission. No matter how talented an individual is, without the support of the team, he or she is likely to fail. (The Marine Corps has a sterling battle history, not because it hires the smartest people in the world, but because it intentionally creates a community of men and women who are committed to each other.)

This is one of the reasons I make such a big point in this book of helping you reach out to a community that you choose—asking for support, spending time with like-minded people, and making it a priority to get along with those who are different from you: because *others are essential to your success.*

Living a meaningful and fulfilling life is in many ways about being able to effectively manage the different aspects of it. You can have all the passion in the world and a fantastic vision for what you want your life to be, but if you lack the skills for applying that passion and implementing that vision, you won't be able to achieve your goals. Instead, you'll remain stuck on the hamster wheel watching life pass by.

Despite the importance of successfully managing our lives, many of us are never taught the skills we need to effectively do so. In primary and secondary schools, we learn reading, writing, and arithmetic. For those of us who go through college, we "learn how to learn." But no one ever teaches us, in a formal venue, how to *manage* our lives successfully. We have to be blessed with parents or mentors who teach us these skills, or we just have to figure it all out on our own. The tools offered in this book will help you become highly skilled at successfully managing your life.

Let's Move Forward Together

So, congratulations! By picking up this book, you've just brought another person into your life to help you solve your present challenges and achieve your goals. And, as I mentioned earlier, I will encourage you to bring even more people into your life to help you become all that you were meant to be. Take a mental bow and give yourself a pat on the back for not giving up on your dreams and for making it to this point in your life. Your desire to continue on the journey of life is both admirable and honorable. And I am here to help you reach your destination.

Next, I want to ask you to put away your fear of failure and disappointment. It will only slow you down, so it's time to let it go. You may be thinking about how you've tried to move forward in the past but have been unsuccessful. Let me reassure you that this time *is* different. Trust me; this journey is going to take you to much better places than you have been before, *because you won't be making this journey by yourself.* You'll be making this journey with others who support you.

So get a little excited! Expect to make some progress! And get ready to move forward!

Part I—Deciphering Your Life Code

1

Knowing Yourself

This book is about helping you gain the tools you need to move forward in life and to achieve your goals and dreams, whatever they may be. Since this is the first chapter (and a foundational one), we're going to start with one of the most fundamental and powerful tools you can have in your kit—knowing yourself well.

Personality Versus Identity

Knowing yourself well—not just the public self that you portray to everyone else, but the inner, private you, what I call your *personality*—is powerful because it allows you to consciously design a life that's in-sync with who you really are—not who others think you *should* be. *And a life that's in-sync with your personality is one that empowers you to pursue and accomplish your goals and dreams as well as brings you satisfaction and fulfillment.*

When your lifestyle is aligned with your personality, things start to flow and move forward for you. Opportunities arise, and you feel comfortable taking them. Inspiration comes, and you have the motivation and courage to follow it. You become skilled at recognizing what you want in life and you begin to achieve it.

> A life that's in-sync with your personality is one that empowers you to pursue and accomplish your goals and dreams, as well as one that brings you meaning and fulfillment.

When the opposite is the case—when you're feeling stuck—it's typically because something is holding you back. It could be that those close to you aren't supportive of you; it could be that you are afraid to try something new; or it could be that you are unskilled at managing your energy so that you never have the "oomph" you need to be proactive about pursuing your dreams. All of these issues are symptoms of the most common obstacle to moving forward—not knowing who you are as a person, or knowing who you are on a subconscious level but rejecting it.

Right now, you might be thinking, "Paul, you're crazy. Of course I know who I am. I didn't get to this point in my life without knowing who I am, what my likes and dislikes are, and what I want to do in this world. In fact, I have been pretty successful so far." And, the truth is, you may know yourself well—on certain levels. But do you know yourself on all levels?

Most of us know ourselves to some degree, but many of us don't know ourselves entirely or we simply push down the parts of ourselves that we don't want to acknowledge. If you're feeling stuck, even in one small area of your life, then it's worth spending some time seeing if you can learn something new about yourself that will help you move forward.

> "I feel like I am slipping away sometimes...it's like I'm becoming more of what I do or what I have and less of who I really am."

Can you identify with the feelings in the previous statement? One of my clients spoke those words at our first coaching session, and they represent the feelings of a lot of my influential clients. While success provides a lot of benefits, it also often causes a few problems, especially when it comes to knowing ourselves.

You don't have to be a celebrity, dignitary, or executive to experience problems with knowing yourself. And I am not talking about mental illnesses like schizophrenia or dissociative identity disorder, but, instead, common issues like the following:

- not becoming who you want to become
- not spending your time doing what you love
- not being surrounded by people who support you
- generally feeling like you are off track.

2

In the case of my client who felt himself slipping away, his issue was that when he asked himself the question "Who am I?" he was beginning to get the answer "I am a famous musician who lives in a multimillion dollar mansion." But this was not the answer that he wanted for that question. He wanted to be more than just his job or his house. He came to me because he wanted to rediscover his true self.

The problem is that for most of us, knowing who we really are is not easy. We lose sight, after years of contending with family and cultural pressures, of the things we once loved or enjoyed doing. Or, as it turns out, we never knew our true selves in the first place. (By the way, in this book I will use *true self* and *personality* interchangeably.) It's not easy for a person to recognize his or her true self because more often than not a person's *identity* masks (or hides) his or her true self.

In this book, we are going to talk about two of the major components that combine to represent your whole person: your personality and your identity.

Figure 1.1: Your Whole Person = Personality + Identity

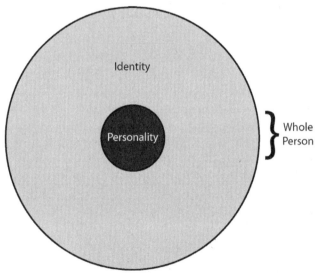

Figure 1.1 shows the relationship between a person's personality and identity. Personality is on the inside because

it refers to those traits, natural inclinations, and temperaments you've had since you were born. Your personality (also known as your true self) is an innate part of you that's unchangeable. Identity, on the other hand, is on the outside because it refers to the elements of you that develop over time in response to the external world and your journey through that world.

Personality vs. Identity

- Your *personality* is made up of those traits, natural inclinations, and temperaments you've had since you were born.
- Your *identity* refers to the elements of you that develop over time in response to the external world and your journey through that world.

In sum, your personality has two characteristics that make it very different from your identity: (a) your personality is innate (you were born with it) whereas your identity develops over time and (b) your personality is immutable (it does not change over time) while your identity can be altered. I have illustrated this for you in Figure 1.2.

Figure 1.2: Characteristics of Personality and Identity

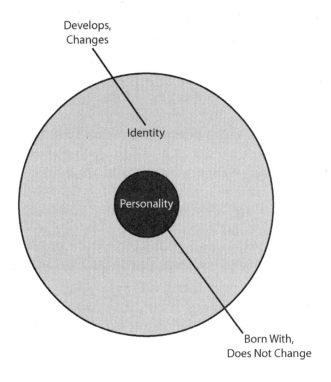

Sometimes, your identity will support your personality, in which case it will be easier for you to move forward in life and accomplish your goals. Other times, and this is the case for many of us until we gain insight into ourselves, your identity will mask your personality. When your identity supports your personality, that indicates an *in-sync identity;* when your identity masks your personality, that represents an *out-of-sync identity.* No matter what, as you grow and develop from childhood into adulthood, you will develop an identity...the question is, will the identity you develop support or mask your true self? One of my goals for you in this book is that you will learn how to develop an identity that supports and is in-sync with your personality. This will be an important part of your ability to move forward in life.

Identity Can Mask Personality

Because personality is the innermost layer of your "personhood," it's easy (and very common) to lose sight of your personality. In fact, most people are unaware of their personalities because from early childhood, they have spent most of their time *adopting out-of-sync identities* that completely mask their natural personalities. More often than not, the environments of our youth (for example, the way our parents raise us, the way society interacts with us, and the way our culture shapes us) mislead us as adults into thinking we are one kind of person—when we are really another!

As children, we are surrounded by families and societies and cultures that are constantly making impressions on us, giving us feedback about how we should be in the world, and teaching us "the right" ways to behave, the "right" thoughts and feelings to have, and the "right" groups to join. Although we come into the world being one way (our personalities), we often receive messages over time, from these outside influences, that there are drawbacks to being our true selves and rewards for adopting identities that are out-of-sync with our true selves. So instead of developing behaviors, thoughts, and relationships that support our true selves, we develop ones that will please the people in our lives. Take Clay, for example:

> Clay grew up in a middle-class suburb where most of his friends and neighbors valued a college education. The high school he attended had a strong academic reputation, and ninety percent of the students went on to college. Clay's parents fully expected him to be one of those students and had originally moved to the neighborhood to help ensure that their son would be accepted into a good college. But Clay hated academics and he couldn't stand being inside all day. School was a chore for him and he dreaded the thought of continuing his education after high school.
>
> Since the eighth grade, Clay had mown lawns to make money after school, and much to his parents' surprise,

he enjoyed the work. He even had visions of starting his own landscaping business after high school. He already had several steady clients that paid him well, and a new subdivision was being built that would probably provide him with some new clients. But when Clay mentioned his exciting business idea to his parents—an accountant and a lawyer—they dismissed it outright. Not only did they insist that Clay go to college, but they pushed him to go for a "practical" degree like business or accounting—nothing having to do with working outside, like landscape architecture.

Like most people, Clay gave in to his parents' wishes. He worried about making it on his own without a college degree and dropped the idea of the landscaping business altogether. He got into a decent college; studied accounting, like his father; landed a well-paying office job after graduation; and was working there when he called me. He called me because he hated his job. Despite his external successes, deep inside, he felt that he'd be happier working outdoors, not behind a desk. But he had the unshakeable feeling that working in a non-office job was somehow "unrespectable."

Does Clay's story sound familiar to you? While every family is unique, Clay's story has a theme that occurs in many families: parents encourage their children to become people who the children really weren't designed to be—to take on identities that do not match their personalities! Although most of these parents have their children's best interests at heart, subtly or not so subtly they reward their sons and daughters for adopting those behaviors, beliefs, and social relationships that are most like their own. And when their sons and daughters don't act, think, or feel like they do, they often penalize them for it.

Clay's personality was clearly oriented to the outdoors. He felt the most peaceful and content when he was outside working with his hands. But, from an early age, his parents convinced him to adopt an identity that was the opposite of his personality (an out-of-sync identity).

As you have no doubt realized by now, we human beings are complex creatures. Nothing about us is simple, including knowing who we are—both our personalities and our identities. I believe that this confusion about who we are is one of the greatest causes of frustration in most people's lives. It is definitely the biggest issue that I deal with in my coaching practice with influential clients. It was certainly the biggest issue that I dealt with when I was an organizational leader. And I suspect it is probably one of your biggest issues, which is why you purchased this book.

Because most of my clients have issues with knowing themselves, I always start the coaching process with a *personality assessment*. The good news is that the assessment process helps my clients understand and discover their true selves. The bad news is that for a whole host of reasons, most people are afraid of finding out who they really are or of making changes in their lives to support who they really are. Happily, we will spend a lot of time in this book helping you get comfortable with your personality. You will also gain several tools for building a life (and an identity) that is more supportive, or in-sync, with your personality.

> To move forward in life, you must be *living in-sync (with your identity supporting your personality)*.

Your Identity—The Three Bs

Now let's spend some time looking more closely at your identity so you can develop a better idea of its role in your life. As I mentioned earlier, your identity is made up of the elements of you that develop over time in response to the external world and your journey through that world. The three elements or layers that make up your identity are what I call the *three Bs*:

- behaviors
- beliefs
- belongings.

Figure 1.3 illustrates the different identity layers and their relationships to each other.

Figure 1.3: The Three Identity Bs

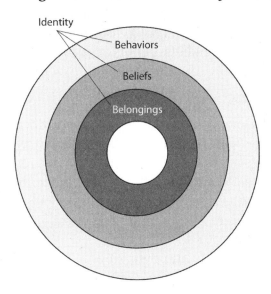

Let's take a closer look at each one of these identity elements to see what they are.

Your Behaviors

The first element of your identity is your behaviors. Your behaviors are the most visible aspect of your identity. I define behaviors as the way we act and conduct ourselves in the world; behaviors consist of the things we *do*. Behaviors include things like the words we use, the clothes we wear, and the actions we take. We can change our behaviors and often do regularly. In fact, it is easier to change our behaviors than it is for us to change any of our other identity elements.

Your Beliefs

The second element of your identity is your beliefs. Unlike behaviors, your beliefs are not usually visible to people around you. (You may *express* your beliefs through your behaviors or even your belongings, but your beliefs themselves are often not seen.) Beliefs are those thoughts, feelings, or ideas that we hold to be true about ourselves and the world around us...regardless of whether they're actually true. Beliefs include things like your philosophy of life, how you feel about yourself, and what you think about others. As with our behaviors, it is possible to change our beliefs. And though we often do change our beliefs, beliefs are much harder to change than behaviors.

Your Belongings

The third element of your identity is your belongings. The term belongings as I use it does not refer to possessions or material things but to the relationships that we form with other people and the communities to which we belong. Belongings are similar to behaviors in that they are very visible to people. Belongings include things like your family, your religious community, and your social network.

As with our beliefs and behaviors, it is possible to change our belongings. But of all the identity elements, belongings is the most difficult element for us to change.

In table 1.1, I provide you with a summary of the three elements of your identity.

Table 1.1: Summary of the Three Identity Elements

	Behaviors	Beliefs	Belongings
Description	What we do in the world	What we think or feel is true about the world	Who we associate with in the world
Visible?	Yes	No	Yes
Changeable?	Yes—Easy	Yes—Difficult	Yes—Most Difficult

Your Personality—The Five Personality Preferences

As I show in Figure 1.4, the three Bs (your identity elements) surround your personality—the natural traits and characteristics of your true self.

10

Figure 1.4: The Three Identity Bs and Your Personality

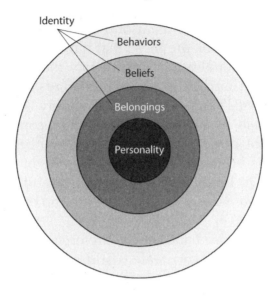

The word I use to describe the natural traits and characteristics of your personality is *preferences* (I also refer to them as *personality preferences*). Preferences can be described as your natural inclinations for "being" in the world. Your preferences refer to the instinctual ways that you function best as a person. Here are the five core preferences of your personality:

1. reenergizing preferences: introvert (I) or extrovert (E)
2. information-gathering preferences: sensor (S) or intuiter (N)
3. information-evaluating preferences: thinker (T) or feeler (F)
4. decision-drive preferences: judger (J) or perceiver (P)
5. communications preferences: direct (D) or indirect (R) communicator.

These five preferences are not the *only* preferences that you have, but they are what I consider to be the most essential ones you should know when it comes to discovering your true self, creating a fulfilling and meaningful life, and enjoying quality relationships with others. Four of the preference groups that I focus on in this book are those that have been defined by a well-known personality assessment tool that you may have heard of or even used, called the Myers Briggs Type Inventory (MBTI). The MBTI has been studied widely and used with great success in both the workplace and people's personal lives. The fifth preference group that I will be introducing to you in this book was developed by one of my mentors and friends, Dr. Linda Berens. Through careful research, Dr. Berens discovered a set of preferences around communication styles.

I myself have used and do use preference information on a daily basis—in the corporate world and my life coaching business, as well as in my personal life. I have seen, time after time, the value of understanding your five personality preferences. This is why we will spend a lot of time in this book getting to know what your personality preferences are. Doing so will help you gain a sharper understanding of your true self, an understanding that you can then use to design a life that is meaningful and fulfilling to you. We will also spend time trying to get to know other people's preferences because this knowledge will help you tremendously in developing and maintaining satisfying relationships with other people. It will also help you in achieving your goals, because 100% of the time, other people are integral to your own progress.

Figure 1.5 shows how the three Bs (your identity) surround your five personality preferences.

Figure 1.5: Your Three Identity Bs and Your Five Personality Preferences

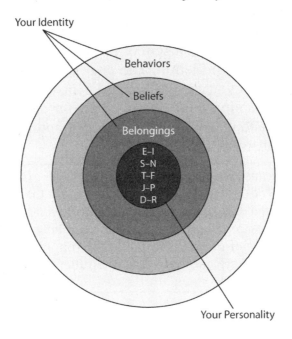

Your Identity

Behaviors

Beliefs

Belongings

E–I
S–N
T–F
J–P
D–R

Your Personality

Your behaviors, beliefs, and belongings have the power to *support* your personality or to *mask* it. For example, if you have adopted your three Bs to please others, then chances are that they don't support your personality (and may be why you're stuck somewhere in your life). If, in contrast, your three Bs have developed as a natural extension of your personality, then they most likely do support your personality (and help you move forward in your life).

As I mentioned earlier, you will soon discover what your personality preference is for each of the five preference pairs of personality. These five personality preferences make up what I call your *life code*. For example, my life code is INTJD. This means that I have a preference for introversion (I), intuiting (N), thinking (T), judging (J), and direct communication (D).

We will look at each preference category in detail as you progress through the book so that you will be able to understand what all those letters in the life code mean. And as the chapters progress, you will not only learn the meaning of each of these preferences, but you will also discover your own life code—*your* five personality preferences.*

While it can be interesting to learn your life code, I want to stress up front that the goal of this book is not just to give you interesting information. The goal is to give you *helpful* information that you can use to build a life that is customized to your personality, your hopes, and your aspirations. This book is not about words on a page, but about strategies to help you transform your life.

> *Note*: Because the reenergizing preferences—extroversion (E) and introversion (I)—are in some ways the easiest to understand and the most self-evident, I will refer to the E–I preference pair in this chapter from time to time for the purpose of giving examples. Later on, you will learn about this preference pair and the other preferences in more detail.

* *I will offer you tips in this book to help you determine your personality preferences. However, if you'd like to take a formal assessment to determine your preferences with certainty, you may do so by visiting this link: http://www.lifechangingcoaching.com/assessments.htm*

Your Preferences Are Your Care Guidelines

Believe it or not, your personality preferences are a lot like the instructions that come with a new plant. Some plants grow best with a lot of sunlight; others get burned if exposed to direct sun. Some plants need water a couple of times a week to stay green; others turn yellow if watered too often. If you came with a set of care guidelines, your five personality preferences would be listed on these guidelines in a similar way. For example, if you are an extrovert, your instructions might read,

> For rest and relaxation, plant in a room full of activity; thrives when surrounded by people, including friends, family, acquaintances, and even strangers.

But if you are an introvert, your instructions might read,

Two times daily, situate in a quiet setting, such as a library or shaded grove, for maximal rejuvenation. Surround with a few close friends for maximum enjoyment.

> *Note*: Throughout this book I will use the name of the preference as a shorthand way of describing the preference. For instance, instead of saying "he has a preference for introversion" or "she has a preference for feeling," I will often say, "he is an introvert" or "she is a feeler." The truth is that there really aren't introverts or feelers—those are one-dimensional descriptions, and we humans are multidimensional beings. So when you see the shorthand preference names used in this book, remember that what I am really saying is that a person has a preference for a certain thing, not that the person is defined solely by his or her preference.

Why Are Preferences an Important Part of Knowing Yourself?

There are two key reasons why it is important to understand what your five personality preferences are. First, *you will thrive best under certain conditions*, the conditions defined by your personality preferences. Once you know these conditions, you can work them into your life, which will lead you to be more effective at achieving your goals. This will probably also make your life more enjoyable, meaningful, and fulfilling.

Just like a plant that needs a lot of sunlight to grow, if you are an extrovert, you will need lots of time with other people to stay healthy and happy. And if you are an introvert, just like a plant that grows best in shade, you will need quiet time to stay healthy and happy. So, to start moving forward in life, you will want to work toward aligning your lifestyle (as well as your identity) with your personality so they are in-sync. In plant terms, if you need more sunlight, you will want to start spending more time in the sun; if you need more shade, you will want to spend more time in the shade.

A key to moving forward in life is recognizing *exactly which conditions you thrive in and designing your environment to be in-sync with those conditions (or personality preferences)*.

Once you've created an identity and designed an environment that are in-sync with your preferences, amazing things will start to happen: you will feel more at ease in your life, you will have the energy you need to pursue your goals and aspirations, and you will find yourself moving forward. You will have a sense of confidence and empowerment because you will be honoring the person who you are, rather than working in opposition to it.

The second reason it's important to understand what your personality preferences are is so that you have a clear understanding of the areas that *lie outside of your natural inclinations*. These areas could be called your weaknesses or blind spots. You will want to become familiar with these blind spots because once you recognize them, you can adjust your behaviors, beliefs, and even belongings to minimize your blind spots, which will ultimately make it possible to achieve more in your life. *Sometimes, you need to be able to flex beyond your personality preferences to reach your goals.*

So there are two bits of counsel I've found to be very helpful in life. First, work to discover the five personality preferences that make up your true self and design a life *in-sync* with them. Second, learn how to behave *outside of* your personality preferences when needed to advance your goals.

Now you may be scratching your head and wondering how these two ideas can really work together. It seems a bit confusing at first to imagine *getting comfortable with your preferences* while also being willing to *behave in opposition to your preferences*. What you need to remember for this to make sense is that you will only need to do *one of these* things at a time. The truth is, there are times when it is best to act in alignment with our true selves, and there are other times when we need to push ourselves out of our comfort zones—for the purposes of advancing our causes—by adopting identity elements that are a little uncomfortable to us and outside of our preferences.

If there is any confusion on this issue, let me specify that *first and foremost, I recommend that you live in-sync with your personality preferences.* I want you to grow comfortable with the fact that you have certain inclinations when it comes to reenergizing, making decisions, communicating, and so forth, and I want you to honor these inclinations through the way you live your life.

But I also know you live in a real world, which demands certain things from you at certain times that may lie outside of your comfort zone. And I recognize that some of your goals may require you to stretch beyond your preferences. So I want you to learn to recognize these times and become skilled at rising to the challenge of flexing beyond your preferences. In summary, you want to design your life in-sync with your personality preferences, but you also want to develop a willingness and an ability to adopt behaviors, beliefs, and even belongings outside of these preferences—at specific times and in service of your goals.

For example, I have a clear preference for introversion. As a result, I have designed my weekly schedule to allow for some alone time each day to help me recharge. Of course, some days life gets too busy and I miss out on that solitude, but most days I'm able to use that down time, even if brief, to press the reset button. As an introvert, occasional alone time is essential to my having the energy to pursue my goals and plans. So whenever I start to feel rundown or stuck, I know to stop and take some quiet time. This often gives me the energy or perspective I need to move forward in my life.

Interestingly, although I'm an introvert, one of my life purposes is to teach. Teaching is an extroverted behavior because it involves spending time with groups of people and, for me, expending a lot of energy in the process. But if I want to fulfill my calling to teach, I have to be willing to adopt the behavior of an extrovert at times. If I don't learn to get out of my comfort zone as an introvert, I will never be able to realize my mission of teaching. So I've learned over the years (not only as a professor, but also as a leader and life coach) how to adopt extroverted behaviors. This doesn't alter my preference from introversion to extroversion, but it does allow me to reach beyond the initial boundaries of my preference for introversion and live the life I want to lead.

In short, because I know the five personality preferences that make up my true self—my life code—I can adopt an identity that is out-of-sync with my personality when I need to. But when I do this, I do it intentionally, in support of achieving my goals. I don't do it because I am confused or because my personality is masked. (We'll talk more about personality masking in the next chapter.)

Before we do, here is a summary of the key points that we have discussed in this chapter.

Table 1.2: Identity and Personality Summary

	IDENTITY			PERSONALITY
	Behaviors	**Beliefs**	**Belongings**	**Preferences**
Description	What we do in the world	What we think or feel is true about the world	Who we associate with in the world	Who we are in the world
Visible?	Yes	No	Yes	No
Changeable?	Yes— Easy	Yes— Difficult	Yes— Most Difficult	No

Important Points

- To move forward in life, for the majority of the time, we must be living in-sync, which means that all of our identity elements (behaviors, beliefs, and belongings) support our personality preferences.
  - Occasionally, to move forward in life, we need to adopt identity elements (behaviors, beliefs, and belongings) that are opposite of our personality preferences.
- There are five personality preferences that make up our true selves:
  - reenergizing preferences: introvert (I) or extrovert (E)
  - information-gathering preferences: sensor (S) or intuiter (N)
  - information-evaluating preferences: thinker (T) or feeler (F)
  - decision-drive preferences: judger (J) or perceiver (P)
  - communications preferences: direct (D) or indirect (R) communicator.

We've covered a lot of new concepts in this chapter: personality, identity, preferences, behaviors, beliefs, and belongings. You may even be feeling a little overwhelmed by all of the information that I have presented or you may be confused about some of the concepts. If so, don't despair, your reaction is completely normal. Take some time to reread and digest the concepts and to process what they mean. If you need to, look back over the diagrams that I presented in the chapter and the key ideas I highlighted in the text boxes. You can also return to this chapter at any time to review these concepts or skim the glossary for definitions of each term.

As we progress through the book, I will spend a lot of time explaining each of these concepts and giving you practical ways to use this information. By the time you are finished reading this book, not only will you have a greater understanding of your own personality and identity, but you will also be able to understand other people's personalities and identities. This knowledge will help improve your ability to interact successfully with the other people in your life, which will ultimately help you move forward.

Congratulations for taking another step along the road to life fulfillment and for making progress toward achieving your goals. Our journey has begun!

2

Understanding the Masks We Wear

Have you ever been to a circus or fair and watched the elephants? Did you ever wonder how the trainers could keep the world's largest land animals under control just by leading them around with those tiny ropes? Have you ever thought to yourself, why doesn't the elephant just break the rope and escape?

The reason why the elephant doesn't break away is because of the way it was trained. As soon as the elephant is born, the trainer ties it to a length of strong rope. At this point, the rope is stronger than the elephant and soon the elephant realizes that no matter how hard it pulls, it can't break the rope. Eventually, the elephant stops trying. It has learned a lasting lesson: the rope is stronger than the elephant.

One day, the elephant becomes stronger than the rope. In fact, once the elephant is fully grown, there are very few materials that can hold an elephant that is determined to break free. But, despite the reality of the situation, the elephant still believes what it learned when it was young: the rope is stronger than the elephant. And so the elephant spends the rest of its life tied to the rope, going wherever the trainer wants it to go and walking around in circles the rest of the time.

Many of us are like those elephants. Somewhere along the way someone has told us something equivalent to *the rope is stronger than we are* and then has gone on to train us using that rope. When we are young, it's important to have the structure of the rope—parents and a society to guide us. But over time, as we grow into adults, we no longer need the rope. Instead, we need the freedom to walk in directions that fulfill us and align with our personalities. We need to learn to break free from the rope or simply to untie it.

The Identity Mask

Unfortunately, many of us are like the adult elephants that are unaware of their strength. We are powerful people who

21

end up walking around in circles because we think we have to stay wherever the rope wants to keep us. Not only are we unaware that we have the strength to break the rope, but we don't even realize that we want to break it. We are living our lives to please the elephant trainer, rather than to satisfy our true selves.

Using the concepts we learned in chapter 1, we could say that in such cases we have taken on identities that run counter to our personalities to please important people in our lives. When this happens, our personalities become obscured or masked by our out-of-sync identities. If you remember from chapter 1, our personalities are the innermost layer of who we are, whereas our behaviors, beliefs, and belongings are more external (see Figure 1.4 in the previous chapter). This means our personalities can get buried or covered up by behaviors, beliefs, and belongings that are *out-of-sync* with our personalities.

I call this *unintentional personality masking*: when your identity masks or covers up your true self. The reason I refer to this concept as *unintentional* personality masking, and not just personality masking, is because by and large we are unaware that this phenomenon is happening to us.

When your identity is unintentionally masking your personality, it looks like some version of the following:

- you act in a way that is out-of-sync with your preferences
- you don't value your preferences owing to your belief system
- the people or groups you spend time with make it difficult for you to honor your preferences, AND
- all of this is happening without you being aware of it on a conscious level.

Bill is a great example of a person who experienced unintentional personality masking:

When Bill started business school, he quickly discovered that extracurricular activities were a large part of the experience. As a student, Bill was not only encouraged to join several clubs but was also expected to regularly attend networking events, guest lectures, and late-night social events with his classmates. By the end of each week, after attending all of these events, Bill was exhausted. He hardly had the energy he needed to keep up with his class work, and he wasn't acting like his usual sharp self at recruiting events for summer internships. Bill wished he could cut back on a few of his clubs and skip all the late-night partying that seemed to be part of his school's culture, but every time he considered scaling back, he heard a voice in his head calling him "lame." His older sister had always given him a hard time for not partying more in high school, and as an adult, he wasn't going to risk letting anyone else do the same—especially in business school, where he knew he was making crucial relationships that would serve him for the rest of his life. He just couldn't risk having his peers thinking he was a social misfit.

Bill, it turns out, has a *personality preference* for introversion, but he has taken on the *identity* of an extrovert (without realizing it, of course). This means that his personality is unintentionally masked. Although Bill would function best (and be happiest) if he behaved, believed, and belonged like an introvert, he is actually behaving, believing, and belonging like an extrovert; as a result, he is exhausted and not functioning well. Bill has no consciousness that his identity is out-of-sync with his personality, and so we can say that he is exhibiting unintentional personality masking.

Let's take some time to understand *why* Bill's identity is masking his personality. First, because of his family background, Bill BELIEVES that it is most respectable and valuable to behave in an extroverted manner. Making things even more difficult, the business school environment he is a part of right now (Bill's BELONGING) also puts a premium on extroverted behaviors. So, without having consciously reflected on it, Bill believes that he must BEHAVE like an extrovert all the time and pays the price for that choice. He attends several clubs, networks often, and parties several nights each week. But because these extroverted activities sap him of his energy, Bill is too exhausted to study, and he has fallen behind in his class work. He shows up at job interviews less prepared than he'd like to be, because he's so tired. Not to mention that he's weary and frustrated with his situation. Bill is experiencing unintentional personality masking and he is floundering.

As soon as Bill realizes that he has a preference for introversion and, even more importantly, *embraces* this preference, things will start to get a lot easier. He will have the freedom to design an environment in which he can thrive as an introvert, not struggle as he forces himself to act like an extrovert. Sure, there will be times when Bill will need to adopt extroverted behaviors (what I call *intentional personality masking*), like the times that he will attend networking events and career-related clubs, to achieve his goal of getting a good summer internship, but he'll be able to eliminate some of the less essential extroverted activities like the late night partying and the non-career-related clubs to have more alone time to recharge and focus on his studies. Instead of responding to the voices of the people who would have him mask his personality (the elephant trainers) and drown out his preference for introversion, Bill will start answering to his introverted personality preference, which calls for solitude and quiet time to regroup.

The change Bill will experience by becoming aware of his personality and designing his life to support it will be dramatic. He will start doing better at academics, he will arrive at his job interviews feeling energetic, and he will have the clarity of mind to make good decisions in pursuit of his goals.

If you are unaware of your personality preferences (for example, you have trouble recognizing one preference over another as your own or you have received conflicting results on personality assessments that you've taken more than once), in all likelihood, this lack of awareness is occurring because your identity is unintentionally masking your personality to some degree. Sometime during your growing-up years, you probably got the message from someone important to you that it just wasn't acceptable to behave, believe, and/or belong in-sync with your personality. Or maybe you were taught that the personality preference opposite to yours was superior. Or your family members simply had different personalities than yours and so you thought that the behaviors, beliefs, and belongings associated with their personalities were the right ones to have and yours were wrong. And now, for whatever reason and perhaps without knowing it, you are living your life in-sync with someone else's personality preferences rather than your own. This personality masking probably didn't occur as deliberately as the way elephants are trained, but the result is the same: someone else, not your true self, has determined the path that your life is taking.

> *Unintentional personality masking* occurs when your behaviors, beliefs, and belongings (your identity) hide your true personality and you have no awareness that this masking is taking place.

This book is about helping you discover your true self, maybe for the first time. It is about liberating you from another person's vision of who you are supposed to be or your perception of how others expect you to be, so that you become free to live life as you were created to live it.

Part of that liberation will come when you have a better understanding of the different ways that your identity elements (behaviors, beliefs, and belongings) interact. For example, the next time you have a job interview or an important meeting, understanding how your beliefs affect your behaviors will allow you to prepare better. Instead of just focusing on the activity (the interview or the meeting), you should also review (and maybe revise) some of your beliefs. Do you believe that you are one of the best candidates for the job? Do you believe that you are able to conduct an excellent meeting? Do you believe that you have something valuable to contribute? Adopting these positive beliefs beforehand is just as important as the clothes you will be wearing and the words you will be speaking because they will lead to positive behaviors that will help you impress the interviewer or the meeting participants. Once you have a good understanding of the way your three Bs interact, you will be free—to make different choices about which behaviors, beliefs, and belongings to engage in; to achieve your goals; and to honor your true self. For this reason, we will examine the way the three Bs interact in the following section.

How Your Identity Elements Interact

Your behaviors, beliefs, and belongings are constantly interacting with each other to form your identity. Figure 2.1 illustrates this dynamic interaction.

Figure 2.1: How Your Three Bs Interact

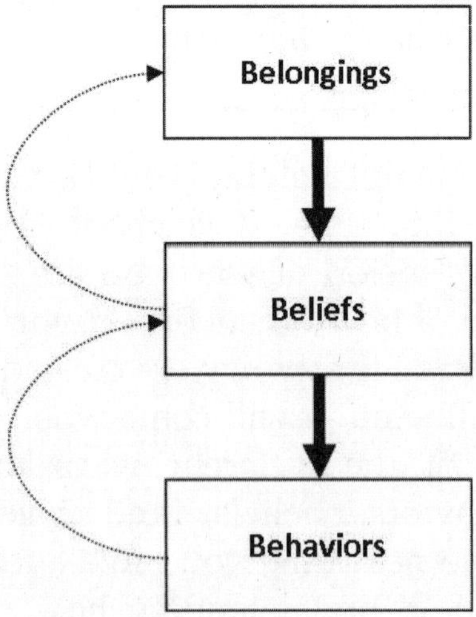

Figure 2.1 essentially lets us know the following:

- Belongings *primarily* influence beliefs.
- Beliefs *primarily* influence behaviors.

26

- Behaviors *secondarily* influence beliefs.
- Beliefs *secondarily* influence belongings.

The relationships among the Bs are not self-evident, so let's break the whole interaction down by each of the identity elements to make it clearer.

Belongings and Beliefs

In chapter 1, we learned that belongings are the relationships that we form with other people and the communities to which we belong. Because we are "hardwired" for connection with other people, our belongings are the primary influencer of our beliefs.**

Belongings are about connection. When we connect with other people in families, through friendship, or through groups and organizations, we create a home for ourselves among others, a feeling that we fit in somewhere, and a sense that we belong.

It is in this environment of belonging that we form our beliefs. Remember, our beliefs are those thoughts, feelings, or ideas that we hold to be true about ourselves and the world around us…regardless of whether they're actually true. While there are a few people whose beliefs emerge after careful study and analysis of different topics, most of us take on the beliefs handed down to us from our parents, teachers, and other authority figures or we adopt the beliefs of our friends or the people we admire. In other words, most of us adopt the beliefs of the groups to which we belong. *This can be good or bad, depending on the belongings and the beliefs these groups hold.*

When we were kids, we called this phenomenon of belonging-influenced belief formation peer pressure. As we got older, we called it nurturing on the positive side and group think or even brain-washing on the negative end. But no matter what we call this phenomenon, it is clear that for most people, their belongings exert the greatest influence on what they believe about themselves and the world around them.

27

> For most people, their *belongings* exert the greatest influence on what they believe about themselves and the world around them.

For example, I had a client who defined himself by his membership in a recovery group. The members of the group had a vested interest in portraying themselves as broken and unable to live "normal" lives ever again. Unfortunately, my client had begun to believe that what the recovery group said about him and others like him was true. Membership in this particular community caused him to believe a certain way (that he was broken). In other words, his belongings influenced his beliefs—and in a way that was unhealthy for him.

Happily, the belongings-affect-beliefs principle works both ways, because after my client and I started working together, he and I formed a new belonging for him (our relationship), and on the basis of our conversations, my client began to believe that it was possible to live a "normal" life and that he did not have to consider himself to be a forever broken person. He eventually quit the recovery group, which was no longer helpful to him, and spent more enjoyable time with his family and friends who supported a healthier concept of his whole person.

** *Recent research has proved what experience has shown — human beings are made for relationships with each other. (See The Institute for American Values, 2003, Hardwired to Connect: The New Scientific Case for Authoritative Communities. New York: Author.)*

Beliefs and Behaviors

Just as our belongings are the primary influencers of our beliefs, so are our beliefs the primary influencers of our behaviors. This means that what we think or how we feel about ourselves and the world around us will often determine how we behave.

For example, children who have been told by their parents time and again that they are "bad" in some way—children who are taught to *believe* that they are bad—will oftentimes act out this belief of "badness" by misbehaving. In contrast, children who are taught to believe that they are good kids will, for the most part, behave in a positive manner. It's as if these kids' behavior unfolds directly from their beliefs.

When I was in the Marines, there was a Private with whom I worked once (we'll call him Jimmy) who was a great example of how our beliefs can shape our behaviors. Jimmy was intelligent, ambitious, and hard-working, yet every time he seemed to be on track for promotion to Lance Corporal, he would do something that would take him out of the running. After observing Jimmy do this a couple of times, I decided to sit down with him and see if I could figure out what was going on with him. After a few times of talking and getting to know him better, I discovered that Jimmy's barrier to moving forward was a phrase his father had repeatedly placed in his head while he was growing up. That phrase was, "You are no good and you will never amount to anything."

Well, you can imagine the damage that kind of destructive belief can end up having on a person's behavior: Jimmy sabotaged himself every time he was about to achieve something. A little voice in his head said he wouldn't amount to anything (his belief), so he acted at times like someone who wouldn't amount to anything (his behavior). Maybe Jimmy didn't expect enough of himself, so he indulged in misbehavior. Maybe he wanted to prove his dad's belief right. (It sounds strange, but we'd often rather sacrifice a positive opinion of ourselves than acknowledge that our parents may have been wrong about something.) But the bottom line was that Jimmy's belief led to him breaking Company rules—in short, misbehaving—and kept him from getting promoted to Lance Corporal.

The good news is that my platoon sergeant and I worked with Jimmy to help him replace this negative belief with a positive belief that was anchored in the truth about who Jimmy was: he was a gifted Marine and natural leader. Three months later, Jimmy was promoted and he continued to excel and grow. And each success confirmed the new healthy beliefs he had about himself and erased the limiting beliefs that his father had implanted in his head many years ago.

The Secondary Pathway

As we have just discussed, the primary way that your identity elements interact is as follows:

> Belongings → *influence* → Beliefs → *influence* → Behaviors.

But there is also a secondary way that your identity elements interact (shown by the curved arrows on the left side of the earlier Figure 2.1 and highlighted in the following text box):

> Behaviors → *influence* → Beliefs → *influence* → Belongings.

Again, let's break this down and look at the specific influences that each B has on the other.

Behaviors and Beliefs

While it's true that our beliefs are the primary influencers of our behaviors, it is also true that our behaviors can influence our beliefs. We don't usually think about our behaviors' impact on our beliefs, but if we stop to reflect a moment, we can see how our behavior is actually continually influencing what we believe.

This is particularly clear when we think about self-beliefs—the ideas that we hold to be true about ourselves. Have you ever tried to lose weight or to watch what you eat? What usually happens when you make healthy behavioral choices about what you are eating? You develop a positive belief about yourself—that you are disciplined, motivated, strong-willed, hardworking, etc.

Now what happens when you fall off the wagon and overeat during a dinner out or succumb to a pint of Ben & Jerry's? You may suddenly embrace a different belief about yourself—that you are weak-minded, undisciplined, unmotivated, or lazy. You are still the same person who two days ago ate grilled fish and asparagus for lunch and skipped dessert after dinner, but somehow you've gone from seeing yourself as hardworking to seeing yourself as lazy. Your behavior has had a dramatic impact on what you believe about yourself.

This behaviors-affect-beliefs phenomenon happens all the time. Here's another example. If you tend to oversleep every morning (*behavior*), you may carry a *belief* about yourself that you are an irresponsible person. But if you turn over a new leaf and start waking up with your alarm clock each morning (*behavior*), you may start *believing* that you are a responsible person. And so on. What's the conclusion here? When you alter your behaviors, you may also change the beliefs you hold about yourself.

Beliefs and Belongings

Just as our belongings influence our beliefs, our beliefs can also influence our belongings. The easiest demonstration of this concept is in the area of religion. When people adopt certain religious beliefs, they tend to form belongings that reflect those beliefs. For example, Christians join churches with other Christians, Buddhists join temples with other Buddhists, and Muslims join mosques with other Muslims. In each case, the spiritual beliefs that the person holds has a great influence over which religious group they belong to. Of course, this phenomenon applies to nonreligious groups as well. For example, if you believe in protecting the environment, you may join a volunteer group that advocates for the environment; if you believe in the importance of democracy, you might volunteer to work at your local polls on Election day. In short, what you *believe* will play a role in the types of groups you join and the people you choose to associate with (*belongings*).

Unintentional Personality Masking

Now that you understand how your identity elements interact, let's take a look at how those interactions can unintentionally mask your personality. Let's go back to our story of Bill and this time look at what is happening to him from a standpoint of identity-element interaction (interaction among the three Bs).

Bill's belongings (his family and business school community) have influenced his beliefs, which have in turn influenced his behaviors. In particular, Bill's sister's teasing (BELONGING) has made him BELIEVE there is something wrong with being an introvert. Furthermore, the fact that many of Bill's schoolmates are extroverts has reinforced Bill's BELIEF that the best way to BEHAVE is like an extrovert. As a result, Bill begins to practice more and more extroverted behaviors. Because Bill values being an extrovert and acts like an extrovert, he thinks that he *is* an extrovert. The truth is that Bill's natural self is an introvert, but it has been *masked* by his out-of-sync extroverted identity.

A lot of us are in the same situation as Bill: our belongings have influenced us to adopt beliefs or to practice behaviors that have masked our personalities. This masking causes us to slow down or get stuck in life. In each of the preference chapters (starting with the next chapter), I am going to show you how to unmask your personality and then form belongings, adopt beliefs, and practice behaviors that will support, rather than mask, your true self or personality. I am going to show you how to break the rope that has been holding you back.

Clarity of Preference

By the way, another way of saying that your personality is masked is to say that you are *unclear* as to what your personality preferences are. If I were to give you a list of all the typical characteristics of your preference type and you didn't recognize or relate to many of these characteristics, then this would be a sign that you were unclear in your preference or largely unaware of it: even though this was your preference (as would be shown by a personality assessment), you would not be aware that it was your preference because your behaviors, beliefs, and belongings would be out-of-sync with it. If on the other hand, you recognized and related to most or all of the characteristics of your preference type, then this would be a sign that you were clear in your preference. The more you identify with your selected preference, the *clearer* in your preference you are said to be.

Researchers of the MBTI, from which four of the five preference pairs we cover in this book are drawn, used to say you were *stronger* in your preference if you identified with more traits in that preference category; but over time, they have discovered that this phenomenon does not indicate *strength* so much as *awareness* or *clarity*. So, if I have a score of 19 I (Introversion) on a scale of 20, that means that I clearly recognize my preference for introversion and that I likely behave, believe, and belong in-sync with that preference. But if I have a score of 3 I on a scale of 20, that means that although I still have a preference for introversion, I am not clear about it (or aware of it) at all and that I likely behave, believe, and/ or belong in a way that is out-of-sync with my preference for introversion.

So you will fall somewhere on this continuum of clarity regarding your preference for introversion or extroversion (and all of your other preferences too), depending on how aware you are of your personality (and likely depending on how in-sync or out-of-sync your behaviors, beliefs, and belongings are with your personality). Figure 2.2 exhibits this clarity scale and shows that although you may have more or less clarity about your preference type, you remain characterized by that preference regardless of your clarity level. (Note that for each preference type—extroversion–introversion, sensing–intuiting, thinking–feeling, judging–perceiving, and direct–indirect communication—you will fall somewhere on this same clarity scale. You may have more clarity regarding some of your preferences than others.)

Figure 2.2: Preference Clarity Scale: Reenergizing Preferences

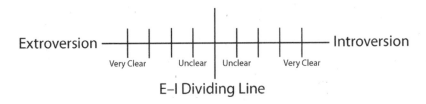

When I teach this concept of clarity to my clients, I talk about the border between California and Arizona. If I am on the California side of the border, one mile from Arizona, I am as much in California as if I was one hundred miles away from the border. I may not realize it because of a lot of factors, but I am in California, not Arizona. The same is true of my preferences…I either have a preference for extroversion or I have a preference for introversion; I can't have a blend of both. Although I may not be completely aware of my preference, I nevertheless fall on either the extroversion or introversion side of the border.

So if you find yourself relating to a few of the characteristics correlating to your opposite preference type, it may mean you lack some clarity on what your preference type really is. As a result, some of your behaviors, beliefs, and/or belongings will probably match up with the opposite preference type. Take the case of Christina, an unclear introvert.

Christina behaved as an introvert in many cases. Sometimes, she'd attend an office party or a social event with her husband, Phil, and his friends, but she mostly loved to spend her weekends at home with Phil and their two daughters. One of Christina's favorite rituals was Saturday morning, before the kids woke up, when she would make herself a cup of coffee and write in her journal. It always reenergized her to spend some time alone with her thoughts.

Unlike some introverts, though, Christina could also be quite talkative, especially when she was out at a party. All this talking actually exhausted Christina, but she felt obligated to make sure social dynamics were flowing well, so she made sure she talked a good deal to carry her load in a social exchange and to make sure there were no awkward silences. Christina had watched her mother socialize in just this way over the years and had picked up this habit from her. It was outside of her preference zone to talk so much, but Christina had sensed by watching her own mother that this was the responsible way to interact with others. (Incidentally, Christina was unaware that she didn't enjoy talking a lot at social gatherings.)

There were some other extroverted behaviors Christina had adopted over the years too (for example, teaching a Sunday school class, organizing school fund raisers). So when she took the MBTI at a work seminar one day, her scores indicated that she was an introvert, but one who lacked some clarity regarding her particular preference.

Christina lacked clarity regarding her preference because of some of her extroverted behaviors. These behaviors were masking Christina's preference for introversion—the most comfortable state for her. As a result, Christina (and incidentally, many of her friends) didn't even realize she was an introvert.

Like Christina, how your preference for either introversion or extroversion plays out in your life will depend on your degree of clarity regarding that preference and whether your identity is unintentionally masking your true self. As we saw in the previous example, Christina had unknowingly reverted to using her adopted extroverted identity when she was socializing. While there were certainly benefits to Christina being able to act in an extroverted manner at social events, this habit also came with its problems. The biggest was that Christina was exhausted by talking so much during her social interactions and didn't know why. She needed to become aware of this fact so that she could better manage her energy. That's not to say she should never behave as an extrovert, just that she should aim to do so consciously and selectively. As you read the upcoming preference chapters, you will have an opportunity to assess your own clarity regarding each of your preferences. If you find that your behaviors, beliefs, and belongings are out-of-sync with your personality preferences, you will be able to spend some time reshaping each B to be more in-sync with your particular preferences.

Intentional Personality Masking

Before we close this chapter, I want to state that not all

personality masking is bad! Now that you have seen the ill effects of unintentional personality masking, let's take a quick look at *intentional* personality masking and its positive effects.

I alluded to intentional personality masking in the book's introduction when I explained to you the five principles of moving forward. Principle number 3 states that sometimes you will need to stretch beyond your natural self to accomplish your goals. This is another way of describing intentional personality masking. *Intentional personality masking* involves deliberately adopting behaviors, beliefs, or belongings that are different than the ones typically associated with your personality preferences to achieve an intended result.

If you want to be able to intentionally mask your personality, then you first need to be aware of your personality preferences. That is, to choose a behavior that is *opposite* of a particular personality preference, you need to first know what your *natural* preference is. For example, if you're not conscious that you're an introvert and that you tend to not speak a lot when you first meet people, then you won't be able to override that preference when you need to—say, at a job interview, when it's important to be able to talk about yourself and verbally sell your strengths and skills. How can you push yourself to talk more during an interview if you are unaware that you have a tendency to be quiet? That's why you need to be aware of your preferences before you will be able to intentionally mask them.

The following is an example of a time when you might use intentional personality masking to advance your goals.

Imagine that you need to study for an entrance exam for law school or medical school. If you have a preference for perceiving, you are likely to be the kind of person who prefers to wait until the last minute to study for a test (judgers prefer to prepare days in advance). (We will describe these and the other preference types in greater detail in chapters 3–7.) This studying delay might work fine for a college midterm, but it won't serve you well on the LSAT or the MCAT, which can take months of preparation to get high scores.

So you have two choices: you can behave in line with your preference by procrastinating or you can alter your behavior and behave outside of your preference (for example, mask your preference) by studying well in advance of the test. If you choose the first option, you are likely to get disappointing results on the exam; if you choose the second option, you will have a high likelihood of doing well on the exam. This is an example of the positive benefits of intentional personality masking: by intentionally and temporarily behaving out-of-sync with your personality, you are able to achieve a specific goal.

> *Intentional personality masking* involves deliberately adopting behaviors, beliefs, or belongings that are different than the ones typically associated with your preferences to achieve an intended result. Intentional personality masking requires you to be aware of your specific personality preferences.

There are lots of reasons why a person might want to intentionally mask his or her personality, for example: I behave differently to achieve a specific goal. I act outside of my preference to be considerate of another person's needs. I adopt a new belief because I am seeking to grow as a person, or I form a new belonging because I want to expand my experiences with people who are different than my true self. Decisions to adjust your behaviors, beliefs, and belongings for these kinds of reasons are usually intentional and conscious; they are also typically constructive: they help you move forward rather than remain stuck.

If we go back to our example of Bill the introvert, we see that when he became aware of his preference for introversion, he still decided to engage in a few extroverted behaviors, like attending networking events and career-related club meetings. He intentionally masked his personality in certain situations to achieve his goal of getting a good summer internship. This is very different from being unaware of one's preferences and continually reacting according to the pressures of one's belongings.

To move forward in life, you will want to become aware of your preferences and then design a life that is mostly in-sync with those preferences. But then, like the new and improved Bill, you will also want to recognize the occasions when you need to act, think, or interact *outside* of your personality preferences—to intentionally mask your preferences—so you can achieve the life goals that require you to flex beyond your preferences. You will learn more about how to intentionally mask your personality in chapter 13 (entitled "Making a Positive Impression").

In the next several chapters, we will describe the different personality preferences and help you to discover your five unique preferences (your life code), but before we do, here is a summary of what we have covered in this chapter.

- Unintentional personality masking occurs when you are unaware of your personality preferences because your behaviors, beliefs, and belongings (your identity) hide them from you.
- The primary way that your identity elements interact is as follows:
  o Belongings → *influence* → Beliefs → *influence* → Behaviors.
- For most people, their belongings exert the greatest influence on what they believe about themselves and the world around them.
- The secondary way that your identity elements interact is as follows:
  o Behaviors → *influence* → Beliefs → *influence* → Belongings.
- Intentional personality masking involves deliberately adopting behaviors, beliefs, or belongings that are different than the ones typically associated with your preferences to

achieve an intended result.

- Intentional personality masking requires you to be aware of your personality preferences.

By focusing less on who others think you should be and more on honoring your true self, you will be able to break the rope of an out-of-sync identity and start moving straight toward your goals. Bye-bye circles, goodbye rope!

3

How Do You Reenergize?

Energy is the fuel supply that keeps you going—throughout the day, the week, the month, and the year—to meet your responsibilities and to achieve your short- and long-term goals. When you are full of energy, you have the oomph you need to get things done; when you're low on energy, it feels like your heels are dragging. When you are full of energy, creative ideas for how to achieve your goals and address life's challenges will flow; when you're low on energy, it's easy to stagnate and see challenges as insurmountable.

The first of your five personality preferences that we are going to learn about is your preference for how you maintain your energy supply for living and for pursuing your goals. I call this your *reenergizing* preference. Let's start our discussion on the reenergizing preference by looking at the importance of having a sufficient energy supply in your life.

When Are You Going to Need Energy?

Living life takes energy, so—it's no surprise to you, I'm sure—that you are *always* going to need energy. But there are times in life when you will need more energy than others. Like when you are working hard to achieve a goal (for example, going back to school, studying for a licensing exam, or completing a big project at work). Or like when you act outside of your preferences—hopefully, by conscious choice, to further your goals.

For example, when I teach—an extroverted activity that is opposite of my reenergizing preference for introversion—I expend a lot of energy. Teaching others is one of my life purposes so I'm willing to flex beyond my preference to do it, but I do so consciously, and I balance my teaching by devoting large chunks of my time to solitude. During this quiet time, I recharge my batteries and store up my energy so that I can use it to enjoy teaching and to be an effective teacher. As an introvert, I expend lots of energy when I am teaching, so I have learned the importance of replenishing that energy by

41

spending time alone after I teach.

Another time you will need to draw on your energy reserves is when you are going through a difficult time in your life (for example, due to a family illness or relationship break-up). Knowing what your energy preference is and incorporating related activities into your life will help you keep up your energy reserves so they are available for you when you need them. If your fuel tank gets low, you will always know what kind of activities you can do to refill it. We can't always "stockpile" enough energy to see us through energy-consuming times, but we usually have the freedom to stop and refuel (even though we don't always feel like we do. Later, we'll talk about making more time for reenergizing.)

You will need to draw on your energy supply when you are working hard to achieve a goal, when you act outside of your preferences, and when you are going through a difficult time in life (like after the loss of a loved one).

Here is a visual example of how powerful good energy management can be. Let's take a look at two people—one who's great at managing his energy, the other who's not doing so well at energy management right now—and let's see how different these two people's lives look.

Mark and Leo have been friends since they were kids and are so close that they are like brothers. The two men have a lot in common—they like the same kind of movies, they both enjoy playing sports, and they even have similar career aspirations. Both of them have talked for years about becoming entrepreneurs and trying to run successful companies. But, while Mark has already jumped ship from the corporate world and started his first successful company, Leo is still struggling to come up with the right business idea so he can leave his corporate job. Leo often wonders why Mark is getting ahead so quickly while Leo feels just plain stuck. Both men are smart, creative, and willing to take risks. But Mark is already running his first business and Leo has no idea how to make the switch to life as an entrepreneur. Is this just a case of bad luck or is there some important difference between the two men?

It turns out that Mark, an extrovert, is expert at managing his energy. He plays on a coed softball team, which gives him at least one night a week out with friends. He is also really good about making plans with friends on the weekends. In short, he has designed his life to include energizing, extroverted activities. So when it's time to focus on his career goals, Mark is ready to take them on. He has abundant energy, he is very motivated, his creativity is flowing, and his mind feels sharp. With his full energy "stores," Mark had the push he needed to start his own company.

Leo, on the other hand, who is also an extrovert, never goes out on weeknights. On weekends, he sometimes goes out, but it is usually with his girlfriend only. It turns out that Leo's girlfriend of several years is an introvert and that Leo has slowly altered his lifestyle to fit with hers. He has given up a lot of the things that once gave him energy— playing team sports, going to happy hours and parties, and meeting new people—because he believed this would make his girlfriend happy. Leo didn't realize that, in the end, he was jeopardizing both his and his girlfriend's happiness. For a few years now, Leo has been in a funk— not clinically depressed, but not very happy either. In his natural state, when he is full of energy, Leo is creative and innovative. This is one of the reasons he knows he could be a good entrepreneur. But these days, the ideas just don't seem to come to him. In spite of his dream of becoming an entrepreneur, Leo feels stuck in the corporate world.

In essence, Mark and Leo are driving the same kind of car, a fast one, like a Ferrari or a Corvette. The difference is that Mark's fuel tank rarely goes below half full so he can cover long distances at top speed, while Leo's tank is often running on nothing but fumes, forcing him to simply crawl along. Mark has the kind of physical and creative energy necessary to run a successful business; Leo, on the other hand, is short on ideas and motivation for getting his own company going.

Everything that he does in his life draws on his shrinking energy supply rather than refills it, so his creativity has gotten blocked.

Are You Managing Your Energy Effectively?

How good are you at managing your energy? If you're like Leo, or most people, you are probably very good at expending energy, but not nearly as good at replenishing it. So take a moment to consider the following questions: Are you taking the time to recharge? Do you know what it takes for you to recharge? Do you spend regular time each day or week engaging in activities that are in-sync with your energy preference? Chances are, if you're feeling stuck in your life, the answers to one or more of these questions is no.

Effective energy management involves renewing your energy supply on a regular basis so you have the power to keep up with your life responsibilities, tackle life's challenges, *and* successfully achieve your life goals. If you're not sure whether you're effectively managing your energy, here are some clues to consider.

If you are effectively managing your energy, you will probably relate to this profile:

- You wake up feeling refreshed.
- You wake up with a sense of purpose.
- You feel that while your goals may be challenging, you can accomplish them.

If you are having some trouble effectively managing your energy right now, you will probably relate instead to this profile:

- You wake up feeling tired.
- You feel like doing other things besides the things you are doing.
- You feel overwhelmed by all of the things you have to do.

If the first profile sounds familiar, congratulations! You are most likely managing your energy effectively. If the second profile sounds more familiar, then this may be a sign that you are not managing your energy as effectively as you could be. In other words, you probably aren't focusing enough in your daily or weekly life on renewing your energy. If you want to move forward in life and to begin accomplishing your goals, it's time to redesign your weekly routine to bring more energizing activities into it.

If you are getting the sense that you are not effectively managing your energy stores, it's essential to figure out what kinds of activities fill you up with energy and what kinds of activities drain you of energy; in that way, you will be able to start consciously managing your energy intake and outflow.

> *Effective energy management* involves renewing your energy supply on a regular basis so you have the power to keep up with your life responsibilities, tackle life's challenges, and successfully achieve your life goals.

Determining Your Reenergizing Preference

We don't all refuel the same way, but we all have to refuel to have the energy to meet our responsibilities and pursue our goals. How you refuel will typically fall into one of two categories: through introverted activities (a preference for introversion) or through extroverted activities (a preference for extroversion). If you have a preference for introversion, you will gain energy by spending time in solitude or with someone you are very close to (say, a spouse or good friend). If you have a preference for extroversion, you will gain energy by spending time with other people, even strangers. Being in a room full of people (at a party, social event, conference) will pump you full of energy if you are an extrovert. In contrast, if you are an introvert, being in a room full of people will drain your energy reserves. This doesn't mean you won't be able to enjoy a group social situation if you are an introvert, just that your interactions will reduce your energy supply rather than

45

refill it.

> *Extroverts* renew their energy by engaging with the external world—talking, socializing, and interacting—whereas *introverts* renew their energy by engaging with their internal world—thinking, observing, and contemplating.

Extroverts tend to be focused on the outer world, whereas introverts tend to be focused on the inner world. What might this look like? Well, let's say you're on a tour bus during a vacation in the United Kingdom, and you're on a day trip to see Stonehenge. If you're an extrovert, you're probably going to be looking out the window on the ride, watching the scenery unfold, and making conversation with your fellow passengers or the bus driver. If you're an introvert, instead, you might be busily skimming a guidebook—reading up on the history of Stonehenge—so you can appreciate the site when you get there. As an introvert, you may be imagining what the setting is going to look like; you might be pondering what times must have been like when Stonehenge was first built.

This isn't to say that an introvert won't ever look out the window or that an extrovert won't carry a guidebook, but instead this is just one example of how an introvert might process experiences internally while an extrovert might process experiences externally. In sum, if you are an introvert, you tend to consider the world from within your mind, while as an extrovert you tend to observe the external world as it moves past you and ideally while in conversation with others. Here, in table 3.1, are some other characteristics that distinguish introverts from extroverts.

Table 3.1: Common Characteristics of Extroverts vs. Introverts

Preference for Extroversion	Preference for Introversion
Energized by others	Energized by self
Dislikes time alone	Needs time alone

Preference for Extroversion	Preference for Introversion
Expends energy	Conserves energy
Large collection of friends	Few friends
Talkative; enjoys discussing things	Quiet; enjoys reflecting on things
Manages by wandering around	Manages by thinking through problems
Likes breadth and variety	Likes depth and specialization
Works at a rapid pace	Works at a slower pace
Thinks out loud	Thinks inside head
Values socializing	Values privacy
Values experiences	Values understanding
Welcomes variety of external stimuli	Selective in external stimuli allowed in
Acts or speaks first, then thinks	Thinks first, then acts or speaks
Appears energetic	Appears calm

So which preference seems to most fit you? Do you find yourself energized by others, do you enjoy socializing, and do you dislike spending time alone, like most extroverts? Or do you cherish your alone time, like to reflect on things internally, and tend to be selective about who you want to spend your time with, like many introverts?

Table 3.2 will provide you with additional helpful information in trying to determine your reenergizing preference. This table lists the common pitfalls that extroverts and introverts can stumble into on the basis of their particular reenergizing preference. Take some time to review the table and see if one side of the table sounds more familiar to you than the other.

Table 3.2: Potential Pitfalls for Extroverts vs. Introverts

Pitfalls for Extroverts	Pitfalls for Introverts
You spend so much time with other people that you neglect the individual attention that needs to be applied to achieving your personal goals.	You don't put enough energy into making or maintaining friendships, so when you need support from others, there are very few people you can turn to for help.
You spend too much time socializing with your work colleagues and neglect your work tasks to some degree. You are so comfortable sharing personal information with others that you share more with your work colleagues than is probably appropriate for the work environment.	You don't give enough attention to developing or maintaining your professional contacts, so when it's time to look for a new job or get support in your career development, your network of contacts for job leads or informational interviews is insufficient.
Because you spend so much time in external conversations, you miss out on insights that you might only gain through quiet contemplation.	You miss out on information or opportunities that would only come to you at social gatherings or in a social setting.
You spend so much time talking that people assume that you aren't interested in what they have to say.	You don't verbalize your thoughts and feelings, so people have to guess at these things or they assume that you have nothing to contribute.

Table 3.2 highlights what might be called the weaknesses of each particular reenergizing preference type. As you read over the table, did you relate to one side of the table more than the other? Even though you know you should be doing one thing in a situation to have better results (for example, talk less or talk more; focus in a quiet place or get out of the house more), do you find that you tend toward doing the opposite because it comes to you much more naturally? If so, reflect on what those natural tendencies are; those tendencies will be an indicator of your preference type.*

If you recognize any of the pitfalls in table 3.2 as being your own, what changes can you make to avoid these pitfalls? If you're an extrovert, maybe you can practice talking a little less and listening a little more when you're in meetings at work. If you're an introvert, maybe you can join a club or group that will give you a chance to meet new people and make more social connections. It might take some time, but with the willingness to try something new and a little problem-solving, you can learn to avoid these pitfalls so you get the most from living in-sync with your preference without being compromised by its potential weaknesses. As we discussed in chapter 2, while we all benefit tremendously from living a life in-sync with our preferences, we sometimes need to flex beyond our preferences to achieve certain goals and to avoid the pitfalls of our preferences' blind spots.

It is important to note that your efforts to identify your reenergizing preference will be more challenging if your identity (your behaviors, beliefs, and belongings) is (are) masking your personality preference for reenergizing. The next section of the chapter will help you get a better handle on whether any masking is taking place.

* You may take an online personality assessment to determine whether you have a preference for extroversion or introversion by visiting this link: http://www.lifechangingcoaching.com/assessments.htm

Is Your Personality Masked?

When you look at tables 3.1 and 3.2 from earlier, you may identify with most of the characteristics for one preference type (extroversion or introversion), while still relating to a few from the opposite category. This is because, as we have talked about before, our behaviors, beliefs, and belongings (our identities) often mask our personality preferences. In other words, even though we have a particular preference (say, extroversion), we may identify with some of the traits of the opposite preference (say, introversion) because some of our current behaviors, beliefs, and/or belongings are out-of-sync with our personality preferences and are thus *masking* a part of our personalities (not just from the world but also from ourselves).

For example, what if you were an extrovert raised by two introverted parents who loved reading books and who often encouraged you to read a book when you needed to recharge? You might have developed a belief that reading books is a great way to relax and that you should read when you need a break. If this was the case, your belongings (parents) may have influenced your belief that reading (an introverted behavior) is a great way for you to relax.

So you take books with you whenever you go on a vacation to recharge, but then when you get there, you never feel like reading. You don't want to sit still; you want to be out exploring the sights and meeting new people. So that's what you do instead. But you feel a little guilty when you see that stack of books in your suitcase. You think there's something wrong with you. Maybe you even wonder if it's a sign that you're not as smart as some people. "Why don't I read books when I finally have the time?" you wonder.

The answer is not that you're less intelligent than other people. It's not that you don't know how to relax. The reason you don't want to read books on your vacation is because you're an extrovert and reading is not how you reenergize! (That's not to say you don't ever like to read, just that, unlike your parents, you don't read to reenergize). Even so, your belief that reading is a relaxing and recharging activity for you has masked your personality to some degree. You can tell this because even though you are engaging in those extroverted behaviors that appeal to you—you're out there sightseeing and socializing—you feel guilty about it and criticize yourself for not reading more. Your sightseeing and socializing are a little less energizing than they would be without that guilt and self-criticism.

This may not be such a big deal if this is a one-time event, but think about the long-term effects of continually second-guessing your attempts to reenergize. Best case, you will be lessening your ability to fully reenergize; worst case, you will be engaging in the wrong activities—those that don't have the power to energize you! That would be like putting diesel gas in your unleaded fuel tank. Your car just isn't going to be able to go with a diesel (or introverted) fill-up.

Let's look at some of the signs that your identity is out-of-sync with (masking) your reenergizing preference.

- You feel pressured to spend your free time socializing when you'd rather be relaxing at home or on your own (masked introvert).
- You feel pressured to engage in quiet or domestic activities in your free time when you'd rather be out socializing (masked extrovert).

If you find that you are pressuring yourself or judging yourself for having a certain preference type—because of messages you've gotten from family, friends, or society (your belongings)—I recommend that you take some time to practice accepting this part of yourself.

One way to foster self-acceptance is to catch your self-critical thoughts when they occur and replace them with more accepting thoughts. So next time you find yourself feeling guilty or thinking critical thoughts about your particular reenergizing preference, take a moment to replace that negative feeling or thought with a supportive one. For example, if as an introvert you catch yourself thinking, "I am so boring for not wanting to socialize on Friday nights," you can stop and replace this thought with, "Staying home on Friday nights is a wonderful way for me to relax so I have the energy I need to be a good friend/spouse/parent/employee/boss and to pursue my life goals."** At first, it might feel unnatural to construct more positive thoughts, but over time, these positive thoughts will actually become integrated into your belief system so that they flow automatically.

Acceptance also often comes with understanding, and you can gain a better understanding of each preference type, including your own, in the "Getting Along With the Opposite

Energy Type" section that comes later in this chapter. Although that section focuses on getting along with people from the opposite energy preference type, it can also be very helpful in learning to understand and accept your own energy preference. For now, let's focus on how you can go about reshaping your behaviors, beliefs, and belongings to be more supportive (or in-sync) with your personality.

**The process of replacing negative thoughts with positive ones is part of a highly effective, well-researched mode of self change used in cognitive-behavioral psychotherapy. For more exercises and support in changing the way you think, consider consulting David Burns' Feeling Good: The New Mood Therapy or his Feeling Good Handbook.

Developing an In-Sync Identity

In chapter 2, when we talked about what it means to have an unintentionally masked personality, I promised that we'd take time in the coming chapters to work on *unmasking* your personality. As a result, each of the preference chapters (chapters 3–7), beginning with this one, has a section called "Developing an In-Sync Identity." In this section, we will focus on the kinds of behaviors, beliefs, and belongings that support each type of personality preference in the chapter's preference pair so that you will have a guide for the kind of Bs you'll want to bring into your life to unmask your own personality and put it in the driver's seat of your life.

As you are probably starting to see, the best way to unmask your personality is to adjust your behaviors, beliefs, and belongings so they flow from your true self (or personality). So that you can start bringing more in-sync Bs into your life, let's look at the kind of behaviors, beliefs, and belongings that support an extrovert versus those that an introvert benefits from.

What Extroverts Need

Behaviors. Extroverts need opportunities to interact with others and to speak out loud rather than just process things in their heads. This means that extroverts gain energy from attending social events and group experiences where opportunities to talk are abundant. Because extroverts value experiences, they also benefit from going out and doing hands-on activities that satisfy their particular interests (horseback riding, rock climbing, sightseeing). Extroverts like to expend energy, so maneuvering the outside world through these different hands-on adventures or just interacting with people for a few hours at social events are wonderful ways for extroverts to expend energy and, ironically, reenergize. In the workplace, extroverts enjoy brainstorming sessions, team-building events, and interaction with customers or other employees. The more people and the more interactions they have, the more energy that extroverts generate.

Beliefs. If you are an extrovert and your beliefs are supportive of your personality, you will value interaction. You will recognize the importance of spending time with others, talking to others, and making a wide group of friends. In fact, you may not even have the concept of "strangers" in your vocabulary. To you, a stranger is simply someone you haven't met, YET. When you interact with people, you will typically enjoy discussing a wide range of topics, because you value breadth of knowledge over depth of knowledge. Similarly, you will value breadth of experience over depth of experience, so you will tend to enjoy engaging in many different kinds of experiences and activities in a given day, week, month, or year. You will also believe that taking immediate action is better than waiting around doing nothing.

Belongings. Extroverts prefer to belong to communities that let them have as many different interactions with as many different people as possible (for example, community service clubs, networking organizations, and professional associations). Extroverts prefer getting to know a little bit about a lot of people, rather than knowing a few people well. They tend to enjoy groups where people feel free to speak and share whatever is on their minds or hearts.

What Introverts Need

Behaviors. If you are an introvert, you will need quiet time or relative solitude to reenergize during the day or week. By having stretches of time with minimal social interaction, you will gain needed space to process your thoughts, feelings, and emotions and to reach an internal state of calm so that you have the energy needed to interact with the external world. Because introverts tend to like conserving energy, good reenergizing activities for introverts are those that allow them to "stay inside" of their heads (for example, watching a movie, reading a magazine, going for a walk, writing in a journal). At work, introverts like activities that will challenge their ability to think through and analyze problems. They prefer job settings or office spaces where they can have the quiet time they need to focus on what's inside their heads.

Beliefs. If you are an introvert and your beliefs are supportive of your personality, you will put a high premium on privacy. You will have clear notions of appropriate and inappropriate types of information that should be shared with "strangers" and will enjoy time spent in solitude or with a close friend or loved one. Because you value depth of knowledge and experience, you will typically enjoy spending a lot of time learning about, talking about, or engaging in a single topic or experience in-depth, rather than jumping from topic to topic or experience to experience. You will also believe that it is better to take your time making sure that you understand a situation rather than rushing into action.

Belongings. Introverts prefer to belong to communities that let them have one-on-one interactions with people (for example, crisis centers, senior citizen homes, or mentoring organizations). Introverts prefer getting to know a few people really well, rather than knowing a lot of people not so well. They tend to enjoy groups where there are processes in place for ensuring that everyone, not just the extroverts, gets an opportunity to participate and share thoughts and ideas.

Now that you see the kind of belongings, beliefs, and behaviors that work well for your preference type, you have a formula for how you can start to live more in-sync with your reenergizing preference. I recommend that over the coming weeks you begin to reshape your out-of-sync behaviors, beliefs, and belongings so they are more in-sync with your particular reenergizing preference. Going forward, you will want to bring activities into your life that support your reenergizing preference, you will want to restructure your beliefs so they are supportive of your reenergizing preference, and, finally, you will want to nurture relationships that are supportive of your reenergizing preference and learn how to manage those that are not.

Table 3.3 provides a list of activities that are energizing to extroverts and introverts. This table can serve as a starting point for discovering what kind of activities you can engage in to keep your energy level high.

Table 3.3: Extroverted vs. Introverted Energizing Activities

Extroverted Activities	Introverted Activities
Calling or visiting a friend	Writing, emailing, or text messaging a friend
Going out with a group of friends	Going out with a close friend or loved one
Engaging in a team sport (softball, basketball, volleyball, soccer)	Engaging in a solo sport (running, swimming, walking, biking)
Going to a party or social event	Going to the library to look for a good book.
Discussing today's news with someone or talking about the latest movie	Watching the news or reading a magazine, newspaper, or book
Hosting a social event for a large group of people	Having a couple close friends over for dinner
Giving a talk, attending a networking event, or going to an association meeting	Writing a journal entry, a story, or an article

Extroverted Activities	Introverted Activities
Volunteering for a group activity at a community charity that interests you (soup kitchen, museum tour guide, senior citizen center, choral group)	Volunteering for one-on-one activities at a community charity that interests you (youth mentoring, literacy programs, crisis phone lines)

Table 3.3 offers some insight into the kinds of activities you can engage in if you are an extrovert or an introvert and you need to reenergize. This table is not meant to say that extroverts or introverts should only engage in extroverted or introverted activities, but is meant instead to highlight which activities are useful for *reenergizing*. For example, introverts may need to attend a networking event (extroverted activity) to get good contacts for career advancement, but they shouldn't look to this kind of event to give them an energy lift. Extroverts may need some quiet time to catch up on reading for work, but this kind of activity won't refill extroverts' energy stores.

How to Find Time to Reenergize

One of the biggest challenges in becoming better at managing your energy supply is finding *the time* to reenergize. The good news is, with a little creativity, prioritizing, and problem-solving, you *can* rearrange your life to make it more supportive of your personality preference for reenergizing. The "bad" news is that you will have to put in some effort to make these life changes.

As you can probably imagine, bringing more reenergizing activities into your life will involve

- planning
- commitment to making a change.

Planning will help you get the right activities on your calendar; commitment will help you follow through. For example, if you're an extrovert and you want to start playing a team sport each week, you will need to investigate what kind of teams are in your area, sign up to play with a team, and rearrange your schedule so you can make practices and games. That's the planning part. The commitment part will involve you showing up for practices and games, even when work or life makes it tempting to cancel. This commitment will have to come from your personal motivation to bring more energy into your life. Happily, once you begin to enjoy the new activity and feel energized by it, it will be easier to honor your commitment. It also helps that others are usually counting on your participation when it comes to extroverted activities; this sense of social connection will help you follow through on your commitments.

If you are an introvert, you will also need to plan and commit to bringing the right kind of energizing activities into your life. Admittedly, it's easier to skip the planning part when it comes to introverted activities because you don't need to sign up with yourself to go for a run, read a book, or write in your journal. But that's exactly why I recommend that you actually schedule your energizing activities right on your calendar, even if they are of the solitary type: to make sure you don't ignore or forget about them. It's also a little easier to skip out on the follow-through of introverted energizing activities because no one is relying on you to show up. Just remember that if you don't follow through, though, in the end you will not only have less energy to achieve your goals and dreams but you will also have less energy to give to those whom you love and care about.

Regardless of whether you're an extrovert or an introvert, I recommend that you add the reenergizing activities to your daily planner, PDA, or whatever means you use to schedule your time. And then make the logistical adjustments to your life necessary to let you follow through on your plans. Maybe this means getting a babysitter, maybe this means rearranging your work schedule to start later or end sooner, or maybe this simply means setting your alarm clock half an hour earlier. There are a thousand excuses not to do these things, but try to remember that putting in this effort up front will pay off when you get to enjoy some reenergizing (which in turn will make you better able to pursue your life goals).

To bring more reenergizing activities into your life, you may have to give something else up—whether it be a hobby that doesn't actually energize you (Internet surfing, watching TV), a project at work that really should be handled by someone else, a friend who is toxic and too demanding of your time, or even a job that requires too many of your hours. In other words, you can give up energy-draining or energy-neutral tasks to gain more time in your schedule. It will probably be hard to give something up to make more time, but once you make the change and get in a new routine, you may forget about what you've given up, or you may find that the benefits of reenergizing make the sacrifice worthwhile.

If you're short on time, a creative way to fit energizing activities into your day is to take care of an errand or task that aligns with your energy preference. If you're an extrovert and you are busy but need a lift, take a break by running to the grocery store where you'll get a sense of interaction with other people but accomplish an errand at the same time. If you're an introvert, jump on the Internet and finish someone's birthday shopping online. With a little creativity and conscious effort, you'll be refueling your energy stores while accomplishing one of your daily tasks.

And remember, even short stints of reenergizing activities can be effective. As an extrovert, you may not have four hours a week to dedicate to playing in a softball league, but you might be able to drop by the park for a game of pick-up basketball most Sundays. As an introvert, you might not have an hour to read before bed, but you might be able to set aside twenty minutes. Even a fifteen-minute phone call to a friend for extroverts or a ten-minute stretch of reading for introverts can give a needed lift. Even short bursts of energizing activities can be restorative.

What happens if you still can't find a way to bring energizing activities in your life? Then, unfortunately, you are probably going to get stuck with the status quo in your life because you will lack the energy needed to pursue your goals. Like I said in the book's introduction, if you keep on doing what you've always done, you'll always get what you always got. And that may be fine for a while, especially if you are in a particularly trying time in your life—say, dealing with a family illness, a major job change, or the birth of a child. But eventually you will want to move out of crisis mode and back into living your life to its fullest. Even if the crisis remains for a sustained period of time, you will benefit a lot from integrating energizing activities into your life. These activities will help you escape life's strains and stresses for a while and then return to your challenges with a renewed sense of energy, creativity, and motivation.

In sum, you now have a plan for how to manage your energy effectively: identify your energy preference, redesign your life to include more energizing activities, and follow through on plans to reenergize. Are you ready to give it a chance? Try out some different activities in your energy preference camp (refer back to Table 3.3 for ideas or brainstorm on your own), and see how these activities make you feel. Figure out which activities are fun for you, work well with your lifestyle, and lift you up—and try to build more of these activities into your life routine. See how much faster you can move when you're running on a full energy supply and how much farther you can actually go.

Getting Along With the Opposite Reenergizing Type

Happily, introverts and extroverts have the ability to get along with each other very well. You've probably heard the saying that opposites attract, right? Well, this can certainly be the case for extroverts and introverts. Here are some reasons why. Extroverts like to talk; introverts like to listen. Introverts admire extroverts' energy; extroverts admire introverts' composure. Introverts may enjoy the adventures that extroverts take them on; extroverts may appreciate the way that introverts help to ground them. So introverts and extroverts can really complement each other.

There are bound to be times, though, when it's hard to

understand someone of the opposite reenergizing preference. It's easy to misunderstand people who interact with the world in a way that varies from yours. So, if you are an extrovert, there may be times in your life when an introvert puzzles you. Similarly, if you are an introvert, there may be times when an extrovert will drive you crazy. Also important to consider, if you hold beliefs or have belongings that don't value your own reenergizing preference, you may find yourself applying negative labels to your own preference type as well. Let's talk about these negative labels, so we can peel them back and better understand what's really going on beneath the surface for extroverts and introverts.

The Negative Labels We Apply to Extroverts and Introverts

If you are an extrovert interacting, working, befriending, dating, or living with an introvert, you might at times see the introverted person as

- uninterested, too quiet
- unsocial
- boring or unexciting
- inaccessible or unknowable.

If you are an introvert interacting, working, befriending, dating, or living with an extrovert, you might at times see the extroverted person as

- too talkative, too social
- domineering
- relaying too much information
- overbearing.

For example, if I have a preference for extroversion, then I am very comfortable with talking about my thoughts and feelings as I experience them. I don't do a lot of filtering. So if I am in a conversation with a person who has a preference for introversion, and I can tell that this person is choosing her words carefully when answering my questions, I may get the impression that she is hiding something from me. While she may be hiding something from me, if she is an introvert, then it is more likely that she is processing the information internally before responding externally. She is probably not hiding information but making sure instead that she is accurately conveying to me her thoughts and feelings.

Or, take the other side of the coin. If I have a preference for introversion, I prefer to keep things private. I am uncomfortable with sharing my successes or failures with strangers. So if I meet someone new who has a preference for extroversion, and this person starts talking to me about the trip that he just came back from, which was a reward for being the best salesperson in the office, I might think that this person is bragging and looking for me to praise him. While that may be true, it is more likely that this person is simply sharing the latest thing that is on his mind, because that's what extroverts do.

Although people may truly possess the negative traits described in these bulleted lists, it is also possible that we simply misinterpret their introverted or extroverted behaviors. We may assume a particular behavior is indicative of a particular negative trait, when it is actually just a sign that someone is processing something differently than we would, according to his or her preference.

What's Really Going on With Extroverts?

Okay, now let's sort through each of the negative labels we tend to give to the opposite reenergizing preference type and explore what's really happening.

Too talkative and too social. Extroverts recharge by social interaction. Talking is a way for them to prime the interaction pump. The more they talk, the more opportunity for response from the other person they get. The more response they get, the more recharged they become. So talking is just a way to get their recharging process started. Extroverts also thrive on the energy present in a group social interaction so they seek it out. Sometimes, it's hard for introverts to understand why their extroverted significant others would want to spend an evening in a room full of acquaintances and strangers instead of snuggling up at home with their partners. But extroverts need time in group settings and with new people to recharge. This kind of interaction stimulates them so they can return to their one-on-one relationships with new things to talk about, creative energy to invest in the relationship, and motivation to be a better person and partner.

Domineering. Energy flows outward from an extrovert into his or her environment. Whereas introverts tend to take in energy from the environment—listening, observing, and processing in their heads—extroverts release energy into the environment, by talking, making jokes, calling over to others, speaking their minds, and so on. At times, it might seem to the introvert like the extrovert is trying to dominate the social exchange when really the extrovert is trying to take the lead and get everyone else involved in the exchange. The healthy extrovert wants everyone to participate in the conversation.

Relaying too much information. Extroverts don't have a value scale for the quantity of information shared. They simply share whatever is on their minds or in their hearts at the moment. If there is a lot going on with them, then they share a lot. If there is not much going on with them at the time, then there will be less shared. Extroverts are truly what-you-get-is-what's-going-on-right-now type of people.

Overbearing. Combine the need to talk with outward flowing energy and introverts may get the impression that extroverts are rude and insensitive. This is not the case; extroverts simply have a different way of being in their worlds than introverts do. Extroverts will ask a lot of questions that the introvert may feel are none of their business to know, and extroverts may share more information than the introvert wants to hear. Again, remember the goal for extroverts is the interaction—the information being shared is just a way to spark the interaction.

What's Really Going on With Introverts?

Now that we have a better idea of why extroverts do what they do, let's go through each of the negative labels extroverts might assign to introverts and see if we can figure out what's really going on for introverts.

Uninterested, too quiet. When an introvert doesn't talk a lot during a conversation or lacks animation when responding, it's tempting to think the introvert is uninterested in the conversation. In truth, it may be just the opposite. To sincerely engage in a conversation with you, an introvert will need to "go inside her head" to process what you are saying. This might make it look like she isn't actively engaged in talking with you. But really, if you could see the neurons firing inside her head, you'd realize that the introvert is fully connected to the conversation. She is hearing every word, noticing every facial expression, and working through your discussion in her mind.

Unsocial. Introverts prefer to be invited to participate in conversations and activities rather than to insert themselves into conversations and activities, which may make them seem unsocial or unsociable. But you might be surprised to see what happens when you reach out to an introvert. If you invite him to join in the conversation, you will help the introvert feel comfortable and open up. It's also helpful to remember that introverts require solitude to recharge. So when introverts turn down social invitations, they aren't meaning to push people away, they are just trying to rejuvenate.

Boring, unexciting. Oftentimes, introverts are only excited about a few things and if you aren't talking about one of those things, they may display little interest or excitement. But if you get them to talk about one of the things that they are excited about, you will see introverts' passion and excitement come to life. Also, because introverts process a lot in their heads, you may not see them demonstrating much energy on the outside; this doesn't mean they lack passion, it's just that their interest in things often gets processed internally, rather than through their speech, facial expressions, or body language.

Inaccessible or unknowable. Because the introvert spends a lot of time listening, observing, and thinking, you may mistake this quietness for the introvert being unknowable or secretive. The truth is, you need to ask an introvert questions, listen, and be patient while the introvert takes time to formulate answers. Most people are flattered when someone else shows interest in them and introverts are no different. If you show interest in introverts and take the time to listen to them speak, you will be able to learn more about them. Just don't expect an introvert to reveal his or her life story the first time you meet. As introverts grow comfortable with you, they will share more.

So now you have some insight into what's going on behind the scenes with the energy preference opposite to yours. You also have more information to help you understand and accept your own extroverted or introverted nature. So the next time you find yourself judging someone else for his or her energy preference—or judging yourself for your own—remember that there are good reasons for the ways that extroverts and introverts act, reasons that help each preference type function best in the world.

Putting Your Best Foot Forward With the Opposite Energy Type

If you want to maximize your relationships with people of the opposite reenergizing type, here are some tips you can incorporate into your interactions with them.

Extroverts...

- Talk less and listen more; introverts will communicate with you, but they need the space to do so.

- Ask for feedback and actively listen when people respond.
- Explain to your introverted friends and family members why it's important for you to socialize beyond your inner circle.
- Understand that your introverted friends and family members will need some time by themselves to recharge.

Introverts...

- Initiate conversations and speak more; experiment with verbalizing your thoughts and feelings instead of keeping them in your head or just writing them down.
- Ask for feedback and verbally acknowledge when people respond.
- Explain to your friends and family members why you need alone time.
- Understand that your extroverted friends and family members will need to socialize in group settings to recharge.

These are some simple adjustments you can make to gain the most from your relationships with people who have the opposite reenergizing preference and to benefit from a life that is in-sync with your preferences without falling into your preference's potential pitfalls.

Intentionally Masking Your Reenergizing Preference

Some of the simple adjustments recommended for introverts and extroverts in the previous section involved masking one's reenergizing preference. This is because as much as embracing your preference through your behaviors, beliefs, and belongings can support you, there will be some times, as we discussed in chapter 2, that intentionally masking your preferences will help you avoid preference pitfalls and advance your life goals.

To review, intentional masking of your personality preference involves adopting behaviors associated with the opposite preference type. The times that you might want to intentionally mask your reenergizing preference include the following instances:

1. when you want to achieve a specific goal
2. when you want to be considerate of another person's needs
3. when you want to grow as a person.

Usually, this doesn't mean that you have to hide your preference altogether, just that you supplement it with the strengths of the opposite preference type. For example, if an extrovert is trying to get a job (that is, achieve a specific goal), his outgoing nature will help him naturally connect with a job interviewer as well as talk about his own job skills and experiences. But the extrovert might also adopt some of the strengths of the introvert (intentional, specific masking), for example, allowing there to be some natural silences in the conversation, so that the extrovert has time to mentally strategize before responding to the interviewer's questions and so that the interviewer has time to process the extrovert's responses.

The purpose of this section in the chapter is not to encourage you to change who you are at your core, but to give you insight into times that you might find it helpful to *support* who you are by incorporating a few of the strengths of the opposite reenergizing type into your interactions. Not only will you get along even better with others, you'll gain valuable skills for moving forward in life—like better communication, more energy, and stronger relationships.

Conclusion

If you find that you're not moving ahead in life, check what kind of reenergizing activities you've been involved in: extroverted or introverted. If these activities don't sync up with your reenergizing preference, it's time to start redesigning your life to effectively manage your energy. If you're an extrovert, try to bring more social activities into your life when you need an energy boost (like calling your friends, going out, playing a team sport, or joining a club). If you're an introvert, try to carve out more quiet time in your week and plan more solitary activities (like going for a walk, meditating, gardening, or even washing your car—whatever it is that will give you some peaceful alone time).

Once you start engaging in more energizing activities, you will have more energy to approach your life goals with vigor and enthusiasm. I don't just mean physical energy, either. You will also have more creative energy. Creative energy is a force that enables you to develop innovative ideas for how to achieve your goals and to come up with novel solutions to problems. When you have creative energy, more things seem possible in life. And because you are capable of coming up with creative strategies for living, nothing seems out of reach. Creative energy can be that special ingredient that helps you be great at something rather than just good at something or that can help you realize all your dreams rather than just some of them. In summary, if you are aware of your particular energy preference, you will have a formula for achieving your life goals: you will know how to refuel when you are feeling fatigued or worn down; and, in turn, you will have more energy to achieve the things that are important to you.

4

What Kind of Information Do You Need?

Have you ever reflected on the process that you use to make decisions in your life? Most of us are so busy making the hundreds of decisions that we face every day that we never stop to consider exactly how we are making those decisions.

If you were to think about your decision-making process now, what would you discover? Do you need a lot of details before you can make up your mind or do you trust your instincts when making a decision? Do you consider only the facts or are other factors important to you in your decision-making? Do you like to have your decisions settled or do you like to leave them open?

All of these questions represent different aspects of the decision-making process. And believe it or not, three of your five personality preferences play a role in how you make decisions. Thus, I call these three preferences your *decision-making preferences*; we will explore the decision-making preferences in this and the next two chapters.

Your three decision-making preferences represent the natural way that you

- gather
- evaluate and
- act on information

in the course of making decisions.

Just as there are typical behaviors associated with your preference for reenergizing (for example, spending time with others vs. spending time in solitude), there are certain behaviors associated with your decision-making preferences (for example, gathering sensory information versus gathering intuitive information). To move forward in life, you will want to align your decision-making *behaviors* with your decision-making *preferences*. When the two are aligned, you will feel more comfortable with the decisions you make and you will be more likely to make better decisions.

Of course, you don't need to contemplate your decision-making preferences and behaviors every time you make a decision, but sometimes—especially when you are feeling stuck in your life or facing a particularly big decision—this process can be a useful way to work through the obstacles you are facing.

Consider Jennifer, whose decision-making *behavior* for gathering information (step 1 of the decision-making process) is out-of-sync with her decision-making *preference* for information gathering.

> Whenever Jennifer has a big decision to make, it's a stressful ordeal for her. She feels pressured to gather lots of information before making the decision because this is what her parents always taught her to do. In truth, Jennifer feels far more comfortable when she skips all the fact checking and just follows her natural instincts. Nonetheless, Jennifer often follows her parents' lead and spends a lot of time considering the pros and cons of a situation and gathering all the details to do so. There is a mismatch between Jennifer's decision-making *behavior* and her decision-making *preference*. In other words, there is a constant tug of war inside Jennifer between her identity and her personality when she has to make decisions. It is not surprising then that Jennifer hates making decisions. And to make matters worse, experience shows that Jennifer tends to make poor decisions for herself.

Why does Jennifer have so much trouble making her decisions? Because her information-gathering behavior is out-of-sync with her corresponding information-gathering preference. In other words, although Jennifer's natural preference (true self) is to gather intuitive information, because of the influence of her parents (belongings) she gathers sensory information instead (a decision-making behavior associated with the *opposite* preference). Until Jennifer learns to adjust her information-gathering behavior so that it matches her intuitive information-gathering preference, she will continue to encounter challenges when making decisions.

The Decision-Making Process

Now let's take a closer look at the actual decision-making process, which involves three distinct steps:

- Step 1: We gather the information needed to help us make the decision.
- Step 2: We evaluate the information.
- Step 3: We decide.

Each step of the decision-making process has two different decision-making preferences associated with it:

- Step 1: information gathering → sensing vs. intuition preference
- Step 2: information evaluating → thinking vs. feeling preference
- Step 3: deciding → judging vs. perceiving preference.

You will have only one preference for each step in the decision-making process. My decision-making preferences happen to be intuition (N), thinking (T), and judging (J; as reflected by my life code: **INTJD**). In other words, I only match up with one preference type for each of the decision-making steps: intuition for step 1, thinking for step 2, and perceiving for step 3. Similarly, you will only match up with one preference type for each of the steps in the decision-making process.

Each of the decision-making preferences has a corresponding decision-making behavior that is supportive of that preference. For example, if you are a sensor, the decision-making behavior that will be *supportive* of that preference is to gather sensory information before making decisions. Being a sensor, though, doesn't mean that you will only collect sensory information. You could also choose to engage in intuitive information-gathering behavior, which is unsupportive of

71

your particular information-gathering preference. In other words, like your other preferences, your decision-making preferences may be unintentionally masked. If you want to move forward in life, you will want to make sure that your decision-making behaviors match up with your decision-making preferences rather than mask them.

```
Decision-Making Preference
+
In-Sync Decision-Making Behavior
=
Good Decisions.
```

I show the decision-making preferences for each step of the decision-making process in table 4.1, along with the decision-making behaviors supportive of each of those preferences. As you progress through this and the next two chapters, you will discover your decision-making preference for each step of the decision-making process and you will also develop insight into whether your decision-making behaviors are in-sync with those preferences.

Table 4.1: Decision-Making Preferences and Behaviors

Step	Aspect	Decision-Making Preferences		Decision-Making Behaviors
1. **Gathering**	*Information type*	Sensing	→	Detailed
		Intuiting	→	Instinctual
2. **Evaluating**	*Evaluation method*	Thinking	→	Logic-based
		Feeling	→	Value-based
3. **Deciding**	*Decision drive*	Judging	→	Closed
		Perceiving	→	Open

So for step 1 of decision-making, you will either have a preference for sensing or intuiting; for step 2 you will have a preference for either thinking or feeling, and for step 3 you will have a preference for either judging or perceiving. If your decision-making behaviors support your decision-making preferences, they will match up with the behavior to the right of your preference in the right-most column of table 4.1. We'll talk about the decision-making behaviors later in the chapter. For now, let's finish examining table 4.1.

In addition to listing the different decision-making preferences and their supportive behaviors, table 4.1 also includes a column labeled "Aspect." This column is there to remind us that each of the different steps of the decision-making process is associated with a different aspect of decision-making.

Information type is the aspect of decision-making that indicates what kind of information you prefer to use to make decisions: sensory (or what I also call *detailed*) information versus intuitive (or what I also call *instinctual*) information. When you align the type of information that you use with your information-gathering preference, you will make better decisions.

Evaluation method is the aspect of decision-making that indicates how you prefer to *evaluate* the information that you have gathered to reach a decision. Those with a preference for *thinking* are best at evaluating information using a logic model, while those with a preference for *feeling* are best at evaluating information using a values approach. When you get comfortable using the evaluation method that is aligned with your preference, you will feel more confident about the quality of your decisions.

Decision drive is the aspect of decision-making that indicates whether or not you like to make decisions. Those with a preference for *judging* have a drive toward achieving finality in their decision-making, while those with a preference for *perceiving* have a drive toward maintaining openness in their decision-making for as long as possible. When you accept the decision drive that is aligned with your preference, you will have a higher degree of confidence in the decisions that you make as well as in the time it takes you to make those decisions (for example, judgers tend to make decisions faster and perceivers tend to take longer to make decisions).

I have devoted the rest of this chapter to step 1 of the decision-making process—gathering information—so you can determine which preference you have for this step of the process and make sure your information-gathering behavior supports your information-gathering preference. We will examine your preferences for step 2 (evaluating information) of the decision-making process in chapter 5, and we will examine your step 3 decision-making preference (decision drive) in chapter 6.

Information-Gathering Preferences:
You Say "Tomato," I Say "Solanum Lycopersicum"*

As a quick review, the first step of the decision-making process is gathering information. There are two kinds of information that you can gather when making a decision— sensory or intuitive. If you have a preference for sensing, you will feel most comfortable and will make your best decisions when you gather sensory (also known as detailed) information. If you have a preference for intuiting, you will feel most comfortable and make your best decisions when you gather intuitive (also known as instinctual) information. Let's look first at the two different information types—sensory and intuitive—and then we will talk more about what the sensing and intuitive preferences look like themselves.

* *Solanum lycopersicum* is Latin for tomato.

Information Types

Information can typically be classified into two categories: sensory and intuitive. Each preference type will feel most comfortable predominantly making decisions on the basis of one of these information types.

Sensory information. Sensory information is the kind of information that can be gathered by using one of the five senses (seeing, hearing, smelling, tasting, and touching). As such, sensory information can be measured and described, which makes it the kind of information that is easy to accept as well as to explain to others. The sensory information used most often when making decisions is the kind gathered through the first two senses: sight (what you can visually observe in the world around you) and sound (what you learn by listening to your environment, including the people in it).

Intuitive information. Intuitive information is information that is perceived through one's intuition or "gut," rather than through the five senses. As such, intuitive information is perceivable, but not quantifiable. It's like a breeze blowing through the air—you can see its effects, so you know it's real, but it's hard to describe and you can't actually see it itself. Because intuitive information is not measurable or concrete, it can be hard to explain. Also, because it can't be described in sensory terms, sometimes people mistrust it.

For more on the differences between sensory and intuitive information, see Table 4.2.

Table 4.2: A Comparison of Sensory and Intuitive Information

Sensory Information	Intuitive Information
Describable: I can see, smell, touch, hear, or taste it.	**Perceivable**: I can't describe it, but it is actual.
Quantifiable: I can measure it.	**Qualifiable**: I can determine its value or whether it's good or bad.
Responsive: It comes as an answer to a specific question: *It costs $30. She arrives at 10 PM. The job pays $75,000.*	**Actionable**: It comes as an action to take: *Move now! Don't buy that! He's a good guy. Avoid her!*

Sensory Information	Intuitive Information
Descriptive: It answers the following questions: Who? What? Where? When?	**Predictive**: It comes as an answer to the questions of why and how?—oftentimes before the question has been formulated.
Present or historic: It is happening now or has happened in the past.	**Historic or futuristic**: It has happened before or it could conceivably happen in the future.

In summary, sensory information provides specific answers to specific questions. These answers can be backed up with tangible evidence. Should I accept this job? No, because the pay is too low. Should I go to the beach today? No, because I have two hours of work to get done before Monday. Intuitive information, on the other hand, informs people of the actions they should take on the basis of their instincts and intuitions. So it can be hard to back up one's answer because there is no tangible evidence to support it. For example, an instinctual decision-maker might say, I'm not going to accept this job—I can't give you hard evidence of why, but it just doesn't feel like the right fit for me. OR, it's a lousy day for me to go to the beach. I can't tell you why; it just is.

Information-Gathering Preference

As with our other preferences, we are born with preferences for gathering one information type over another. Just as we can't change our eye colors, we can't change our information-gathering preferences (although we may be *unaware* of our preferences or we may mask them).

As we have seen, you will have either the sensing or the intuitive preference for information-gathering. Those with a preference for sensing are most comfortable gathering sensory information to make decisions, while those with a preference for intuiting feel most comfortable when they gather intuitive information to make their decisions.

Does this mean that everyone with a preference for sensing

is actually using only sensory information to make all of their decisions and that all those with a preference for intuiting are always relying only on instinctual information to make decisions? Not at all.

As we have discussed throughout the book so far, there will be times in every person's life when he or she will need to act outside of his or her preferences. Information gathering is no different. There will be times when people with a preference for sensing will need to gather intuitive information and those with a preference for intuiting will need to gather sensory information. What's important is knowing your preference and determining when it will be most helpful to you to act in-sync with that preference and when it will be most helpful to mask it. You will gain this knowledge as the chapter progresses.

But first, to help you understand the difference between those with a preference for sensing versus those with a preference for intuiting, I'm going to give you a visual example of the difference between each preference type: when I'm teaching a class on preference types, I often raise a Sharpie marker and ask the audience to describe it. Those with a preference for sensing answer very differently than those with a preference for intuiting.

The sensors typically yell out words that describe the appearance of the pen:

"It's 6 inches tall."
"It has a black, circular cap."
"It has a white cylindrical body with black writing on it."

The intuiters usually just say something like the following:

"It's a pen."
"It's a marker."
"It's a Sharpie."

In other words, the sensors list the sensory details that

they observe about the pen—its size, shape, and color—while the intuiters are looking at the bigger picture—they see the writing instrument as a whole and describe its purpose.

> Those with a preference for *sensing* are most comfortable gathering tangible, factual (sensory) information to make decisions, while those with a preference for *intuiting* feel most comfortable when they gather intangible, instinctual (intuitive) information to make their decisions.

Put another way, sensors tend to process information in terms of an object's (or person's) *material essence*, while intuiters often process information in terms of an object's (or person's) *conceptual use*.

For example, my wife has a preference for sensing and when she is getting ready to buy a new car, she looks at the tangible aspects of the cars she's considering: color, size, cost, potential expenses. Conversely, as an intuiter, I tend to look at cars in terms of what they will give me: comfort, prestige, durability, power, or speed. Here's how my wife versus my own information-gathering process would look when we are considering buying a black, Dodge, Durango, with a 5.6 L Hemi engine.

Pam, a sensor, gathers sensory information:

- Black color = Shows dirt easily. Will need to be washed more often.
- 5.6L Hemi Engine = Definitely less miles/gallon than the 4.8L standard engine. Will cost more to drive.
- Dodge reputation = Quality cars. Should cost less to maintain and service.
- Large size = Good for growing boys. Good for seeing over other cars. Will cost more to clean. Will it fit in the garage?

Paul, an intuiter, gathers intuitive information:

- Black Color + Hemi + Dodge Reputation + Large Size = Very Cool Truck! Powerful! Fast!

In this example, my wife, a sensor, is gathering sensory information about the vehicle that we are interested in, while I, as an intuiter, am focusing on the intuitive impressions having such a vehicle will make on myself and others. My wife and I may or may not come to a similar decision about whether to buy the Dodge Durango, but the information we'll use to come to our decision will definitely be different.

Determining Your Information-Gathering Preference

Perhaps you are already developing an idea of whether you have a preference for sensing versus intuition. To gain an even better understanding of your information-gathering preference, take a look at Table 4.3, which provides a side-by-side comparison of how sensors versus intuiters like to gather information when making decisions.

Table 4.3: How Sensors vs. Intuiters Gather Information

Preference for Sensing	Preference for Intuiting
Take in information through five senses: see, hear, touch, taste, smell	Take in information through sixth sense: intuition
Pay attention to what they are experiencing at the moment	Make future and past connections and associations with present experiences
Gather information in a linear fashion	Gather information in leaps
Prefer tangible proof	Accept theories
Comfortable with the familiar	Drawn to the new and different
Interested in practical information	Interested in theoretical information

Another way to get a sense of your preference is to look at

Table 4.4, which shows the pitfalls that sensors versus intuiters sometimes encounter. You may recognize yourself as being prone to the pitfalls on one side or other of the table, which is another way to identify your preference for information-gathering.

Table 4.4: Potential Pitfalls for Sensors vs. Intuiters

Pitfalls for Sensors	Pitfalls for Intuiters
You always insist on getting explanations for everything, which makes it hard for you to take advantage of the unexplainable.	You don't explain any of your reasons for the decisions you make, causing people to mistrust you.
You don't place too much value on the imagination, which causes you to be less creative than you could be.	You place too much emphasis on the creative aspects of life, causing you to add little practical value to projects.
You spend so much time focused on the details that you miss important strategic implications.	You spend so much time developing grand strategies that none of your ideas ever get implemented.
You get so locked into how things used to be that you find it hard to accept new ideas.	You are always proposing so many new ideas that people feel you don't value their past contributions.

Which pitfalls do you tend to gravitate toward? The answer to this question will not only help you determine your information-gathering preference; it will also point to the blind spots of your preference. Being more mindful of these blind spots will help you achieve more of your goals and lead a more meaningful and fulfilling life.

Unlike the fairly straightforward reenergizing preference of extroversion versus introversion, the sensing–intuiting preference can be a difficult one for people to decipher for themselves. As a result, you may want to take a personality assessment, such as the Majors PTI (or another personality assessment) to help you determine whether you're a sensor or an intuiter.* Alternately, you can continue to decipher your information-gathering preference on your own, but if you choose this method, you will probably need to take plenty of time to make your discovery and will want to pay careful attention to distinguish whether you are masking your information-gathering preference.

If you take this latter approach, in the coming week or month, pay attention to several of the decisions that you make and take note of the kind of behavior that you use to make your decisions: sensory or intuitive. For example, when you decide which movie to see, do you research the reviewers' ratings (sensing behavior) or do you go with your gut (intuitive behavior). When you choose your next vacation, do you break out the guide books and use sensory information to help you make your decision (sensing behavior) or do you pick a place that strikes your fancy (intuitive behavior)? When you decide whether to hire a service provider, do you evaluate the stats on a person (credentials, references, past experiences), a sensing behavior, or do you go with your sense of whether the person seems trustworthy and good at what they do after interviewing the person (intuitive behavior)? In other words, are your information-gathering behaviors predominantly sensory or intuitive? Another option in this self-assessment process is to look back over the *previous* week or month and reflect on whether you used sensory or intuitive information to make your decisions.

Of course, the previous exercise assumes that your information-gathering *behavior* is in-sync with your information-gathering *preference*. If it is not, looking at these behaviors won't be very helpful to you in determining your particular information-gathering preference. To address this possibility, the following section will help you sort out whether your information-gathering behavior masks your information-gathering preference. If it does, you will learn some techniques for determining your particular information-gathering preference in spite of this masking.

* *You may take an online personality assessment to determine whether*

81

you have a preference for sensing or intuiting by visiting this link: http://
www.lifechangingcoaching.com/assessments.htm

Is Your Personality Masked?

Do you remember the earlier example of Jennifer? If you recall from her story, a person's decision-making behavior will not necessarily be supportive of his or her decision-making preference. In other words, decision-making behavior can mask a person's decision-making preference. In Jennifer's case, she had a preference for using intuitive information to make decisions, but she masked this preference and collected sensory information instead because her parents (her belongings) had encouraged her throughout her growing-up years to rely on sensory data to make decisions and she thought this was the "right" way to make her decisions. Similar to Jennifer, it's possible that you are unintentionally masking your information-gathering preference because you are trying to behave in the "right" way.

Before we look at out-of-sync information-gathering behaviors, let's review what the in-sync information-gathering behaviors are. If you refer back to Table 4.1, you will see the in-sync decision-making behavior for each decision-making preference, as indicated by the right-most set of arrows. In the case of information-gathering, the matchup is as follows:

- sensing preference → detailed behavior
- intuiting preference → instinctual behavior.

In other words, if you have a sensing preference and it is not masked, you will tend to gather sensory information to help you make a decision. If you have an intuitive preference and it is not masked, you will go ahead and gather information for a decision using your intuition. In contrast, if you have a masked preference for intuition like Jennifer, you will actually use sensing behavior to make your decisions; if you have a masked preference for sensing, you will use intuitive behavior to make your decisions.

The big question is...how do you know whether your

preference is being masked? I recommend that you use the following test: if you are comfortable and confident with the information you are using to make your decisions, your information-gathering preference is probably not masked; if you feel uncomfortable or less confident with the kind of information you use to make your decisions, your information-gathering preference may be masked. Exercise 4.1 is based on this test and can help you assess whether your information-gathering behavior is masking your information-gathering preference.

Exercise 4.1: Is Your Information-Gathering Preference Masked?

Instructions: Work your way from left to right in Table 4.5 to discover whether your information-gathering preference is masked. Specifically, look at column 1 and select which behavior-type describes what you do most often: information-gathering behavior #1 or information-gathering behavior #2. Then look at the options in column 2, either (a) and (b), for that particular preference. For whichever option you select, look to the right of that option in column 3 for information as to whether or not your preference is being masked by your behavior.

Table 4.5: Masked Status Exercise

Column 1	Column 2	Column 3
Information-Gathering Behavior	**How I View My Information-Gathering Behavior**	**Masked Status**
(1) I tend to use sensory information to make my decisions.	(a) I like gathering sensory information and feel reassured when I use it to make my decisions. I have a high degree of confidence in the decisions that I make when I use sensory information.	True self
	(b) I use sensory information to make my decisions, but I have to force myself to gather it. I don't have a high degree of confidence in the decisions I make using sensory information.	Masked

Column 1	Column 2	Column 3
Information-Gathering Behavior	How I View My Information-Gathering Behavior	Masked Status
(2) I tend to use intuitive information to make my decisions.	(a) I am very comfortable going with my instincts or using my insight to make decisions. I have a high degree of confidence in the decisions I make even though I can't always explain why I reached a particular conclusion.	True self
	(b) I am not comfortable relying on my instincts or "gut" when making decisions. I would have a higher degree of confidence in my decisions if I had a few more details.	Masked

If Jennifer completed Exercise 4.1, she would select option (1b) since she only uses sensory information because she thinks she "should," not because it reassures her. This is a sign that Jennifer's information-gathering preference is masked and her behavior is out-of-sync with her preference. As a result, Jennifer finds the decision-making process stressful and, a lot of the time, she tends to make poor decisions.

Many of us are like Jennifer when it comes to our information-gathering behaviors and preferences being out-of-sync or masked. As children, most of us learn from our belongings (parents or caregivers) which information-gathering behavior we should use. This is fine if the *behavior* that our belongings teach us matches our *preference*. When this occurs, our identity supports our personality and we will tend to make better decisions. But, in a lot of cases, our belongings' preferences are different than our own, which means that our belongings probably use different decision-making behaviors than we should. And because we want to please our belongings, we often adopt their style of behavior, which conflicts with our preferences.

Like Jennifer, instead of listening to the recommendations

of our preferences, we listen to the recommendations of our belongings, and this causes our personalities to become unintentionally masked. When this occurs, we will tend to make poorer decisions because we are not gathering the type of information that we naturally need to begin the decision-making process.

> *Note*: If you have a preference for intuiting, you may feel particular pressure to adopt the opposite decision-making behavior: sensory (that is, detailed). This is because the majority of people in the world have a preference for sensing. In other words, those with a preference for intuiting are more likely to have a different decision-making preference than most of the people around them (unless they happen to be in an intuiter support group)! Interestingly, K-12 schools teach detailed information-gathering behavior because the majority of K-12 teachers have clear preferences for sensing. So intuiters may need to make special efforts to stay true to their preference for information gathering, given the external pressures they face on a daily basis.

If you continue to have trouble discovering whether your information-gathering behavior masks your information-gathering preference, look at the following statements. If you identify with either of them, you may be unintentionally masking your information-gathering preference.

- You feel pressured to justify your decisions to yourself or others by citing supportive facts when it's really just your instincts telling you that your decisions are right (masked intuiter).
- You feel like you are guessing rather than actually having tangible data to work from when making decisions (masked sensor).

After you complete Exercise 4.1 and examine the preceding bullet points, do you have a sense of whether your information-gathering preference is masked? If not, give yourself some time to figure out the answer to this question. Start paying more attention to the kind of information you use to make decisions and spend some time assessing whether this information is useful to you.

If you realize that you are behaving in-sync with your preference, congratulations! You are on your way to making good decisions that will help achieve your goals and bring you meaning and fulfillment in life. From time to time, you will want to check back in to make sure that you are staying in-sync.

If you are out-of-sync and your information-gathering behavior and preference are not aligned, don't worry; there are some things that you can do to get in-sync and gather the type of information that you need to make better decisions.

Developing an In-Sync Identity

So far in this chapter, we've focused on only one of the three identity Bs—behaviors—and the importance of aligning your information-gathering behavior with your information-gathering preference. In reality, you will benefit from aligning not just your behaviors with your information-gathering preference but your belongings and beliefs as well. If you discovered in the previous section that your information-gathering preference is masked, you will benefit greatly from the descriptions in this section, which will show you what kinds of behaviors, beliefs, and belongings will best support your particular information-gathering preference. Even if you don't suspect that your information-gathering preference is masked, you will still benefit from learning more about the identity Bs that help you function best in life.

Let's look, then, at the kind of behaviors, beliefs, and belongings that support a sensor versus the belongings, beliefs, and behaviors that support an intuiter.

What Sensors Need

Behaviors. When it comes to making decisions, sensors will do best collecting concrete, tangible, or measurable information to inform their decisions. Beyond decision-

86

making, sensors need to be involved in activities that allow them to interact with their world using their five senses.

Beliefs. Sensors value practicality and place a premium on what is actual: things that can be seen, measured, and explained. As a result, when sensors make decisions, they value tangible information as the major source for their decisions. Sensors are fine with information that comes from either the present or the past, as long as that information is real rather than conceptual. Sensors may discount the value of their own or others' intuitive feelings, since these cannot be measured or proven.

Belongings. Sensors benefit from belonging to communities that will support their preference for gathering sensory or concrete information. They tend to enjoy groups that allow them to physically interact in some way with the world around them (for example, gardening clubs, sports teams, and neighborhood clean-ups).

What Intuiters Need

Behaviors. When it comes to making decisions, intuiters will do best using their gut instincts to guide them. Instead of focusing only on sensory information (data, statistics, pros, and cons), intuiters will benefit from focusing on their internal insights. Beyond decision-making, intuiters need to be involved in activities that allow them to interact with their world using their sixth sense. Intuiters prefer gathering and interrelating with intangible information like concepts and ideas.

Beliefs. Intuiters value what is possible and thus prize the new or unimagined. Similarly, intuiters place a premium on the future and creating what does not yet exist. When it comes to making decisions, intuiters feel it is important to listen to the voice in their heads or the feeling in their stomachs. That voice or feeling gives them insight into the decision that is right for them: Go for it! Call her. End this relationship!

Belongings. Intuiters enjoy belonging to communities that discuss concepts and ideas (for example, research institutes, university-level academic forums, and science fiction or fantasy clubs). They tend to benefit from groups that allow them to use their insight and imagine a world that could be.

Now that you see the kind of behaviors, beliefs, and belongings that work well for your particular information-gathering preference type, you have a formula for how you can start to live more in-sync with your information-gathering preference. I recommend that one by one over the coming weeks you begin to reshape your belongings, beliefs, and behaviors so they are more in-sync with your particular information-gathering preference. For example, try to join a group that supports your preference, or practice making some of your decisions using the right kind of information for you. Take a look at Table 4.6 for some activities related to each of the information-gathering preferences and think about how you might bring more of the activities related to your preference type into your own life.

Table 4.6: Sensor vs. Intuiter Activities

Sensor Activities	Intuiter Activities
Participate in activities that engage your five senses: sports, gardening, martial arts, cooking.	Participate in activities that engage your imagination: reading, writing, debating, designing.
Study history, economics, finance, chemistry, biology, or any of the more factual disciplines.	Study psychology, mathematics, humanities, creative writing, or any of the more theoretical disciplines.
Read books on how to build something or how to fix something.	Read books about the future or fantasy stories.

These are just some of the examples of activities that you might enjoy as a sensor or an intuiter. If none of these activities match up with your interests, take out a piece of paper and brainstorm on other behaviors or belongings that might support your particular information-gathering preference and think about how you can work one or more of these new behaviors or belongings into your life.

If you find yourself struggling to unmask your personality preference for information-gathering, you may want to take some time to practice accepting your preference type. As mentioned in the previous chapter, one way to do this is by replacing self-critical thoughts with self-supportive ones. For example, if you are a sensor and you tend to think things like, "I am so unimaginative," you can practice replacing this thought with something like, "As I sensor, I am at my best when dealing with things I can see and touch. My ability to ground projects in reality is a strength."

Acceptance also often comes with understanding, and you can gain a better understanding of each preference type, including your own, in the following section on getting along with the opposite information-gathering type. Although this section focuses on getting along with *others*, it can also be very helpful in learning to understand and accept your *own* information-gathering preference.

Getting Along With the
Opposite Information-Gathering Type

Now that you have insight into what you can do to live more in-sync, let's spend some time reflecting on the people in your life who have an information-gathering preference that is opposite of yours. Perhaps you've already begun to think of these people as you've been learning more about each of the preference types in this chapter: parents, friends, significant others, coworkers? As we did in the previous chapter, let's look at some of the negative labels we may project onto the opposite information-gathering preference type.

The Negative Labels We Apply to Sensors and Intuiters

If you are a sensor interacting, working, befriending, dating, or living with an intuiter, you might at times see the intuiter as follows:

- out of touch with reality
- hiding something
- not detail-oriented enough.

If you are an intuiter interacting working, befriending, dating, or living with a sensor, you might at times see the sensor as follows:

- unimaginative, uncreative
- mistrusting of you
- too mired in the details.

As you reflect on the different people in your life, do any of these labels sound familiar? Do you find yourself frustrated by people for any of the preceding reasons? If so, you may be experiencing friction because you value a different kind of information than the people who frustrate you. Let's peel back these negative labels so we can understand more what's going on with the opposite information-gathering preference type.

What's Really Going on With Sensors?

Unimaginative, uncreative. Sensors tend to tie everything back to concrete data, and this may make you feel like they are limiting your ability to dream up new ideas that can't be supported by concrete evidence. But remember, once you learn to get along with sensors, they can be a great balance to you or your team, helping you turn your ideas into a reality by grounding them in the practical.

Mistrusting of you. Because sensors feel most comfortable proceeding based on detailed, sensory information, they will spend a lot of time picking your brain to gather this kind of information. You may feel like this means that sensors don't trust you, when in reality, they are just trying to gain the information they need to make good decisions.

Too mired in the details. Because sensors value detailed

information, they will probably want to share with you all of the concrete information they collect when it comes time to make a decision. This may feel like information overload for you, but try to remember that it helps sensors be better decision makers to sort through this kind of information. You don't need to process all of this information yourself, but try to be respectful of sensors' approach.

What's Really Going on With Intuiters?

Out of touch with reality. Intuiters use their imaginations to come up with novel ideas and they are not bound by the conventions of reality. Although this means that intuiters will risk coming up with harebrained schemes at times, it also gives them the freedom to invent new ways of doing things and creative ways of solving problems, something that will help you and your team overcome challenges and adopt powerful new strategies.

Hiding something. Because intuiters don't need sensory information to make their decisions, they probably won't realize that you need this kind of information to make your decisions. If intuiters don't offer up sensory information, try to remember that they probably aren't hiding anything; they just don't realize that you need this information to make a good decision.

Not detail-oriented enough. You may feel frustrated when intuiters seem to provide you with only big-picture information when you need the tangible facts to assess a situation. Try to remember that intuiters can be a valuable part of your team because they can help you be more creative about solving challenging problems and expanding into new territories. Also, if you need to, you can encourage the intuiter to provide you with more of the information you need, but be willing to explain how this is helpful to you so the intuiter doesn't think you don't trust him or her.

The goal as I see it is not for us all to have the same

information-gathering type; it is for each of us to behave in-sync with our own preference types so we can together generate a complete information picture. In fact, things work quite well when people of both types interact together in a work environment, relationship, or community, because small details plus a big-scale view provide the whole information picture.

In other words,

$$\text{Sensory Information} + \text{Intuitive Information}$$
$$=$$
$$\text{Complete Information Picture.}$$

The previous equation underscores the value of each preference type when it comes to gathering information. Although it helps at times to be able to intentionally mask your information-gathering preference, much of the time your natural personality preference will be an asset to your life and your environment.

Putting Your Best Foot Forward With the Opposite Information-Gathering Type

If you want to benefit fully from your relationships with those who have a different information-gathering preference than you do, here are a few suggestions.

Sensors...

- Avoid demanding that intuiters provide you with facts and details for all of the decisions that they make; these details may have been processed at a subconscious level, but the intuiter often does not need to be conscious of all the facts and details to make a sound decision.
- Don't instantly dismiss an intuiter's idea as impractical; you can work out the details later, but at first the intuiter needs breathing room to brainstorm and invent.
- Learn to value the intuiter's sixth sense, even if

you don't understand it.

Intuiters...

- Provide sensors with the details and facts they need to make their decisions.
- Don't discount the importance of past or present information.
- Ask sensors to provide you with concrete feedback as to the practicality of your ideas and theories; they will appreciate the opportunity to share their thoughts with you and you will probably benefit from their feedback in the process.

These suggestions probably won't require you to make any radical changes to how you normally act, but they will net you great gains in terms of improving your relationships with those whose preference is different than yours. Give these suggestions a try and watch how your relationships improve.

Intentionally Masking Your Information-Gathering Preference

Some of the simple adjustments recommended for sensors and intuiters in the previous section involved masking one's information-gathering preference. This is because as much as embracing your preference through your behaviors, beliefs, and belongings can support you, there will be some times, as we discussed in chapter 2, that intentionally masking your preferences will help you avoid potential pitfalls and achieve your life goals.

To review, intentional masking of your personality preference involves adopting behaviors associated with the opposite preference type. The times that you might want to intentionally mask your information-gathering preference include the following instances:

1. when you want to achieve a specific goal
2. when you want to be considerate of another person's needs
3. when you want to grow as a person.

Here's an example of an adjustment I made in my own intuitive behavior to achieve a specific goal at work—convince my boss I was contributing to the organization—and the benefits that resulted.

One day at my former job, during my regular update meeting with my boss, he asked me, "How is your division?" "Great," I said simply. But my boss wasn't satisfied with this answer, and he proceeded to grill me for the next hour, asking me about specific aspects of my division. Because I didn't initially provide facts and details to my boss, he started to wonder if I was hiding something from him (when in truth, it just isn't my natural tendency to communicate sensory information). In turn, I started to get the feeling that my boss didn't trust me. As he continued to pepper me with questions, I became more reluctant to provide answers.

Then, suddenly, a light went on: I realized that my boss had a preference for sensory information-gathering, in contrast to my intuitive information-gathering preference. It wasn't that my boss didn't trust me so much as that he needed sensory information, not the big-picture intuitive information that I was giving him, to make his decisions.

In response, for our next meeting I created a 15-page report with a list of my division's current projects and initiatives. My boss responded wonderfully to the sensory information. As a result, our meeting was done in 15 minutes. My boss now had the sensory information he needed to make his decisions regarding my division and could see how I and my team were contributing to the organization.

What happened here exactly? I intentionally masked my personality by adjusting my information-gathering behavior to match my boss's so that he would have the information he needed to make good decisions. I did not have to compromise myself in the process, as it was my boss here who was making decisions, not me. If my boss needed sensory information to make his decisions, there was no reason I couldn't provide that to him. I simply had to shift gears and take some time to formally prepare for our meetings, being sure to rely on a sensory format. And in the process, I strengthened my relationship with my boss. He felt he could trust me and was able to assess the true value I was bringing to the organization. Without sensory information, he would have had difficulty making this assessment. Similarly, there will be times in your life when you will want to adjust your information-gathering behavior to match another person's information-gathering preference, to achieve a specific goal or be considerate of that person's needs.

As you can see from the previous example of how I adjusted my intuitive behavior to improve my interactions with my sensing boss, there will be times when it will be helpful to your relationships to intentionally mask your information-gathering preference. You wouldn't want to be in a relationship with someone where you had to mask your preference all of the time, because that would be uncomfortable and unsustainable, but in the right situations and for short periods of time, intentional personality masking can be very useful. Not only can intentional masking of your personality preferences be helpful to your relationships, intentional preference masking can also help you achieve your personal and professional goals.

Conclusion

As you begin to align your information-gathering *behavior* with your information-gathering *preference*, you will discover some wonderful benefits. You will find that it is much easier for you to make decisions. When you begin to gather the type of information that comes naturally to you, decision-making will be less stressful for you. Not only will it be easier for you to make decisions, but the quality of your decisions will improve. Because you will be gathering the type of information that you are naturally suited for, you will be able to make better decisions and you will have the information you need to move you successfully through the next two steps of the decision-making process.

5

How Do You Evaluate Information?

Now that you have a better sense of your information-gathering preference—sensory or intuitive—it's time to focus on the second step of the decision-making process—evaluating that information.

As we learned in the previous chapter, although it seems that when we make decisions there is only one step involved—making the decision—it is helpful to think of decision-making as a three-step process. That is, we...

- gather the information needed to make the decision
- evaluate the information
- make the decision.

Your preference for sensing or intuiting will guide step 1 of the decision-making process (as discussed in chapter 4). What will guide step 2 of the process is whether you have a preference for thinking versus feeling, what's called your information-evaluating preference. Of course, how you gather information (step 1) has some influence on how you evaluate it (step 2) as well as how you make a final decision (step 3). We will discuss the way each of the decision-making preferences affects each other in chapter 6, but for now, let's spend some time exploring how you evaluate information (by thinking vs. feeling) and what it means to have a preference for thinking or feeling.

Some Use Their Heads, Some Use Their Hearts

All of us have thoughts and all of us have feelings, but some of us are most comfortable evaluating information based on impersonal principles (the thinking preference), while others of us are most comfortable evaluating information based on personal values (the feeling preference).

It's important to define what I mean by *thinking* and *feeling*. You probably already have some sense of what these terms mean since you've heard them many times before in other contexts in your life. Some of the associations you already have with these terms will apply to the present discussion on preferences and decision-making, while others may not. Read on to learn more about what it means to have a preference for thinking versus feeling.

Thinkers

Do you remember the original Star Trek series? Mr. Spock, played by Leonard Nimoy, was a great example of a person with the thinking preference. If you ever saw him on the screen, he appeared to be emotionless and almost robotic when it came to decision-making. As his character developed through the subsequent episodes and movies, we discovered that Mr. Spock did have some very powerful emotions, but he didn't let them influence his decisions, good or bad.

Like Mr. Spock, thinkers tend to give weight to objective facts and principles (as opposed to values) when making decisions. Thinkers focus less on the people involved in a situation when making a decision and more on the facts of the situation as well as the principles they see as being relevant to the case. In other words, thinkers depersonalize the situation in their minds. This often leads them to act in ways that make the people involved feel like they are being analyzed and dissected, while the personal parts of them are being ignored. This can give the appearance that thinkers are cold or unempathetic, when in actuality they are just trying to fairly and impartially evaluate the different situations they find themselves in. This impartiality often makes thinkers good referees or judges. You can count on them to give an unbiased opinion about the subject that they are asked to analyze.

Thinkers are generally better at confronting others regarding their misbehaviors than feelers. If done diplomatically, this can be helpful in both professional and personal life. If done without care, it can cause relationship problems.

Feelers

Have you ever heard someone say, "That person's thinking with her heart"? This statement points to the 60% of us who make our decisions based on our feelings. Interestingly, when people say someone is thinking with his or her heart, it tends to have a negative connotation, as if to say that the person who's using his or her heart to make a decision is making a big mistake. But for the 60% of us who have a preference for feeling, making decisions with our "hearts" is often what works best for us.

Feelers tend to give weight to values, subjective concerns, and personal considerations. They focus less on the objective facts involved in a situation and more on subjective issues such as personality traits, background, and circumstances. Because feelers consider the personal aspects involved in a situation, they portray warmth to those involved and may advocate for compassion or mercy. Feelers are generally better at maintaining relationships and encouraging social harmony than thinkers.

Feelers' focus on the personal makes it hard for them to confront others regarding their behavior. This can be limiting at those times that feelers need to address a problematic behavioral issue in their interpersonal relationships or with their work colleagues. On the positive side, feelers' focus on the personal usually allows them to promote harmony at home and at work.

Determining Your Information-Evaluating Preference

When I work with clients and groups to help them determine whether they have a preference for thinking or feeling, I ask them to imagine that they are a member of a jury and tell them to write down a list of the information they need to assess the defendant's innocence.

Thinkers will typically indicate that all that they need to hear are the facts of the case, including the content of the law and whether or not the defendant broke the law. Thinkers are not interested in extenuating circumstances or why the defendant broke the law. For the thinker, the only way that the charged person can be found innocent is if he or she did not commit the crime.

In contrast, feelers indicate that in addition to the facts, they need to hear the defendant's background, history, and personal story. Feelers want to hear the defendant speak so they can tell whether or not the person is being sincere or whether the person is showing remorse. Feelers want to know why the person committed the crime and what drove him or her to break the law. Feelers take all of this information into consideration when deciding whether to charge the defendant with guilt. In other words, even if a feeler believes that a defendant committed a crime, the feeler may believe that because of extenuating circumstances (for example, poor education, no parental influence, substance abuse history, etc.) the defendant does not merit a verdict of guilty.

Table 5.1 depicts some of the key differences between thinkers and feelers. Take some time to identify which side of the table most represents the way in which you typically evaluate information.

Table 5.1: How Thinkers vs. Feelers Evaluate Information

Preference for Thinking	Preference for Feeling
Logic rules	Concern for others rules
Appreciate competence	Prize relationships
Objectify or depersonalize decisions	Subjectify or personalize decisions
Decide with their heads	Decide with their hearts
Tackle unpleasant subjects head on	Avoid unpleasant subjects
Value directness	Value tact
Advocate justice	Advocate mercy
Promote truth	Promote harmony
Cite the facts	Cite extenuating circumstances
Appear insensitive	Appear emotional
Are good at critiquing	Are good at appreciating

Preference for Thinking	Preference for Feeling
Usually don't take things personally	Usually take things personally

Which side of the table do you relate to more—thinking or feeling?

> *Thinkers* tend to give weight to objective facts and principles when making decisions, while *feelers* give weight to values, subjective concerns, and personal considerations.

If you are having trouble figuring out whether you are a thinker or a feeler, look at the two sample dialogues that follow for more information. The first dialogue represents how a thinker might have a conversation with someone when making a decision regarding a possible disciplinary action against him or her. The second dialogue represents the conversation a feeler might have in the same situation.

Thinker: *Did you do X?*
Defendant: *Yes.*
Thinker: *That's against company rules. You are suspended from work without pay for a week, per company policy.*
Defendant: *But there was a good reason for me to do X.*
Thinker: *I am sure there was, but the bottom line is that you did X, right?*
Defendant: *Yes.*
Thinker: *And X is against company policy, right?*
Defendant: *Yes.*
Thinker: *So you can see why I have no choice but to suspend you, right?*
Defendant: *I guess so.*

Feeler: *Did you do X?*
Defendant: *Yes.*
Feeler: *Why did you do it?*
Defendant: *Because of Y.*
Feeler: *Well, as you know, doing X is against company policy, but I see why your circumstances made it hard for you to follow*

the rules in this case. Maybe we can make an exception here. How will you do things differently next time?

Defendant: *I will do Z.*

Feeler: *Okay, I understand why you broke company policy and I see that you plan to do things differently in the future. You've already been punished enough through the stress of your personal life and this ordeal. Let's move on from here and get back to work.*

As you can see from these two example dialogues, the thinker evaluates the information he received by comparing it to the facts and the rules. The fact is the person did X. The rules are that X isn't allowed. So the thinker applies punishment to the person for breaking the rules. The feeler, on the other hand, evaluates her information differently. She obtains the facts but then gathers more information. What were the circumstances under which the person did X? What were the reasons the person did X? Does the person show remorse for breaking the rules and have a plan for doing things differently in the future? Depending on how these questions are answered, the feeler will know whether and how to discipline the person involved.

You may have noticed that in the preceding example, a man is cast as the thinker and a woman as the feeler. Or maybe you didn't notice at all, because it seemed so natural that a man would have a thinking preference and a woman would have a feeling preference. The information-evaluating preference is a preference in which gender stereotypes often apply. That is, men (57% of them) tend to have a preference for thinking, while women (76% of them) tend to have a preference for feeling.

This being said, there are still plenty of men who have a preference for feeling and plenty of women who have a preference for thinking. You may be one of them. If you are, you may have noticed that there is a cultural bias against men having a preference for feeling and women having a preference for thinking. This is one of the cases where pressure from society or your workplace (your belongings) may cause you to unintentionally mask your actual preference (your personality) to your personal detriment.

For example, one of my students was a senior police officer for a large police agency. When I first met the man, I sensed that he had a preference for feeling. He was warm, friendly, and personable. When we came to the part of class where we sorted between thinking and feeling, he automatically went over to the thinking side of the room. During a break I shared with him my sense of his preference and asked him to process my observations and talk to me later about it.

To my surprise, he called me the next day at my office and asked if we could meet for lunch. I agreed, and at lunch he told me that for the past few years he had been depressed and unhappy with his life and he couldn't understand why. He had a great wife, had good kids, and really loved his job, but something fundamental wasn't clicking. He had even talked to a therapist but couldn't find the answer.

As he started to process the information that he had learned in class, along with my sense of his preference, he felt that he had identified a big piece of the puzzle. He talked to his wife about it and she had the same sense of his preference that I did. And then he realized that he had been masking his preference at work, especially once he started to get promoted, because he didn't think that he would be respected or taken seriously if he let his preference for feeling be known. As a result, he was pretending to be a thinker, when really he was a feeler. This was causing him to ignore all of the personal concerns at work that he normally paid attention to in all of the other areas of his life where he was making decisions—home, coaching his son's basketball team, and so on. We talked about this, and eventually he was able to embrace his preference for feeling in his workplace and became an even more effective and successful leader because of it—and his depression went away.

Table 5.2 lists some of the possible challenges of each

preference type. If you find yourself identifying with one side of the table more than the other, that may be an indication of your preference type for evaluating information.

Table 5.2: Potential Pitfalls for Thinkers vs. Feelers

Pitfalls for Thinkers	Pitfalls for Feelers
You are overly critical of others.	You don't make your feelings or needs known.
You frown or have a neutral look on your face when evaluating information, and people perceive this as you being angry with or disappointed in them.	You avoid conflicts, even when it would be appropriate to engage.
You ignore the human element of interpersonal communications.	You take personally criticism and observations about you or your work.

Which pitfalls do you tend to gravitate toward? Table 5.2 will offer you one more clue into which preference is yours—thinking or feeling.* You will also want to use this information to help you steer clear of the pitfalls associated with your preference type. Doing so will help you achieve more of your goals and lead a more satisfying life.

* *You may take an online personality assessment to determine whether you have a preference for thinking or feeling by visiting this link: http://www.lifechangingcoaching.com/assessments.htm*

Is Your Personality Masked?

Now that you've gained a word to describe the way you evaluate information—thinking or feeling—are you feeling validated? Surprised? Enlightened? Does your new understanding of the way you evaluate information when making decisions confirm that you have been living in-sync with your true self, or does it instead reveal that you've been living out-of-sync, like my client described previously, who had been trying to act like a thinker in his career as a police officer? If the latter, you will want to spend some time examining why you have chosen to mask your personality and then work toward embracing your preference in your daily life so you can reap the benefits of living in-sync with your true self.

Remember, if you find that you are living out-of-sync, this means that your decision-making *behavior* for information evaluation is in opposition to your decision-making *preference*. If you recall from Table 4.1 (in chapter 4) in the previous chapter, the decision-making behavior that works best for those with a thinking preference is logic-based, while the decision-making behavior that works best for those with a feeling preference is value-based. This is just another way of saying that if you have a preference for thinking, you will feel most comfortable making decisions using logic, while you will feel most comfortable making decisions using your personal values if you have a preference for feeling.

Let's look at some of the signs that your identity (behaviors, beliefs, and/or belongings) is (are) out-of-sync with (that is, masking) your information-evaluating preference.

- You feel pressured to base your decisions on facts and to ignore extenuating circumstances and people's feelings (masked feeler).
- You feel pressured to consider others' feelings when making a decision, but you'd feel most comfortable relying on the facts and rules of the situation for guidance (masked thinker).

Do you relate to either of the previous statements? If so, this may mean that your identity is unintentionally masking your preference for information-evaluating. Let's spend some time exploring why you might be unintentionally masking your information-evaluating preference.

Perhaps you live or work in an environment that encourages a preference type opposite of yours, so you feel pressured to behave in line with that preference. Or perhaps you simply have a false idea of others' expectations for you.

You may assume that others want you to act in-sync with the opposite preference type, when in fact, others would accept you just as you naturally are. Oftentimes, this happens when we were raised by parents or caregivers who encouraged us to behave out-of-sync with our preferences. We then project onto others the belief that they are just like our caregivers when in fact they are very different people.

Take some time to reflect on the areas (environments or people) in your life in which you feel pressured to act opposite of your natural preference. Over time, as you become more conscious of the sources of this pressure, you will be able to analyze what's really taking place and make a conscious choice to avoid giving in to that pressure. The more you give yourself permission to act in-sync with your information-evaluating preference, the more easily you will be able to make decisions and move forward in your life.

Developing an In-Sync Identity

To begin adopting an identity that is supportive of your information-evaluating preference, you will want to begin to shape your behaviors, beliefs, and belongings so they match up with the three Bs that your preference type is most comfortable with. Let's look, then, at the kind of behaviors, beliefs, and belongings that support a thinker versus a feeler.

What Thinkers Need

Behaviors. Thinkers prefer to engage in activities that allow them to analyze and evaluate situations and people. In the sports world, thinkers are often referees and analysts. In the business world, they are often accountants, project managers, and supervisors. When thinkers need to make a decision, they will feel most comfortable evaluating the objective facts of the situation.

Beliefs. The world needs to make sense to thinkers, and thinkers believe in the value of logic. Thinkers believe that objectivity is the fairest way to evaluate a person or a situation.

Belongings. Thinkers benefit from communities that allow them to analyze problems, critique events, and use their logic to achieve their ends (for example, legal associations, *empirical* research institutes, and management organizations). Thinker communities will not display much outward personal warmth, but they will have passion around their principles.

What Feelers Need

Behaviors. Feelers prefer to express their emotions and state their positive feelings toward events and people. In the sports world, feelers are often the "heart" of the team or the person on the sidelines encouraging the others on to victory. In the business world, thinkers are often counselors, teachers, and other kinds of helpers.

Beliefs. Feelers believe that people matter most of all. The world needs to "feel right" to feelers and they are most comfortable when the people around them are happy. Feelers believe fairness requires considering the whole situation, not just the facts.

Belongings. Feelers gravitate to communities that let them connect with other human beings in a sincere and intensely personal way (for example, counseling associations, *qualitative* research institutes, and human resources organizations). Feeler communities will often be involved in helping others in need or providing support to those in distress.

Now that you have an understanding of what behaviors, beliefs, and belongings are supportive of thinkers versus feelers, you can start shaping your own Bs to be in-sync with your information-evaluating preference. Take a look at Table 5.3 to get a clearer picture of some of the activities (behaviors) that you may want to start incorporating into your life depending on your preference.

Table 5.3: Thinker vs. Feeler Activities

Thinker Activities	Feeler Activities
Join a debating club or team and practice and develop your skills in arguing and defending your points of view.	Join a support group that allows you to express your feelings about issues you are struggling with.
Study law, philosophy, mathematics, or physical sciences.	Study humanities, psychology, or social sciences.
Volunteer to take on analytical assignments at work or in your other organizations.	Volunteer to take on social assignments at work or in your other organizations.

These are just some of the examples of activities that you might enjoy as a thinker or a feeler. If none of these activities match up with your interests, take out a piece of paper and brainstorm on other behaviors that might support your particular information-gathering preference and think about how you can work one or more of these new behaviors into your life.

If you find yourself struggling to unmask your personality preference for information-evaluating, you may want to take some time to practice accepting your preference type. As mentioned in the previous chapters, one way to do this is by replacing self-critical thoughts with self-supportive ones. For example, if you are a feeler and you tend to think things like, "I am such a softy when it comes to people," you can practice replacing this thought with something constructive like, "As a feeler, one of my strengths is my ability to consider other people's needs and feelings."

Acceptance also often comes with understanding, and you can gain a better understanding of each preference type, including your own, in the following section on getting along with the opposite information-evaluating type. Although this section focuses on getting along with others, it can also be very helpful in learning to understand and accept your own information-evaluating preference.

Getting Along With the
Opposite Information-Evaluating Type

It can be particularly hard to understand and get along with someone who has a preference opposite to yours on the thinking versus feeling spectrum. In fact, this is the spectrum where differences in preference tend to lead to the most divisive and lasting conflicts of all. This is the case because evaluating information is at the heart of how we make decisions. For those with a preference for feeling, disagreements tend to make them feel like they aren't being appreciated. For those with a preference for thinking, disagreements tend to make them feel like they aren't being respected. Both of these misunderstandings can lead to personal and bitter conflict. So it's important to understand that preference is not personal, it's just preference.

> For example, Jill is a feeler and her husband, Tom, is a thinker. Jill had to pick their son Andy up from school early today because he had been in a fight with another student. When Tom got home, he was furious at Andy and wanted to ground him for at least a month for fighting at school; but Jill felt that Andy shouldn't be punished. She tried to explain to Tom that she had talked to Andy and learned that he had been picked on by the kid, had gone to the teachers who did nothing, and didn't feel like he had any choice but to defend himself to stop the bullying. Tom called Jill a "softy" and said that none of that mattered. The only thing that mattered is that Andy broke the rules and needed to be punished for it. Jill told Tom to stop acting like a robot and start acting like a human being.

Let's look at this scenario from each person's perspective and see what we can learn about the difference between the preferences. Let's start with Tom. As a thinker, Tom tends to disregard the value and people concerns of feelers. Thinkers usually say that feelers are being "irrational" or acting "soft" and that feelers don't stick to the facts. This causes the feeler to feel disrespected, underappreciated, and hurt. Jill's feelings about what should happen to Andy are perfectly valid, but Tom doesn't value them.

Now, let's look at Jill. As a feeler, Jill tends to personalize the actions of thinkers, which makes Tom, a thinker, feel misunderstood, unfairly judged, and unappreciated. Feelers tend to characterize thinkers as insensitive and uncaring. Thinkers don't understand why they are perceived this way, because in most cases they are sensitive and they do care; they just don't allow their emotions "to cloud their judgment." Tom doesn't understand why Jill called him a robot because he cares about his family very deeply.

The Negative Labels We Apply to Thinkers and Feelers

Here are some of the negative judgments that we might make about the opposite preference type.

As thinkers, we may believe that feelers are…

- too emotional
- too sensitive
- pushovers.

As feelers, we may believe that thinkers are…

- cold and unfeeling
- overly critical
- overbearing in their directive behaviors.

Are these judgments accurate or inaccurate? It depends. Sometimes, a feeler or thinker *does* act too far in the extreme— and then one of his or her blind spots shows up. Maybe a thinker ends up being unfairly critical of someone or a feeler has trouble making a good decision because emotion gets in the way. But is it fair to describe all thinkers as cold or all feelers as hypersensitive? No. In truth, we may simply be perceiving the other person that way. Let's look at the case of Mary, a thinker, who was perceived as being cold.

Mary is a police officer with a preference for thinking. She is assigned to the traffic division. All day long she spends her time observing motorists and writing citations for those who break the traffic laws. She appears to be unsympathetic to all the different excuses that motorists give her to explain why they were speeding or ran the red light or didn't stop at the stop sign.

One mother (who had a preference for feeling) thought Mary was very cold when Mary stopped her for speeding. The mother explained how she was running late in picking her daughter up from school and didn't want her daughter to think that she had forgotten about her. Mary listened politely but wrote the mother a ticket anyway. The mother left the encounter feeling like Mary didn't believe her. And couldn't she lighten up a bit?

After citing the mother, Mary wrote a few more tickets for other motorists and then went to pick up her own daughter from daycare. The Mary that was with her daughter appeared to be a completely different Mary than the one who was writing tickets a few minutes ago: Mary was warm and caring and visibly excited to be with her daughter. It turns out that Mary wasn't cold and unfeeling at all; it's just that when she was at work, she did not rely on feelings to make her decisions, just facts and the law.

As you can see from this example, it's easy to draw a false conclusion about someone when you don't understand his or her preference. Let's zero in on each of the negative labels we tend to give to thinkers versus feelers and see if we can understand the motivation for why people in each type act as they do.

What's Really Going on With Feelers?

Too emotional. If you are a thinker, you may feel frustrated when feelers use their emotions to evaluate decisions, but try to remember that for feelers, their emotions are like a compass that helps them make effective decisions. By tuning into their emotions, feelers are able to tap into their capacity for empathy and work to create social harmony, something we

111

all benefit from. You may worry that feelers sacrifice fairness in their decision-making, but its important to remember that feelers want to be fair too, it's just that their understanding of fairness differs from yours.

Too sensitive. Feelers are highly attuned to their own and others' emotions. While this allows them to consider the personal when making decisions, it also means that they are more vulnerable to having their own feelings hurt. Since a top priority of feelers is to maintain social harmony, they may be offended when a thinker doesn't return the favor and consider the feeler's emotions in a situation.

Pushovers. When you see feelers deviate from following rules or abiding by logic when dealing with someone else, you may assume that feelers are doing this because they are afraid to assert themselves. And while feelers don't want to hurt other peoples' feelings, this isn't usually the main principle guiding their decision-making. Feelers honestly feel it's most fair to consider the personal components and extenuating circumstances of a situation when making a decision, so they use this philosophy to guide their decision-making.

What's Really Going on With Thinkers?

Cold and unfeeling. Because thinkers put a premium on using logic to make their decisions, this means that logic will prevail over personal considerations. It's not that thinkers don't care about people; it's just that thinkers believe that it's important to follow rules and logic to keep order in the world and be fair to others.

Overly critical. Thinkers tend to provide others with feedback because they want to be helpful and they would want someone to do the same for them. Thinkers don't usually take feedback personally and so they don't realize that they might need to make an effort to deliver feedback to others in a way that's considerate of people's feelings.

Overbearing in their directive behaviors. If you are a feeler, you may think that thinkers are being overly "pushy" when they interact with you. This is because thinkers value efficiency and have an overriding need to get tasks accomplished. This need to get things done doesn't often take other people's feeling into consideration, which is why feelers may end up feeling bossed around. Try not to take thinker's efficient approach personally, and if something bothers you, tell the thinker.

Some of the formula for getting along with those of the opposite preference is learning not to attach negative judgments to what are for them natural and effective behaviors. The other part of getting along with people of the opposite preference is recognizing that all preferences—your own included—have blind spots and that you will find more success in getting along with others if you are willing to address your own blind spots. Usually, this means learning to flex out of your preference from time to time and to borrow some behaviors from the opposite preference type.

For example, if you are a feeler, you will likely find it hard to confront others regarding their misbehaviors. This can be problematic. Not only does it handicap you from getting what you want in life, say from your significant other, or what you feel needs to be done at work, say from your colleagues or employees, but it also frustrates those around you who have thinking preferences, making it harder for you to get along with them.

Amanda, the finance manager for a group of five people, had a preference for feeling. One of her employees, Carolyn, wore jeans every day, even though this went against the company's dress policy. Carolyn's dress bothered everyone in the group, Amanda included, but as a feeler, Amanda was uncomfortable pulling Carolyn aside and communicating that she needed to dress more professionally. Amanda worried she would embarrass Carolyn by confronting her on something as personal as her dress. Plus, she knew Carolyn made a low salary, which probably made it hard for her to afford work clothes. But Amanda's inability to counsel Carolyn was frustrating the others in her group who were thinkers. They couldn't understand why Amanda wouldn't deal with the issue when company policy clearly gave her guidelines to do so. They also felt like it wasn't fair to let Carolyn wear jeans when no one else was allowed to. The thinkers in the group lost some respect for Amanda's ability to lead and took her less seriously when she delegated work to them. She sensed the difference in them but didn't understand why.

Amanda's story is a good example of a time when it would be helpful to borrow behavior from the opposite preference type. As group manager, it is Amanda's role to step in and clearly set the dress expectations for Carolyn. She doesn't have to enjoy confronting Carolyn regarding her work clothes, and she probably won't, but she does need to address the issue head on. It's only fair to Carolyn to be straight with her and it's only fair to the other employees in the group.

That's not to say that Amanda has to throw all of her feeling skills out the window. The fact that she has a preference for feeling will actually help her talk to Carolyn about the issue in a kind and diplomatic way. She will naturally be sensitive to Carolyn's feelings during the discussion, reducing the chances she will lower Carolyn's morale and positive feeling for her job. If Amanda can enhance her feeling skills with the strengths of a thinker, she will end up being a very good manager—effective in her tasks and respected by her employees.

Here are some tips on how you can improve your interactions with those of the opposite preference, which will in turn help you achieve your goals and enrich your relationships.

Thinkers…

- Listen carefully to the advice of people with a preference for feeling and take some time to process what they are telling you. Feelers will help you remember that there is more to decision-making than just gathering facts and data.

- Offer words of appreciation from time to time to those around you. When people feel appreciated, they are often motivated to invest more in their work or their relationship with you.
- When delivering bad news, begin with a compliment or a positive observation. This will let people know that you see the whole picture, not just their flaws.

Feelers…

- Listen carefully to the advice of people with a preference for thinking. Thinkers will help you remember the facts and principles you need to be aware of when making decisions.
- Consider the logical reasons for why you are making a decision and be willing to share these with your thinking friends and colleagues. This will help the thinkers understand you and support you better.
- When something a thinker has said hurts your feelings, don't take it personally. Remember that the thinker is not disagreeing with *you*, he or she is just disagreeing with your conclusion or method of evaluating information.

The more you are able to get along with others of the opposite preference type, the more benefits you will enjoy. Your own decision-making will be improved, and you will have valuable people in your life who are willing and able to support you in the decision-making process.

Intentionally Masking Your
Information-Evaluating Preference

Some of the simple adjustments recommended for thinkers and feelers in the previous section involved masking one's information-evaluating preference. This is because as much as embracing your preference through your behaviors, beliefs, and belongings can support you, there will be some times, as we discussed in chapter 2, that intentionally masking your preferences will help you avoid potential pitfalls and achieve your life goals.

To review, intentional masking of your personality preference involves adopting behaviors associated with the opposite preference type. The times that you might want to intentionally mask your information-evaluating preference include the following instances:

1. when you want to achieve a specific goal
2. when you want to be considerate of another person's needs
3. when you want to grow as a person.

For example, if you have a preference for thinking and your feeling life partner just lost her job and is sharing her frustrations with you about the current poor job market, instead of responding with logical ideas on how she can beat the market and get a job, you might practice some feeling behaviors, like telling your wife you empathize with her frustrations and giving her a hug. Because your wife has a preference for feeling, this is probably the kind of behavior she needs right now from you, so you temporarily adopt some feeling behaviors. This doesn't compromise you as a person; it simply enriches your relationship with your life partner.

Intentional personality masking is meant to help you get more out of your life, without giving up the core of who you are. If you are conscious of when you use intentional personality masking and your reasons for using this technique are to achieve a specific goal, be considerate of someone else, or grow as a person, you will be able to benefit from the strengths of the opposite preference type without compromising your personality.

Conclusion

Whether you are a thinker or a feeler, you have the innate tools needed to evaluate information and make good decisions. You just need to trust your natural preference and align your behaviors, beliefs, and belongings with it. This doesn't mean that everyone you know should have the same preference as you, but that you want to choose friends, workplaces, and communities that are supportive of your true self and your information-evaluating preference. In turn, your aim can be to learn from those around you who have an opposite preference and to use their strengths to overcome your own blind spots when it comes to decision-making.

Once you align your information-evaluating *behavior* with your information-evaluating *preference*, you will discover how much easier it is for you to make decisions. Your decisions won't feel forced or cause so much stress. Instead, you will enjoy making decisions because you will feel that you are making better decisions and achieving better results.

6

What Is Your Decision Drive?

When you have a decision to make, do you feel a little agitated or off balance until you make that decision? Is there an impulse inside of you to sort through what you want to do, so you can either commit to or pass on an opportunity and, in either case, move on with your life?

Alternately, do you instead revel in the freedom of remaining undecided about a decision, loving the sense of possibility and being unwilling to commit to a single option? When you finally make a decision—because time is running out—do you feel pinned down or hemmed in?

The way you answer the preceding questions—and whether you tend to relate more to the first paragraph versus the second paragraph—has to do with your preference for the third and last step of the decision-making process: committing to your final decision after gathering and evaluating information.

The preference pair associated with the last step of the decision-making process is the *judging* versus *perceiving* preference. This preference refers to what I call your decision drive: the impulse you feel to either make a decision quickly or to draw out your decision-making for as long as possible.

Closed or Open?

We all make decisions every day of our lives, regardless of our preferences. In fact, most of us make hundreds of decisions a day—What will you wear? What will you eat for breakfast? Which route will you take to work or the store? Which airline will you fly? Which hotel will you stay at? And then there are the really significant decisions, like, which job will you accept? Which school will you send your child to? How will you end a relationship? How will you handle an ethical challenge at school or at work? And the list goes on and on. The judging–perceiving preference does not indicate whether or not you make decisions but whether or not you like finality (that is, closure versus openness) with the decisions that you make. Here's an example.

119

My brother Michael and I meet at the same restaurant for lunch every week. We have been doing this regularly for the past ten years. I have a preference for judging, so I don't want to take a lot of time with the menu, because I can't really relax and enjoy our get-together until I've settled on what I'm eating (that is, finalized my decision). So I usually order the same thing because it allows for an easy and quick decision.

My brother Michael on the other hand, has a preference for perceiving, so every time that we go to the restaurant, for him it's like we are going for the first time. He takes his time and reviews every item on the menu to see what he would like to order. Although he usually ends up getting the same thing, steak and the salad bar, Michael has not decided on that before he starts looking over the menu. Whereas I can't fully enjoy our get-together until I've decided what I want to eat, Michael won't be able to enjoy our get-together unless he takes time making his lunch decision to ensure that he orders something he is in the mood for and will enjoy.

Do you see the difference in how my brother and I make our decisions? As a judger, I prefer finality (or closure) to my decisions, so I make my decision as quickly as possible, sometimes even before I sit down with the menu. Once I find a menu choice that I like, I am likely to keep making that same selection until either my tastes or the menu changes.

In contrast, Michael, a perceiver, prefers to leave his decisions open, so no matter how many times he has had the same selection in the past, he does not know whether he will want it again in the future. Each and every time we go to the restaurant, he likes to consider all of his options. This allows him to keep his decision open until the last minute. While I feel most comfortable with a sense of certainty to what I'll be ordering, Michael feels most comfortable being able to explore all the choices available to him.

Have you ever been to a restaurant with a really big menu? You've seen them—probably at a diner—you know, the ten-pager. My brother Michael, a perceiver, would be thrilled by all these menu choices, but I'd feel a little overwhelmed. So many choices! What to choose? I prefer a much simpler menu.

This example is not to say that if you look at the whole menu before ordering at a restaurant that you are necessarily a judger. It's just a simple example of how the judging versus perceiving preference might play out. Now let's take a closer look at both of the decision-drive preferences—judging versus perceiving—so you can gain a greater understanding of each.

Judgers

Judgers tend to push for finality and closure in their decision-making. They don't like having too many options, because this makes it more difficult for them to come to a final decision quickly. When decisions are left unmade, judgers feel unsettled. It's like the frustration that results when you have a word on the tip of your tongue, but you can't think of it or when you were going to say something, but you forgot what it was. This is a little bit like how judgers feel when a decision is left hanging and unmade—as if there is something that still needs to be done, remembered, or taken care of, and they can't fully move on to the other matters in their lives until that item is taken care of.

Judgers' desire for certainty and finality often results in them speaking as if they are the authority on different issues. For example, if a judger has been assigned to a group project at school or at work, he might start directing how the group should proceed because this helps the group move past the decision stage into the action stage and this makes judgers feel most comfortable. Because of this approach, judgers can be seen as pushy or forceful in their relationships with others, especially perceivers, who have a different approach.

Perceivers

Unlike judgers, perceivers resist finality in their decision-making. They prefer to leave things open and undecided until the exact moment that a decision needs to be made.

Whereas having a decision made gives judgers a sense of peace or comfort, settling on a single option (making a final decision) tends to make perceivers feel hemmed in or even claustrophobic. Perceivers feel limited by final decisions—what if they change their minds or they make the wrong choice? It excites perceivers to have a lot of options and they are very reluctant to trade in possibility for certainty.

Of course, perceivers do eventually have to make decisions, but that doesn't mean that they will enjoy the moment of committing to certain choices. Just as judgers feel a sense of *relief* the moment after a decision is made, perceivers often feel a sense of *limitation* the moment after a decision is made. Suddenly, all of the options that had excited the perceiver have been eliminated and replaced by a single certainty. Because perceivers prefer to consider as many options as possible when making their decisions, they can be seen as indecisive or vacillating in their decision-making, especially by judgers.

Determining Your Decision-Drive Preference

The best way for me to help my clients and students sort between judging and perceiving is to ask them this question: you have decided to go on a vacation to the beach—what will you need to do to prepare for your trip? Take a few minutes to answer this question, mentally or in written form.

How did you answer? My clients with a preference for judging immediately begin to make a long list of the things they need to do. They write down such things as *make a budget; plan an itinerary; make arrangements for pets, mail, and newspapers; research weather conditions; make a list of items to pack; research places to stay; find flights and rental cars; make a list of activities to enjoy;* and on and on. My clients with a preference for perceiving have a much shorter list. They usually write down three things: *go, have fun, come back* (maybe). It's even more dramatic when I do this exercise in class or at a seminar. The perceivers are done with the exercise in a couple of minutes, while the judgers are still writing when I tell them that time is up. And when I have the perceivers read their list, the judgers are horrified at the lack of planning and preparation that the perceivers put into their trip—judgers could never enjoy such an unstructured experience. And when I have the judgers read their list, the perceivers eyes immediately start to glaze over; they comment that there is no way anyone could enjoy a trip like that, with all of those plans and constraints.

> *Judgers* prefer finality and closure in their decision-making, while *perceivers* resist finality in their decision-making and prefer to leave things open.

Which category do you seem to relate to? Are you starting to identify with one preference over the other? The following table depicts some of the key differences between judgers and perceivers. Take some time to identify which side of the table most represents you.

Table 6.1: Common Characteristics of Judgers vs. Perceivers

Preference for Judging	Preference for Perceiving
Prefer to make a decision	Prefer to keep things open
Seek closure to things	Seek openness to issues
Feel tension until an issue is decided	Feel tension when forced to decide
Speak with authority	Speak with ambivalence
High value on rules	High value on freedom
Planners	Adapters
Settled	Spontaneous
Comfortable with authority	Rebel against authority
Ask permission before	Seek pardon after
Step in and take charge	Wait for things to develop
See things as black or white	See things as shades of gray
Energized when completing a project	Energized when starting a project
Well organized	Less organized
If in doubt, throw it out	If in doubt, keep it
Work now, play later	Play now, work later

Table 6.1 shows in detail how a preference for judging

versus perceiving tends to manifest itself in a person. Which side of the table do you find yourself relating to most—judging or perceiving? Are you comfortable with rules and authority (as judgers are), or do you prefer to make your own rules when needed (as perceivers do). Do you start and end your day by organizing your work space (a judger), or are you comfortable with your own chaotic piles of paper on your desk (a perceiver)? Do you enjoy life most when you get your work done first (a judger), or do you prefer to squeeze in some fun before settling in to your work (a perceiver)?

Perhaps it is becoming very clear to you what your decision-drive preference is. If not, you may want to take the Majors PTI (or similar personality assessment) to help you determine whether you have a preference for judging or perceiving.* And remember, if you find yourself straddling the preference-pair line—identifying with traits on both sides of Table 6.1, you are probably experiencing unintentional personality masking. Another way of saying this is that your decision-making *behavior* for step 3 of the decision-making process may be different than your decision-making *preference*. As Table 4.1 (see chapter 4) indicates, those with a preference for judging benefit most from a closed decision style, whereas those with a preference for perceiving benefit most from an open decision style.

Table 6.2 lists some of the possible challenges of each decision-drive preference type. You will want to be mindful of these potential pitfalls so you can get the most out of your life. If you are still working to figure out your decision-drive preference, this table will also give you an opportunity to spend more time assessing which preference resonates with you.

* *You may take an online personality assessment to determine whether you have a preference for judging or perceiving by visiting this link: http://www.lifechangingcoaching.com/assessments.htm*

Table 6.2: Potential Pitfalls for Judgers vs. Perceivers

Pitfalls for Judgers	Pitfalls for Perceivers
You miss out on a good opportunity that comes up unexpectedly because you were too committed to your plan.	You miss out on a good opportunity because you wait too long to act.
You make a decision that isn't right for you because you didn't give yourself enough time to think through the decision.	You don't accomplish much because you are unable to commit to a particular plan or decision.
You offend others because you speak with too much authority on an issue.	You irritate others because you are unwilling to take a position on a topic.
You're adherence to conformity and rules limits your ability to come up with novel solutions to problems.	Your desire for freedom makes it difficult for you to get along with others and function within a system.
Your unwillingness to adapt to change causes you to forgo opportunities or resources that could move you closer to meeting your goals.	Your unwillingness to stay the course in a stable environment makes it so you never cross the finish line of your goals.
You seldom find time to relax or reenergize because of your work-now, play-later attitude.	You seldom find time to accomplish things because of your play-now, work-later attitude.

Do you find yourself being vulnerable to one set of pitfalls versus the other? As a judger or a perceiver, you will tend to gravitate more toward one set than the other. Identifying these pitfalls and being on the lookout for them will help you avoid the limitations of your preference and benefit from its strengths.

Is Your Personality Masked?

If your decision-drive behavior and your decision-drive preference are synced up, the speed with which you make decisions will reveal this. If you have a preference for judging and are living in-sync with it, you will make your decisions as quickly as possible and, when involved in a decision with someone else, you will probably encourage that person to help you bring closure to that decision as quickly as possible. In contrast, if you have a preference for perceiving and are living in-sync with it, you will probably string out your decisions for as long as possible. When making joint decisions, you will want your decision partner to be patient with you and allow you ample time before finalizing things.

Table 6.3 lists some signs that the opposite is the case—that you are living out-of-sync with your preference for judging or perceiving (that is, that your decision-drive behavior is masking your decision-drive preference).

Table 6.3: Signs You Are Living Out-of-Sync

Masked Judger	Masked Perceiver
You lead a life of spontaneity and last-minute decision-making, but this keeps you in a constant state of discomfort and stress.	You lead a life of predictability and you make your decisions quickly, but this makes you feel hemmed in and a bit claustrophobic.
You follow all the rules, but it frustrates you to be subject to someone else's guidelines.	Your work, relationships, or environment encourages you to bend the rules, which you do, but this makes you nervous and uncomfortable.
You force yourself to keep your physical surroundings organized, but doing so doesn't bring you any sense of satisfaction.	You're not keeping your physical environment tidy or orderly, and this is driving you crazy.

As table 6.3 reveals, you will know that your decision drive behavior is out-of-sync (or masking) your decision-drive preference if you are living your life like the opposite preference type, but this way of living makes you feel uneasy, uncomfortable, stressed, or frustrated.

Let's look at a visual metaphor for the out-of-sync experience. When you are living out-of-sync with your preferences, it's like dressing for the wrong weather. If you are wearing a wool coat but the temperature outside is 80 degrees, you're bound to feel hot and uncomfortable. Likewise, if you're wearing only a windbreaker in 30-degree weather, you're going to suffer from the cold. It's the same thing when you're living out-of-sync with your preferences. Because you're wearing a "costume" (that is, identity) that doesn't fit the "weather conditions" of your life, you're going to have trouble functioning at your top capacity as long as you wear that costume or identity. If you have discovered that your identity is unintentionally masking your personality, you will benefit from bringing more in-sync behaviors, beliefs, and belongings into your life. This will be much like dressing for the right weather, which lets you function at your top capacity.

Developing an In-Sync Identity

To begin living a life that is in-sync with your decision-drive preference (either judging or perceiving), you will want to begin to shape your belongings, beliefs, and behaviors so they match up with the three Bs that your preference type is most comfortable with. Let's look, then, at the kind of belongings, beliefs, and behaviors that support a judger versus those that support a perceiver.

What Judgers Need

Because judgers prefer to have finality in their decision-making, their three identity Bs will look very different from the identity Bs of the perceivers.

Behaviors. Judgers prefer to be conformists in their behaviors. If there is a right, normal, or accepted way of behaving, then judgers will tend to act that way. They tend to dress conservatively or fashionably. They pay attention to grooming and often appear neat and tidy. They usually arrive on-time or early to meetings; if they arrive late, it makes them very uncomfortable. Judgers tend to govern their lives through the use of calendars and schedules; and they are usually good planners, often knowing months in advance what they will be doing.

Beliefs. Judgers tend to believe in the importance of time. They tend to focus on the finite aspect of time and therefore want to use it as efficiently as possible to be productive. Judgers also believe in the importance of rules. They tend to emphasize following rules and complying with authority, even at the expense of personal individuality.

Belongings. Judgers prefer to be members of communities that have clear and established rules for how the members of the community interact with each other. They prefer to belong to groups with well-defined hierarchies (who's in charge?) and contingencies (what do we do if a certain thing happens?). If judgers are interested in advancement within the community, they like to know what the requirements, time frames, and expectations for advancement are.

What Perceivers Need

Perceivers look nothing like judgers because of their preference to maintain openness in their decision-making. The three identity Bs for perceivers reflect their core needs for possibility and freedom.

Behaviors. Perceivers behave in ways that tend to express their individualities. They are less concerned with what is right, normal, or acceptable and are more interested in what is comfortable, convenient, or expressive of their thoughts and feelings at the particular time. They tend to dress casually and may not be fashion conscious. They are usually late to appointments, having found something or someone that engaged their attention while they were on their way to the scheduled event. Except when required to by occupational constraints, perceivers tend to not use calendars or day planners, preferring instead to keep things open so that they can experience life as it comes at them. They usually don't know until the last moment what they will be doing at any given time because they like being random and spontaneous.

Beliefs. Perceivers also believe in the importance of time, and like judgers, they tend to focus on the finite aspect of time. But, unlike their judging counterparts who focus on productivity, perceivers want to maximize their use of time to get as much enjoyment out of life as is possible. Perceivers are less interested in efficiency and more interested in experience. They believe in the importance of freedom. They tend to emphasize following one's own inner drum beat, even at the expense of communal conformity.

Belongings. Perceivers prefer to be members of communities that are open and free-flowing. They prefer to belong to groups that have flexible membership requirements and as few rules and regulations as possible. They want to be able to adapt themselves to current situations as they arise, so they don't like groups that have rigid structures or concrete ways of interacting.

Now that you have an understanding of what behaviors, beliefs, and belongings are supportive of judgers versus perceivers, you have valuable information to help you start bringing more in-sync Bs into your life. You can also read through the activities in table 6.4 for ideas on what kind of in-sync activities (behaviors) you can begin incorporating into your life.

Table 6.4: Judger vs. Perceiver Activities

Judger Activities	Perceiver Activities
Schedule time each day or week to organize your world so you have a structure and plan to follow. Avoid becoming overcommitted in ways that make you too busy to keep up with planning and organizing your life.	Don't over-schedule yourself. Leave plenty of room in your life for travel, adventure, and exploring. Avoid prolonged experiences without any creative or spontaneous outlet.
Volunteer to work on the planning team for your organization's next big event.	Volunteer to work on the implementation team for your organization's next big event.
Spend some time organizing your files, work area, and home. This will help you feel more settled and less stressed.	Spend some time rearranging your work area and your home, try out different "looks," and don't be afraid to change it again when the mood strikes you.

If you find yourself struggling to unmask your decision-drive personality preference, you may want to take some time to practice accepting your preference type. As mentioned in the previous chapters, one way to do this is by replacing self-critical thoughts with self-supportive ones. For example, if you are a judger and you think, "I am so uptight for wanting to plan my schedule every week," you can practice replacing this thought with something like, "As I judger, I am best able to live the life I want by planning in advance and building structure into my life." Coming up with a constructive thought and saying it to yourself—or even writing it in a journal or notebook, will help you get better at accepting your particular preference. This is one of those cases in which your behavior (your thinking) will affect your beliefs (your acceptance of your preference).

Acceptance also often comes with understanding, and you can gain a better understanding of each preference type, including your own, in the following section on getting along with the opposite decision drive type. Although this section focuses on getting along with others, it can also be very helpful in learning to understand and accept your own decision-drive preference.

Getting Along With the Opposite Decision-Drive Type

As with all cases in which people have opposing preferences, challenges sometimes arise when people with a preference for judging and a preference for perceiving interact. Areas of joint decision-making can cause particular friction: in the personal realm, things like trying to decide where to go on vacation, whether to buy a particular house, and even a simple thing like which movie to go see; in the work realm, things like struggling over who to hire, how to restructure a department at work, or how to plan the activities for your upcoming holiday party. In the end, judgers and perceivers may agree on the same decision, but each will want to take a very different approach to coming to that decision.

Let's look at the following scenario to understand more about what kinds of challenges may arise between judgers and perceivers.

One Saturday afternoon at a coffee shop, Tim and Karen began to discuss the idea of going on a special trip to celebrate their 15th wedding anniversary (which was going to occur in six months). They both loved to travel and were excited by the idea of going somewhere in Europe. They talked about all the possibilities—Paris, Rome, Madrid, or some more out of the way places in the same countries, like Aix-en-Provence, Finale Ligure, or Seville. As Tim and Karen finished up their coffee, Karen asked excitedly, "So, which is it going to be? Let's decide so we can start planning!" Tim gave her a look of surprise—"Isn't it a little early to decide? We just started talking about the trip. Plus, our anniversary isn't for another six months…we have time!" Karen rolled her eyes. "Oh no, not this again. Can't you ever make a decision? If we leave it up to you, the trip won't even happen. By the time you decide, all the hotel rooms will be booked!" Offended, Tim replied, "Well, if we leave the trip up to you, we won't have any fun! You'll have us committed to the dates and times we have to take our showers and brush our teeth!"

After nearly fifteen years of being married, Tim and Karen still got irritated with each other when it came time to make joint decisions. Karen would go on to badger Tim for the rest of the weekend as to where they were going to travel for their anniversary, and Tim would get more and more distant, telling Karen to "chill out" and stop being so uptight. Now that the idea had been put on the table for discussion, though, Karen, a judger, felt unsettled. She wouldn't be able to fully relax until the matter was settled. Plus, she wanted to be able to start planning all the details of the vacation. For her, much of the fun was in the preparation.

Alternately, as a perceiver, Tim felt threatened by Karen's attempts to make him commit to a particular location for their anniversary trip. For him, much of the fun was in the exploration of possible destinations. Why would he want to forgo the part of the decision-making process that involved looking at all of his options? To commit too early, would rob him of that enjoyment; plus, how could he know where he'd want to vacation six months from now? Karen and Tim actually had something in common—they both wanted to enjoy the process of planning their anniversary vacation. It's just that for Karen to enjoy herself, she needed to make a decision sooner rather than later; and for Tim to enjoy himself, he needed some time to explore all of his possibilities.

The Negative Labels We Apply to Judgers and Perceivers

You can see by the way Karen and Tim's conversation at the coffee shop ended, they are having trouble understanding each other's decision-drive preference and that this causes them to insult each other rather than get along.

Here are some of the negative judgments that Karen and Tim, and anyone else, might make about the opposite preference type.

If you are a judger interacting, working, befriending,

dating, or living with a perceiver, you might at times see the perceiver as...

- ineffective at getting things done
- lazy
- indecisive.

If you are a perceiver interacting, working, befriending, dating, or living with a judger, you might at times see the judger as...

- too trigger-happy
- obsessed with productivity
- a know-it-all.

As you've seen from the previous preference chapters, these negative labels don't necessarily apply. Let's spend some time looking at what's really going on for judgers versus perceivers.

What's Really Going on With Perceivers?

Ineffective at getting things done. Judgers with a need to have closure in their decisions may be quick to assume that perceivers will never move from the decision to the action phase simply because they move at a different pace than judgers would. Judgers, try not to confuse perceivers' need for time and space in decision-making with an inability to make a decision. Healthy perceivers will *eventually* make a decision; they just need more time to make decisions than judgers to feel comfortable and certain about those decisions.

Lazy. Because perceivers put a high value on enjoying life, this means they are willing to delay errands, chores, and obligations in favor of fun. This doesn't mean that perceivers are lazy; they just need to relax first to get the energy and motivation that they need to get their work done. Perceivers may irritate judgers when they relax first and work later, but judgers may benefit from perceivers' influence to enjoy life more.

Indecisive. Perceivers are very good at seeing all of the options in a given situation; this makes them reluctant to commit to a single option because they can see the value of each option and want to be sure to make the right decision. While it may appear to judgers that perceivers are incapable of making a decision, what's really going on is that perceivers are willing to invest a lot of energy in making the right decision. This may frustrate judgers, but it also can help balance judgers so that they avoid making premature or regrettable decisions.

What's Really Going on With Judgers?

Too trigger-happy. Perceivers may feel that judgers are irresponsible in their quickness to make decisions, but judgers have a lot of practice at making decisions quickly and are usually good at it. Occasionally, judgers may be too quick to make a decision, just to reduce stress, but on the other hand, they can be a great balance to perceivers, helping them move projects and goals forward rather than getting stuck in the decision stage.

Obsessed with productivity. Judgers do tend to place a higher value on tangible outputs and productivity than perceivers, but this doesn't mean they're robots. Judgers still enjoy life, but they can enjoy it most after they have put in some hard work and shortened their to-do list. Also, although it may be hard for perceivers to believe, judgers get pleasure out of being productive, so this is one of the ways that judgers enjoy their lives.

Know-it-all. To bring closure to decisions and relieve their own stress, judgers have a tendency to jump in and settle issues as quickly as possible. In a group setting, this may mean that the judger takes control of the project at hand without being officially given that authority or without considering the perceivers' needs. Judgers don't usually realize that they are imposing their decision preference on others and instead think they are doing the group a favor by helping it "move forward." Perceivers should feel free to express their needs to judgers to take more time with making a decision and will have the most success if they allow the judger to retain some feeling of control and closure in the situation (for example, by setting timelines or creating to-do lists).

Now that you have a better understanding of what's really going on for judgers versus perceivers, let's return to our earlier example of Tim and Karen to see how the two might be able to resolve their disagreements in planning their anniversary vacation.

First, Karen needs to understand that Tim needs some time to make his decision so he can feel comfortable with it and enjoy the decision-making process. In return, Tim needs to understand that he will eventually need to commit to a decision, maybe a little earlier than he may have liked, so that Karen can gain the sense of closure that will put her at ease and allow her to enjoy the planning process that leads up to the trip. Tim and Karen will need to negotiate a reasonable time frame between the two of them.

Once Karen understands how Tim operates, she will be more likely to see how it isn't reasonable to expect him to make a decision just a few days after the subject of the vacation has come up. Once Tim understands the stress an open-ended decision causes Karen, he will hopefully understand that it is unreasonable to expect her to wait until the last minute to make a decision.

While Karen waits for Tim to become ready to commit, what can she do? She can begin enjoying the planning process without actually committing to any plans. She can start doing the research on the costs of the different destinations so that she and Tim can know the different price ranges for the different destination possibilities. She can start making a list of all the things that they will need to take, including making sure that both of their passports are up-to-date. She can do all of the things that need to be done, no matter which destination they choose. This will allow her to feel like she is moving toward closure and being productive with her planning time and still give Tim the space he needs to think about where he would like to go.

Tim, on the other hand, can help Karen by narrowing down the selection to either a range of activities or a particular country. For example, say that Tim really enjoys scuba diving and would like to make sure that they had the opportunity to do that, then that would help Karen eliminate all of those destinations that did not have good scuba diving activities. Or maybe Tim would like to go to eastern Europe for their anniversary, because he has never been there. Letting Karen know this would help her narrow the choices down to a few eastern European locations. By selecting a broad category of an activity, experience, or geographical area, Tim still keeps his options open but also lets Karen feel like they are making progress to reaching an ultimate decision.

So, getting along with others of the opposite preference type does involve some compromise and understanding, but it *is* possible to get along with others. And don't forget that you can learn from the opposite type as well!

For example, judgers, there may be times in your life when you will benefit from temporarily taking on the approach of the perceiver. Let's say you've had an exhausting week at work and when you come home, you're judging preference causes you to jump right into your housecleaning, when what you really need is to relax first and work later.

Perceivers, you may find that certain areas of your life call for judging behavior—perhaps you have a job that requires you to make quick decisions or to be more organized. In another example, you may have a big project that requires you to put off relaxation for a week and work really hard now. Perceivers can benefit from bringing this aspect of the judging preference into their behavioral style. It's important to stay true to your preference, but it's also important to know when to intentionally mask your preference to make progress toward your goals.

Putting Your Best Foot Forward With the Opposite Decision-Drive Type

The key to getting along with the opposite preference type is to remember that preference conflicts are usually not personal. People with preferences that are different than yours simply see the world differently than you do. Judgers find comfort in making decisions and are reluctant to change once their decisions are made, while perceivers find comfort in change and variety and are reluctant to limit their options by making decisions.

Here are some recommendations that you can follow to improve your interactions with those of the opposite preference.

Judgers...

- Give perceivers more time to make decisions. Don't rush them into a decision simply because you have a need for closure.
- Be open to changing your decision if a perceiver presents you with a better option.
- Spend more time being spontaneous with your perceiver friends. Learn to enjoy a few moments of unscheduled fun.

Perceivers...

- Be respectful of the judger's time. Avoid arriving late to meetings and missing important deadlines.
- If you are sharing workspace or living space with a judger, make an effort to be more organized or tidy.
- Practice closure with your judger friends and colleagues. Create short to-do lists and finish a few tasks before starting new ones.

Intentionally Masking Your Decision-Drive Preference

Some of the simple adjustments recommended for judgers and perceivers in the previous section involved masking one's decision-drive preference. This is because as much as embracing your preference through your behaviors, beliefs, and belongings can support you, there will be some times, as we discussed in chapter 2, that intentionally masking your preferences will help you avoid potential pitfalls and achieve your life goals.

To review, intentional masking of your personality preference involves adopting behaviors associated with the opposite preference type. The times that you might want to intentionally mask your decision-drive preference include the following instances:

1. when you want to achieve a specific goal
2. when you want to be considerate of another person's needs
3. when you want to grow as a person.

For example, if you have a preference for judging, your tendency will likely be to want to finish work projects quickly. While the action-oriented aspect of your nature can be very useful in a work setting where tangible results are valued, you may also choose to adopt perceiving behaviors when you are getting ready to print handouts for a big meeting. Instead of hitting the Print button on your computer as soon as you finish your first draft of a presentation, you may instead override this tendency and proofread your work before you print it out, ensuring that your handouts are polished and finalized. In other words, you know yourself well enough to avoid the pitfalls of your particular preference and keep moving forward at work.

Conclusion

As you become more familiar with the different decision-making preferences...

138

- sensing–intuiting,
- thinking–feeling and
- judging–perceiving

...you will gain greater insight into the process you and others use to make decisions as well as the reasons for those decisions. This will help you trust your natural preferences for the decision-making process and embrace its strengths. It will also provide you with valuable insight into what your blind spots may be so you can adjust your behaviors to reduce or eliminate these blind spots.

As with the benefits described in the previous chapters, when your decision-drive behaviors are in-sync with your decision-drive preference, you will start making better decisions. You won't feel unnecessarily rushed or prematurely forced to make decisions that you are really not comfortable with. The decisions you make will feel more natural to you as they will be springing from your personality rather than your identity. And as you make better decisions, you will be able to achieve better results.

Finally, your awareness of all the different decision-making preferences will most likely make it easier for you to get along with others who have preferences opposite to your own. Not only will you understand why others process decisions as they do, you will have special insight into how to engage with them during that process, by meeting them on their own terms. This will empower you to work together and move forward in your life.

7

How Do You Communicate?

When you speak to other people, do you come right out and say exactly what you're thinking, or do you find a way to soften what you're saying to make sure you don't hurt anyone's feelings or make anyone feel imposed upon? Some of us communicate plainly, maybe even bluntly, while others of us find ways to imply our points without coming right out and saying them.

How you communicate will depend on your preference for communications—direct or indirect—and whether you are behaving in-sync with that preference or masking it. The direct–indirect preference pair is the last of the personality preferences we'll be focusing on in this book, and this chapter will provide you with an opportunity to learn more about each communications preference and determine which preference is yours.

Communications are made up of the words, gestures, and body language that you use to express your thoughts, ideas, wishes, and requests to other people. If you communicate effectively, other people will understand what you are trying to say and will remain positively engaged with you. If you communicate ineffectively, other people will not understand what you are trying to say and/or may be offended by what you say. As a result, effective communications are essential to advancing your goals and maintaining rewarding social and professional relationships.

Let's look at a simple example of communications between two people with different communications preferences: myself and my wife, Pam.

One day Pam and I were riding the shuttle bus to the Hollywood Bowl to attend a concert. Earlier in the day we had gone to the grocery store to pick up some food to bring to the event. We had purchased salad, snacks, drinks, and a pack of gum. On the bus, I was carrying the bag that had all of the food, and the gum was in my pocket. My wife looked at me and asked, "Did you remember to bring the gum with you?" Years ago, my answer would have been a simple, "Yes." And this simple answer would have led to an argument or hurt feelings. But I was enlightened now; I knew that my wife wasn't just asking to see if I'd remembered to bring the gum—she was asking for a piece of gum right then! So I reached in my pocket and offered her a piece. She accepted the gum, thanked me, and the evening continued on its pleasant path.

Was this interaction magical? Or was it simply the fact that Pam and I had been married for nearly fifteen years so I could read her mind? Neither, actually. Our effective communications resulted from my awareness of the fact that my wife has a preference for indirect communications. I know that when Pam has a request, she couches it in passive language, which in this case was a question. I have a preference for direct communications, so I have had to learn about Pam's different communications style. Since I've begun to understand how Pam communicates, our relationship has improved. This interaction regarding the gum was simple, but being able to understand my wife's communications preference enabled me to meet her (indirect) request for gum and keep the mood positive on our way to the concert.

As shown by the previous example, understanding other people's communications styles affects how we respond to them. And, of course, how we communicate to others affects how they will respond to us. Let's take some time now to learn more about each communications preference type so you can get a sense of which preference reflects your natural personality.

Direct Versus Indirect Communications

So, just as we all have preferences for how we reenergize and how we make decisions, we also have preferences for how we communicate. Some of us have preferences for direct communications (D); others of us have preferences for indirect communications (R).* Direct communicators prefer to say what they mean plainly and clearly, because they are focused primarily on communicating efficiently and this style of communications is the most efficient method. Indirect communicators, in contrast, state things in roundabout ways that imply what they want, or they take time to reveal what they want.** Indirect communicators use this approach because they are primarily focused on maintaining harmony among the needs of the group—themselves and others.

On the one hand, indirect communicators tend not to initiate communications; when they do, it usually focuses on informing others of their needs, and then others are expected to interpret that this information means a request is being made. This approach allows indirect communicators to make their needs known in a diplomatic way—one that invites the other person to address it, rather than commands him or her. This helps social dynamics continue to run smoothly.

On the other hand, direct communicators tend to initiate conversation and make direct requests. They have no problem asserting themselves and asking for what they want. This approach enables direct communicators to maximize the chances that their needs will be met, because there is no confusion about the content of their requests. Unlike the indirect communicator who only invites, the direct communicator compels.

> *Direct communicators* prefer to say what they mean plainly and clearly because they are focused primarily on communicating efficiently, while *indirect communicators* prefer to state things in roundabout ways that imply what they want because they are primarily focused on maintaining harmony among the needs of the group.

Here are some examples of how direct versus indirect communicators might make the same request using different language. Which of these categories sounds most like you?

Table 7.1: How Direct vs. Indirect Communicators Make Requests

Situation	Direct Language	Indirect Language
A light bulb has burned out and needs replacing.	"Please change the light bulb."	"The light bulb burned out."
It's lunchtime and the person wants to eat.	"I'm hungry. Let's get something to eat."	"Are you hungry?"
A couple is out to dinner and one person wants to try the other's dish.	"Can I have a bite?"	"Mmmm. That looks good."
Two friends are shopping together at the mall, and one of them sees a shirt she likes but realizes she doesn't have any money on her.	"Oh shoot. I left my wallet at home. May I borrow $30 to buy this shirt?"	"Oh, shoot, I really like that shirt, but I left my wallet at home."
An employee turns in a sloppy report.	"You made several mistakes in your calculations. Go back and proofread your work."	"It looks like there were some errors in the report. Could you look it over a couple more times before finalizing it?"
The boss needs two employees to work late.	"Bob and Jane, I am going to need you to stay late tonight."	"There is still some work that needs to be done. Bob and Jane, do you have any plans for this evening?"

The difference between the two communications styles starts to become clear when you look at examples of each type side by side. As you can see, direct communications are really effective at making its point known. The request being made is plain and clear.

144

- "You need to change the light bulb."
- "It's time to eat."
- "I need to borrow some money."

With direct communications, there is little room for misunderstanding.

Indirect communications are not as clear, particularly for direct communicators, who assume that everyone else will be making their needs known in a direct way. If I am a direct communicator, I may miss the request that is being implied by the person's indirect communications because I'm not aware that I need to do some interpretive work. The onus is on me to figure out that...

- My wife saying, "The light bulb burned out" (information) means she would like me to change the light bulb (request).
- When my friend asks me if I am hungry (information), he is probing to see if this is a good time for him to mention that he's hungry and he'd like to stop for food (request).
- My friend notices a shirt that she likes (information), but because she left her wallet at home (additional information), she might be interested in borrowing some money from me (request) to pay for it.

The requests being made here are not necessarily obvious—particularly to the direct communicator—but they do help maintain social harmony. How so? Because these communications do not compel the other person to address a request but merely invite him or her to consider it. For example, I don't have to offer to lend my friend money to buy the shirt, and I don't have to offer her a bite of my meal. So if I don't want to do these things, my friend, the indirect communicator, has allowed me a graceful exit: if she doesn't directly ask to borrow money or taste a bite of my meal, I don't have to come right out and say "no." That makes my life easier and the social dynamics between my friend and me more pleasant. Of course, the indirect communicator may feel offended when I don't offer, but, at least overtly, social dynamics will continue to flow well.

Now, as a direct communicator, I may not even realize any of these requests are being made when an indirect communicator is talking to me. But when two indirect communicators are talking with each other, they understand each other quite well. They are used to using indirect language and know how to interpret it without blinking an eye. If you are a direct communicator, it might take some practice learning to interpret the requests being made by an indirect communicator.

Now you may also be wondering...do indirect communicators ever come right out and ask for what they want? Actually, they do. But when they make a specific request, they often couch the request in "soft" (invitational) rather than "hard" (compelling) language. For example, my wife might come right out and ask me to change the light bulb, but she'd probably phrase it in an invitational way, like "It would be great if you could change the light bulb when you have a chance, honey." For purposes of comparison, if my wife were a direct communicator, she would be more likely to say, "Honey, would you please change the light bulb?" You can probably see the difference between these two cases: the first case is phrased like an open-ended request; the second is phrased more as a directive. In both cases, though, my wife wants me to change the light bulb; how she is asking me to do so is what differs.

The preferences for direct communications and indirect communications are shared equally between men and women, although cultural norms may encourage women to adapt to using indirect communications regardless of their natural preference and men to adapt to using direct communications.

* I draw my understanding of direct versus indirect communication

146

from Linda Berens' work on interaction styles (see Berens, L.V., 2000, Understanding Yourself and Others: An Introduction to Interaction Styles. Huntington Beach, CA: Telos.).

** *Berens refers to indirect communicators as informing communicators.*

Determining Your Communications Preference

Perhaps you are starting to get a sense of whether you are a direct versus an indirect communicator. Completing the following exercise will provide you more insight into which is your preferred form of communications.

Exercise 7.1: Determining Whether You Are a Direct vs. Indirect Communicator

Instructions: For the next seven days, pay attention to how you ask for things that you want from other people and keep a log of the way you word things. For example, how do you ask for support or assistance at work? When you are in a retail store, how do you request assistance from the salesperson? When you call a service provider or credit card company to manage your services or bills, how do you word your request when speaking to the phone representative? When you want to ask a friend or loved one for a favor, how do you state it? When someone has upset you, how do you communicate this to the person? (Do you communicate this to the person at all?)

Shortly after you notice how you word something, write it down in a notebook or journal. At the end of the week, look over your notes and take some time to analyze how you have worded things when making requests. Does your language seem direct or indirect? Here are some questions to ask yourself.

- Have I come right out and asked for what I want?
- Have I used compelling language when asking for what I ·want?
- In moments of conflict, have I been direct?*
- When interacting with those I don't know well, have I been direct?*
- When giving someone feedback, have I been direct?***

An answer of "yes" to most or all of these questions probably means you are a direct communicator. Alternately, if you answer "no" to the preceding questions, you are most likely an indirect communicator. Here are some more questions to ask.

- Do I tend to provide information and expect the other person to interpret that a need is being requested when I provide that information?
- Have I softened the language of my requests to make sure I invite rather than compel someone to do something?
- In moments of conflict, have I been indirect?*
- When interacting with those I don't know well, have I been indirect?*
- When giving someone feedback, have I been indirect?*

If you answer "yes" to the preceding questions, you are likely an indirect communicator; an answer of "no" means you are probably a direct communicator.

***Remember, direct communication is when you make your request known—up front—in clear and specific language. Indirect communication is when you provide information that implies a request is being made or when you soften your request with passive language. Refer to Table 7.1 for examples of the difference between direct and indirect language.

After completing Exercise 7.1, which type of communicator do you think you tend to be? The goal is to figure out which type of communications you most often use. Note that if you are an indirect communicator, you might occasionally use direct communications, and if you are a direct communicator, you might occasionally use indirect communications. For example, if you are an indirect communicator, you might come right out and ask your spouse for a bite of his or her food. This is because you don't worry about imposing on your spouse—you know your spouse will come right out and tell you no if he or she doesn't feel like sharing.

In reverse, if you are a direct communicator, say in the business world, you may have learned over the years how to provide feedback to your employees who are indirect communicators using indirect communications. Maybe you saw early in your career how some indirect communicators reacted negatively to your use of the direct communications style, and you learned how to adjust your behavior to match their preference.

If you are having trouble determining your communications preference because you use both kinds of communications behaviors (direct and indirect), consider what kind of communications behavior you use in the following three contexts:

- with those whom you don't know well
- in times of conflict
- when providing someone with feedback.

If you usually use indirect communications in these circumstances, then you most likely have a preference for indirect communications. When you are interacting with those you don't know well, dealing with a conflict, or providing feedback, these are the times that positive social dynamics are most at risk. So if you have a preference for indirect communications, it will kick in here.

On the flip side, if you use direct communications when you don't know people well, when you are in conflict with a person, or when you are providing feedback to someone, chances are that you are a direct communicator. These are times of potential stress or confusion so you will feel it is particularly important to express yourself efficiently and clearly.

Here is one more tool you can use to determine your preference type. Look at Table 7.2 for a list of some of the possible challenges of each preference type. Do you find yourself falling into the pitfalls on one side of the table? Reviewing this table may provide you with additional insight into whether you are a direct or indirect communicator.

Table 7.2: Potential Pitfalls for Direct vs. Indirect Communicators

Pitfalls for Direct Communicators	Pitfalls for Indirect Communicators
You are unaware of the effect you are having on your listener (for example, upsetting him, hurting her feelings) because you may not be paying attention to social dynamics.	You may not get what you want because your message or request is unclear.
You may come across as stubborn, bossy, or closed to others' ideas because you are telling people what to do rather than asking for their input.	You may not command respect in a leadership role where clarity and decisiveness are valued.
You may needlessly escalate conflicts, when the other person was willing to choose from a menu of acceptable alternatives.	You may get taken advantage of in a conflict (for example, if you offer a choice that you really don't want the other person to choose, the other person may take you up on it).
You may give others the impression you are selfish or insensitive.	You may give others the impression you are wishy washy or unconfident.

Do you find yourself relating to one side of Table 7.2 more than the other? If so, this may point to your particular preference for communications: direct or indirect. In addition, having awareness of the pitfalls of your preference will give you insight into times you may want to flex out of your preference and intentionally adopt behaviors from the opposite communications preference.****

We will talk more in depth later in the chapter about when and how to modify your communications style. But first, let's focus on determining whether you are currently living your life in-sync with your communications preference so you will have the information you need to determine whether you want to make any adjustments to your behaviors, beliefs, and belongings.

*** *If you need extra assistance determining your communications preference, you can take the Majors PTI (or similar personality assessment) by visiting this link: http://www.lifechangingcoaching.com/assessments. htm. Direct communicators are those with any of the following life codes: INFJ, ENFJ, INTJ, ENTJ, ISTJ, ESTJ, ISTP, or ESTP. Indirect communicators are those with any of the following life codes: INFP, ENFP, INTP, ENTP, ISFJ, ESFJ, ISFP, ESFP.*

Is Your Personality Masked?

If you find that you don't feel authentic when you are communicating with other people, it's possible that you've been using the communications style that is opposite to your actual preference. Here are some signs that you are behaving out-of-sync with your preference for communications.

- You give direct instructions to people, but you have to work to keep your communications simple and straightforward (masked indirect communicator).
- You give people information only, but you want to give them instructions also (masked direct communicator).
- You are direct about telling people what to do, but it stresses you out (masked indirect communicator).
- You ask people for input, but you feel very impatient when they respond (masked direct communicator).

As these bullet points reveal, you will know that your personality is unintentionally masked if you are living your life like the opposite preference type, but this way of living makes you feel uneasy, uncomfortable, stressed, or frustrated. While it's definitely helpful to be able to use the opposite communications behavior at times to achieve specific goals, you will find the most satisfaction in your life if you are generally behaving in-sync with your communications preference (as we've seen for all the other preferences). If you think of your opposite communications preference type as a mask or a costume, you can see how it would be uncomfortable to wear that mask or costume hour after hour, day after day. Not only would it be uncomfortable or tiring, it would probably feel strange, disorienting, or even disconcerting to consistently present yourself to the world as someone that you're not.

If you have discovered that your identity is unintentionally masking your personality, you will benefit from bringing more in-sync behaviors, beliefs, and belongings into your life. Let's spend some time examining the three Bs that best support direct communicators versus indirect communicators.

Developing an In-Sync Identity

To begin living a life that is in-sync with your particular communications preference, you will want to begin to shape your behaviors, beliefs, and belongings so they match up with the three Bs that your preference type is most comfortable with. Let's look, then, at the kind of behaviors, beliefs, and belongings that support a direct communicator versus those that support an indirect communicator.

What Direct Communicators Need

Behaviors. Direct communicators are most comfortable when they are providing direction and telling people what to do. They prefer activities that allow them to influence other people and move things ahead. They tend to physically move toward others and use definitive language.

Beliefs. Direct communicators value efficiency. They want to get things done as quickly as possible in the most efficient manner. They prize action over diplomacy.

Belongings. Direct communicators would benefit from belonging to communities that match their interests and allow them to function in the roles of providing structure and direction to the communities' events and activities (for example, planning committee member, finance chairperson, organization president). Direct communicators tend to gravitate toward communities of other direct communicators because of the shared interaction style.

What Indirect Communicators Need

Behaviors. Indirect communicators prefer to draw forth cooperation from other people. They would much rather provide information and have someone reach their own conclusions, than suggest what a person should think or do. They tend to physically hover and use open language.

Beliefs. Indirect communicators value harmony. They want things to run as smoothly as possible, with the least amount of interpersonal conflict. They prize diplomacy over action.

Belongings. Indirect communicators would benefit from belonging to communities that match their interests and allow them to assume roles that use their skills of drawing out information, inspiring others, and seeking input from others (for example, group facilitator, social director, motivational speaker). Indirect communicators tend to prefer relationships that allow them to express their needs without imposing their views on others.

Now that you have an understanding of what behaviors, beliefs, and belongings are supportive of direct versus indirect communicators, take a look at Table 7.3. If you have discovered that you are masking or behaving out-of-sync with your particular communications preference, this table will give you some activities that you can incorporate into your life that correspond to your preference.

Table 7.3: Direct vs. Indirect Communicator Activities

Direct Communicator Activities	Indirect Communicator Activities
Providing instruction to others	Providing inspiration to others
Telling people what to do	Asking people for their input

Direct Communicator Activities	Indirect Communicator Activities
Organizing events and activities	Brainstorming to come up with ideas for events and activities
Ensuring that tasks get completed on time	Ensuring that the process runs smoothly

Table 7.3 lists the general kinds of activities that you will find fulfilling as a direct or an indirect communicator. Take some time to reflect on your particular interests, and see if you can come up with direct or indirect (depending on your preference) activities that incorporate your interests. For example, if you are a direct communicator who enjoys painting, you could volunteer to teach an art class at your local community center (allowing you to provide instructions to others). If you are an indirect communicator who enjoys painting, you could volunteer to give a talk at your local community center on the healing effects of painting (allowing you to inspire others).

If you find yourself struggling to unmask your personality preference for communications, you may want to take some time to practice accepting your preference type. As mentioned in the previous chapter, one way to do this is by replacing self-critical thoughts with self-supportive thoughts. For example, if you are a direct communicator and you tend to think things like, "I am so bossy," you can practice replacing this thought with something like, "As a direct communicator, I feel most comfortable stating my needs and thoughts plainly and clearly. As long as I am considerate of other's feelings, my communications will be effective, not domineering."

Acceptance also often comes with understanding, and you can gain a better understanding of each preference type, including your own, in the following section on getting along with the opposite communications type. Although this section focuses on getting along with others, it can also be very helpful in learning to understand and accept your own communications preference.

Getting Along With the Opposite Communications Type

Since all of our interactions with other people in life are based on communications, it's truly helpful to be able to recognize and understand others' preferences for communications. Once you successfully identify someone's communications type, you will have valuable information for improving your interactions with that person and ultimately enriching your relationship. You will have the tools you need both for making yourself understood by others and for understanding what it is they are trying to say to you! When communications run effectively, everyone involved is able to move forward.

> For example, imagine you are the manager of a sales department and you are an indirect communicator, while the rest of your sales team members are direct communicators. Every time you have your monthly team meeting, you say, "It'd be great if you could begin making sales calls by 8 AM each day." But later when you look at the phone records, you see that half of the team doesn't start making their calls till 9 AM. You scratch your head and wonder, "Why are they defying me?"

In reality, your sales people are not defying you. Your team of direct communicators simply doesn't realize that you are saying it's mandatory that they start their sales calls at 8 AM. Why? Because you have said, "It'd be great if..." rather than "Everyone needs to start making their sales calls by 8 AM...," making it sound to the sales team as if they have a choice.

The truth is, as an indirect communicator, you want people to feel like they have a choice—because giving people choices is a way to keep social dynamics running smoothly—but what is important to direct communicators is knowing exactly what you want them to do. As a result, when you are dealing with a situation in which there's no choice involved (for example, sales calls must begin at 8 AM), you need to be clear with direct communicators on exactly what you want them to do: "Everyone on the team needs to start making sales calls at 8 AM."

By learning to adopt direct communications behavior for this particular issue at work, you will find that your sales team will understand the new policy and be empowered to adopt it. In short, your department will run more smoothly and will keep moving forward!!!

The Negative Labels We Apply to Direct Versus Indirect Communicators

You probably already know from experience how people with the opposite communications preference can exasperate you. If you're a direct communicator, you've probably been bewildered when an indirect communicator has gotten mad at you for being "so blunt" or for not accurately interpreting their attempts to request something from you. Similarly, if you're an indirect communicator, you may have resented a direct communicator's way of running one of your office or volunteer club meetings when they seem to order everyone around instead of working toward group consensus. It can be challenging to understand why those opposite of us communicate as they do, especially when it involves an issue that's important to us. So let's spend some time deconstructing why direct and indirect communicators tend to act as they do.

If you are a direct communicator interacting, working, befriending, dating, or living with an indirect communicator, you might at times see the indirect communicator as...

- a poor leader
- afraid of conflict
- overprotective of others' feelings.

If you are an indirect communicator interacting, working, befriending, dating, or living with a direct communicator, you might at times see the direct communicator as...

- bossy, overbearing

156

- confrontational
- insensitive.

While it's true that the preceding can be pitfalls for each preference type, oftentimes direct and indirect communicators are simply expressing themselves in ways that work best for them, and we have misunderstood them. If we learn more about how the opposite communications type works and what motivates them, we will have a better chance at understanding what people are communicating to us and avoiding frustration that holds us all back. Let's spend some time looking at what's really going on for direct versus indirect communicators.

What's Really Going on With Direct Communicators?

Bossy, overbearing. Because direct communicators value efficiency, they don't beat around the bush when expressing themselves. They want to communicate their ideas as quickly and clearly as possible, so they come right out and state their needs. This can make it seem to indirect communicators, though, that direct communicators are expecting their own needs to be met in a vacuum, without considering others' needs. In reality, direct communicators expect everyone else to make their needs known plainly too and then they figure issues can be addressed and resolved by sorting through everyone's (clearly expressed) interests. So if you are an indirect communicator, instead of assuming that the direct communicator means to boss you around, try to understand that he or she is just trying to communicate clearly and efficiently. The direct communicator fully expects you to reciprocate and make your needs and opinions known as well.

Confrontational. Direct communicators are not afraid to express their opinions or state their needs plainly, even when around others who have differing opinions or needs. If you are an indirect communicator, you may interpret direct communicators as being argumentative when really they are simply trying to be clear about stating their needs or ideas.

157

Direct communicators do value action over diplomacy, so it's possible they are neglecting the social dynamics of a group in favor of moving that group forward, but on a positive note, you will usually know what direct communicators are thinking and you won't have to guess at it.

Insensitive. Because direct communicators value action over diplomacy, they don't usually attend to people's feelings in the way that indirect communicators do; their focus is instead on the question of how they can make their points quickly and clearly so everyone can keep moving forward. Direct communicators don't want or mean to offend others; they just don't usually take the time to consider the way their direct statements might impact other people. As a result, direct communicators may come across as insensitive, when in fact their goal is not to alienate others but instead to be effective when they communicate.

What's Really Going on With Indirect Communicators?

Poor leaders. When indirect communicators are in leadership roles, they tend to lead by consensus. They want to make sure that everyone in the group feels heard and valued, so they will take time to listen. This can be frustrating to direct communicators who want to spend less time talking and more time acting, but try to remember that indirect communicators' ability to connect to the group will help foster a loyal followership. Sometimes, indirect communicators' typical way of providing *information* rather than direct instructions can make it hard for people to know what is being requested of them. If needed, be willing to ask the indirect communicator for instructions or clarification.

Afraid of conflict. It's not so much that indirect communicators are *afraid* of conflict as that they want everyone in the group to be happy. In fact, indirect communicators' willingness to step into the middle of a conflict and mediate shows that they aren't scared off by disagreement but instead that they are adept at helping to diffuse conflict. In one-on-one situations, indirect communicators may hesitate to tell you exactly what's on their minds, but remember, their reason for holding back is a considerate one: to make sure that they don't offend you or make you uncomfortable. Be willing to probe a little with indirect communicators to see how they feel or think about something. Chances are, if you're patient, you will be able to learn what's going on inside their minds.

Overprotective of others' feelings. Direct communicators may get frustrated with indirect communicators, who put a special emphasis on looking out for others' feelings. A direct parent, for example, might get upset that the indirect parent doesn't come right out and tell their son that some recent behavior was wrong. What the direct communicator may not realize is that the indirect parent is still communicating the same message to the child, just in a different way. True, there may be times when direct communications is most effective, but it will help direct communicators to remember the value of the indirect communicator's people skills.

Putting Your Best Foot Forward With the Opposite Preference Type

Here are some tips and tricks to getting along well with those of the opposite preference type for communications.

Direct communicators…

- Try to bear in mind that, even though indirect communicators' requests are couched in soft or passive language, you are still expected to understand that requests are being made. If you don't understand the requests or are confused, go ahead and ask. Explain to indirect communicators that you want to support them but that you need more help understanding what they mean.
- When indirect communicators seem to be offering you a choice, they may or may not really mean you have a choice. There are times that indirect communicators are leaving decisions up to you

and times that they really do want you to meet their implied requests. If you are uncertain about the situation, ask the indirect communicators to clarify.

- The closer you are to indirect communicators, the more they might expect you to recognize and meet their needs without having to explicitly state them.
- While indirect communications can be used as a passive form of manipulation, indirect communicators are often simply trying to phrase things in a diplomatic way.

Indirect communicators…

- Remember, direct communicators can't read your mind. If they don't seem to be responding to your request, try stating it more directly or specifically.
- Direct communicators don't mean to offend you with their direct language. They speak the way they do because it seems logical and efficient.
- Even if direct communicators don't solicit your feedback, they may still be interested in hearing it. Don't be afraid to tell them what you are thinking or feeling.
- Avoid using indirect communications as a form of passively expressing your anger or displeasure at something. This will confuse direct communicators and make it harder for them to understand your intentions or desires.

In other words, when interacting with the opposite communications preference type, try to put yourself temporarily in the mindset of that preference so you can understand what that person is really trying to communicate. Also, be willing to flex out of your own preference at times to improve communications with someone else. When people understand what you are trying to communicate to them, they'll be more likely and capable of supporting you and helping you move forward in your goals and joint projects.

Intentionally Masking Your Communications Preference

Like our other preferences, we are *born* with our preference for communications; it's not something we choose or can change. However, we can learn to adopt the opposite communications behavior for a period of time when a particular situation calls for it.

> As I mentioned earlier, I'm a direct communicator. Over the years, I've learned how to modify my communications to make them more indirect when I am communicating with someone who has a preference for indirect communications. For example, I use the tool of writing and rewriting my communications to make them more indirect when I know that I will be talking to an indirect communicator. Sometimes, it takes several revisions to get it close to right. I also seek input from other indirect communicators before I send my communications out. This helps me avoid accidentally upsetting the indirect communicator with direct language that might be misinterpreted as brash.

When you encounter a challenge in getting along with, understanding, or communicating with another person, take some time to decipher what his or her communications style is and how it interacts with your own. Once you get a handle on the other person's communications style, consider adapting your behavior to communicate in the opposite way, particularly when a conflict or misunderstanding starts to arise. If you are an indirect communicator, this will help ensure that the other person understands your wishes. If you are a direct communicator, this will reduce the chances that you will be seen as too forceful or a poor listener.

Since one of the times you will want to adjust your communications style is to communicate with those of the opposite preference type, I recommend that you take some time to identify the communications style of those with whom you work, spend time, and live—coworkers, employees, and bosses; friends, teachers, and service providers; spouses, children, and roommates. This may be particularly helpful if you are encountering a relationship challenge with someone.

Exercise 7.2: Assessing Other Peoples' Communications Styles

Instructions: For the next week, pay attention to how others in your life ask for things that they want from you or other people and keep a log of the way they word things.

Shortly after you notice how the person words something, write it down in a notebook or journal. Be sure to write down who said the phrase and the context in which they said it. At the end of the week, look over your notes and take some time to analyze how others you know have worded their requests. Does their language seem direct or indirect? Here are some questions to ask.

- Has the person explicitly asked for what he or she wants?
- Has the person been specific about asking for what he or she wants?
- Has the person compelled someone to do something rather than invited him or her?
- In moments of conflict, has the person been direct?*
- When interacting with those whom the person doesn't know well, has he or she been direct?*
- When giving someone feedback, has the person been direct?*****

An answer of "yes" to most or all of these questions, probably means the person is a direct communicator. Alternately, if the answer is "no" to the preceding questions, the person is most likely an indirect communicator. Here are some more questions to ask.

- Does the person tend to provide information and expect the other person to interpret that a need is being requested when he or she provides that information?
- Has the person softened the language of his or her request to invite rather than compel someone to do something?
- In moments of conflict, has the person been indirect?*
- When interacting with those the person doesn't know well, has he or she been indirect?*****

- When giving someone feedback, has the person been indirect?*****

If you answer "yes" to the preceding questions, the person is likely an indirect communicator; an answer of "no" means the person is probably a direct communicator.

***** *Remember, direct communication is when someone makes a request known—up front—in clear and specific language. Indirect communication is when someone provides information that implies a request is being made or softens a request with passive language. Refer to Table 7.1 for examples of the difference between direct and indirect language.*

After spending some time reflecting on others' communications styles, what have you discovered? Are your interactions with others starting to make more sense? Maybe now you understand why your partner (a direct communicator) hasn't been addressing your needs when you provide him or her with related information (indirect communications). Or maybe you have insight into why your coworkers have told your boss they don't want to be on projects with you (because they feel you are overbearing). If you've been communicating too directly with them, they may feel bossed around. You now have valuable information to help you adjust your own communications behavior in specific situations and to figure out the most effective way to communicate with others.

Conclusion

Each communications style has its strong points. The direct communications style is most effective when a person needs to make his or her point clear, while the indirect communications style is effective for maintaining social harmony.

Given this reality, the direct communications style tends to work well when you are in leadership positions because it's important to be clear when giving instructions to those you are managing. It also works well in situations where you need to give careful instructions to people, such as classroom settings or when helping people fix problems with their computers. This is true regardless of whether your audience is direct or indirect in their communications preference.

The indirect communications style typically works well when you are in counseling or facilitation roles. This style of communications encourages people to speak candidly and respond authentically because they don't feel imposed upon by the person they are interacting with. Actually, this style works well in any role where you're developing people and helping them discover the answers to questions themselves. This is true regardless of whether your audience is direct or indirect in their communications preference.

Working with others is an essential ingredient in being able to move forward and accomplish our goals. Effective communications is a vital part of that process. At times, it can be frustrating to speak to someone with the opposite communications preference. At other times, we admire others for their diplomatic skill or their ability to really speak their minds. So value the gifts you have as a direct or indirect communicator, and know that you have the power to adjust your communications style when the situation calls for it. As you master your skill at communicating effectively, you will be able to interact more effectively with the people in your world.

8

Your Place in This World

One of my favorite movies is called "About a Boy," starring Hugh Grant and costarring Nicholas Hoult. It is the story of a rich, single, Londoner named Will (Grant's character), who learns how to form meaningful relationships by helping a weird kid named Marcus (Hoult's character) cope with life. As the opening credits roll, we see Will living all alone in his expensively furnished apartment. "In my opinion," Will says, "all men are islands." As the story unfolds, we watch Will waste his life in selfish pursuits and meaningless social encounters. Then Marcus comes into his life. As a result, Will realizes how selfish and empty his life has been. By helping Marcus, Will winds up helping himself. As the movie ends, we see that Will's apartment is now full of people. There is Will and his new lady, Marcus and his girlfriend, and several other friends and family members. As the closing credits roll, we discover that Will has modified his opening position as he says, "Every man is an island. I stand by that. But, clearly, some men are part of island chains. Below the surface of the ocean they are actually connected."

Will is right: we are all connected. Now we may not be able to see these connections, because some of us are like Will—linked beneath the surface of things, while others of us are more visibly attached. But whether our connections are apparent or hidden, they are there, binding us to each other. There is a Cameroonian proverb that says, "Rain does not fall on one roof alone." This is a wonderful way of illustrating the truth about the communities in which we live: when the rain falls, all of the houses get wet; when the sun shines, all of the houses become dry. That is, the conditions of the world affect all of us, not just one of us. If we work to improve the conditions of the world, each of us will benefit.

I have modified this Cameroonian proverb a little and tell my clients and students that "All boats rise together." For example, when a community works together to keep its streets clean and safe, say through a neighborhood clean-up or night-watch association, everyone in the neighborhood benefits. Families stay safer, children have a more pleasant neighborhood to play in, and home values may even rise.

Or look at it in a business context: when an organization works together to manufacture a quality product or deliver excellent service, everyone in the organization benefits. As more people buy the product or service, revenues increase. As revenues increase, so does job security and the opportunity for increased compensation and benefits.

In both examples, because of the inherent connection that we have with each other in neighborhoods and organizations, when the water level rises, all the boats rise together.

We Need Other People

The all-boats-rise-together concept is helpful to keep in mind when you are trying to move forward in your life. I believe that the reason that so many people stay stuck is because they mistakenly believe that all human beings really are islands—that essentially we are all alone in this world. And so, armed with this false belief, instead of reaching out to others for support, they head off to their local bookstores to purchase the latest *self*-help book. They scour its pages for remedies to their lifelong dilemmas and diligently begin to implement the recommended strategies. And maybe they get some traction for a little while. They change their diets, they join gyms, they begin to give themselves positive self-talks. They start to move forward a little…and then they come to a crashing stop. They can't sustain their progress. They toss out that book and head off to the store to buy another self-help book, with a different "secret to success."

Well, no matter how many books people buy or how many seminars they attend, if their formula for progress does not factor the human community into the equation, then people's efforts are doomed to fail. This sounds harsh, but it's true. As Mark Twain said, "the universal brotherhood of man is our most precious possession." *We are each other's best support; we are each other's best resource.*

This book is unashamedly about helping people find their place in this world by connecting with the people around them. I have found that this is the only way to make real and sustained progress in life. One of my clients, Ron, offers a good example of this.

> Ron was depressed when he hired me to be his coach. He wasn't suffering from clinical depression, but he did feel sad most of the time, and he didn't really know why. We did his personality assessment and he discovered that his life code was INFPR. I observed that some of his identity elements were out-of-sync with his true self, so we developed a plan for getting them into alignment.
>
> As Ron began working on the plan, he still felt depressed about life in general. I asked him to tell me more about his belongings. He mentioned that he didn't really have any. I told him that I was pretty sure that his disconnectedness was part of his depression. I recommended that he volunteer at a local teen crisis center. He resisted at first, telling me that he felt too sad to be of any real help to anyone. I asked him to trust me and try it for two weeks. He agreed reluctantly and went to a center near his house that trained him to answer phones and help the teens who were calling in.
>
> The next time I talked to Ron he seemed like a different person. He felt energetic and was excited about life. I asked him what had caused the change. He told me that by working at the center, not only did he find purpose in helping others, but he had also found a community of people like himself with whom he was able to relate and begin to make connections.

Ron learned firsthand that as the water level in the lives of the teens he was helping rose, because he was connected to them, his boat rose with theirs. Although Ron and I spent some time helping him focus on himself—by aligning some of his behaviors with his preferences—it was only when Ron reached outward and began making connections with other people that his sadness lifted and he started moving forward in life. The same is true for all of us. *We need to be connected to others to get the most fulfillment out of our lives and to have the support we need to accomplish our goals.*

The Three Types of Relationships That We All Need

What I taught Ron and what I teach all of my clients and students is that to make continuous progress in life, each one of us needs to have at least one of each of the three different types of relationships that exist in the world, what I call receiving relationships, mutual relationships, and giving relationships. I also call these Type I, Type II, and Type III relationships.

- Type I receiving relationships are relationships in which we predominantly receive from others.
- Type II mutual relationships are relationships in which we and our partners contribute equally to the relationship.
- Type III giving relationships are relationships in which we predominantly give to others.

Table 8.1 illustrates the different relationship types.

Table 8.1: The Three Types of Relationships

Type I Receiving	Type II Mutual	Type III Giving
Receiving more than giving	Mutual giving and receiving	Giving more than receiving

Most of us have a variety of relationship types in our lives—some Type I, some Type II, and some Type III. A Type I receiving relationship is the kind we would have with a school teacher or college professor, whose sole focus when we are together is to educate us without expectation of receiving anything from us in return. Type II mutual relationships often occur within a marriage or friendship, in which two equals work together to care for and support each other. A common Type III giving relationship would be that of a parent with a child, in which the parent is the predominant giver in the relationship.

In the case of my client Ron, by volunteering to work at the teen center, he went from having no relationships (zero belongings) to having one of each of the three types of relationships.

1. During the phone counselor training, Ron was in a Type I receiving relationship with his instructor—he received more than he gave.
2. Becoming a part of the organization, Ron developed new Type II mutual relationships—mutually giving to and receiving from his peers.
3. During the phone calls with his teen callers, Ron engaged in Type III giving relationships—he gave more than he received.

By linking in to the community related to his local teen crisis center, Ron found his place in the world and began to experience the positive energy that comes from being connected to the people in the world around him.

> We need to be connected to others—both giving and receiving—to get the most fulfillment out of our lives and to have the support we need to accomplish our goals.

Ron's case represents an example of the positive dynamic of giving and receiving in the world. But what happens when we break that dynamic and all we do is receive, but we never give anything back? Think about the Colorado River, which sources the water supply for many states—such as California, Nevada, and Arizona. If each state continues to draw from the river without finding a way to replace that water (or at least conserve it better), the river will eventually run dry.

The same is true with relationships. Sometimes, we can rely on others to replenish the world's river of love and care (Type I receiving relationships). Sometimes, we can take turns replenishing the river (Type II mutual relationships), and sometimes we need to be the ones to step in and replenish the river ourselves (Type III giving relationships). The world works best—as do our individual lives—when we take turns giving and receiving. None of us can do everything all alone—we have to be willing to seek out and accept the support of others at times. But if *all* we do is take and never give back, the river of love and care in the world—and our relationships—will soon run dry. We can't just take without giving back; if we do, eventually there will be nothing left for us to receive and love won't be returned to us.

When to Receive and When to Give Back

None of the relationship types—Type I receiving, Type II mutual, and Type III giving—is inherently good or bad. What matters is…

- the *context* in which we are doing the giving and receiving
- the *degree of balance* between giving and receiving that we achieve in our lives.

The *context* of giving and receiving and the *balance* of giving and receiving are the two key factors that let us know whether we need to make adjustments to the kind and degree of giving and receiving we are doing in our lives.

Let's look at *context* first. If you are recovering from surgery at home and a friend offers to take care of your laundry, feed your pet, and make you dinner, this is a perfect time for you to accept the offer of help and to receive. If, in contrast, you are in good health but want to go out with your other friends and you ask a different friend to wash your laundry, pick up groceries, and make you dinner, this would be a poor context to expect that kind of help. It's not an appropriate time to ask for this kind of support because you are asking for something you can do yourself, and you are asking your friend to be something other than a friend in this context. This example is a simplistic one—since most of don't expect our friends to do our laundry—but it makes the point clearly: sometimes it's appropriate to ask for help; other times, it's not.

Now let's look at the second factor: your *balance* between giving and receiving. How do you know what constitutes the right balance between giving and receiving? Well, it's different for different kinds of relationships. If you are friends with someone (a Type II mutual relationship), the balance of giving and receiving between the two of you should be roughly equal. In contrast, if you are a parent, your role is to be the giver in the relationship with your child (Type III giving relationship) so the giving and receiving will be unbalanced, with you giving much more than your child. The child's role is to receive and to engage in only minimal giving (Type I receiving relationship). So the best mix of giving and receiving in a relationship will depend on the kind of relationship we're talking about. As you read through the rest of the chapter, you will learn the appropriate balance of giving and receiving for each of the different relationship types (Type I receiving, Type II mutual, or Type III giving).

You will then have an opportunity to reflect on the kind of relationships you have in your life—receiving, mutual, or giving—and assess whether your giving and receiving dynamic is in balance. Does one relationship type predominate for you? Do you find yourself giving to others all the time and not feeling comfortable receiving? Or, if you're honest with yourself, will you discover that you tend to take a lot more from your relationships than you give?

When you are experiencing an imbalance in your giving and receiving, you are likely to encounter road blocks that make it hard for you to reach your goals. For example, if one of your goals is to find a lifelong romantic partner, but you tend to take more from romantic relationships than you give, you may have trouble finding someone willing to stay in a relationship with you for the long-term. Or, if you are the kind of person who likes to give a lot but is uncomfortable receiving, you may find it challenging to develop an intimate relationship with someone. By not accepting gifts (of time, listening, caring, etc.) from others or by being unwilling to ask for support, you may be keeping people at a distance.

When you make adjustments to the mix of relationships you have—say, add more Type III giving relationships to your life or learn how to be in equal partnerships with more people (Type II mutual) rather than to receive from others all the time (Type I receiving)—your boat (and those connected to it) will start to rise. Sometimes, like Ron, to receive, we have to give first. Other times, we need to stop giving so we can receive. As you continue to read, you will begin to figure out which prescription applies most to your current life situation.

Type I Receiving Relationships

Type I receiving relationships are those in which you receive more than you give. When you're on the receiving end of a relationship, the net energy flow is inward.

Healthy Type I Receiving Relationships

There are lots of positive, healthy Type I receiving relationships out there. For example, children who have healthy relationships with their parents will receive more than they give. These children receive love, support, guidance, and physical care from their parents, without needing to give their parents the same in return. Sure, these children may give their parents love and happiness, but they are not expected to run the household or manage the upkeep of their parents' emotional lives. They are not responsible for the majority of giving in the relationship.

Another example of healthy Type I receiving relationships are those you typically have with service providers. Whether you are seeing a doctor, dentist, attorney, life coach, psychologist, physical therapist, hair dresser, or personal fitness trainer, you will be in the role of receiving from the service provider, and the service provider will be in the role of giving—information, advice, or care. Yes, you pay your service provider (a form of giving), but in terms of the relationship dynamic between the two of you, you will be on the receiving end and the service provider will be on the giving end.

Healthy Type I receiving relationships also occur in

relationships characterized by learning. This occurs when you are a trainee at a seminar, a professional being mentored by individuals more experienced in your field, or a student in college or graduate school. In these cases, your teachers are the predominant givers in the relationships.

Limiting Type I Receiving Relationships

The previous examples represent times when it is appropriate and healthy to have a Type I receiving relationship. As you can probably imagine, though, sometimes it can be limiting to be in a Type I receiving relationship. If you have a Type I receiving relationship with a friend, for example, in which you receive or take more than you give, this isn't healthy for either of you.

There are two scenarios in which a Type I receiving friendship might play out: what I call the *fizzling friendship* and the *inauthentic friendship*. If you fall prey to the fizzling friendship, you might be the kind of person who starts new friendships only to have trouble sustaining them. Once people catch on that you want to take more than give, they will quickly decide to end their friendships with you (because it's exhausting for someone to give support and care without receiving the same in return.) Sometimes, fizzling friendships happen without you even realizing it! That's because friends usually don't break up with each other like couples do. Instead, friends just stop calling you or tell you they're too busy every time you ask them to get together. Any chance that this sounds familiar? If it does, the people around you may be telling you that you are engaging in a limiting Type I receiving friendship. If you want to sustain deep or true friendships, you will have to adjust the balance and start giving more.

In the second limiting Type I receiving friendship, the inauthentic friendship, someone *is* willing to stick around and to give more than he or she receives, but by nature, this unequal balance of giving and receiving undermines you and your friend's ability to have a real or authentic friendship. True friendships are always based on mutual giving and receiving. There may be times that you step in and give more or receive more, but the net balance of giving and receiving is roughly equal over time. So if you are in a friendship where the other person gives far more than you do, you are in an inauthentic friendship.

If you are in Type I receiving inauthentic friendships, you have to ask yourself, Why are the relationship partners willing to give you so much? Are they getting something in return for giving so much—like having their identities defined by their friendships? And if they are depending on their friendships to define their identities, are they going to be unbiased in supporting you at all times or will they instead be biased, only giving support when it keeps your Type I receiving friendship intact? This was the case with Elizabeth and her friend Mia, which I describe next.

Any time Elizabeth was feeling down, which was often, she could count on Mia to be there for her. When Elizabeth called, Mia would listen as Elizabeth complained about her job, vented about her boyfriend, and philosophized about life. Elizabeth rarely asked about Mia's life; when she did ask, she was bad about listening to Mia's answer. Mia wished that Elizabeth was a better listener, but she also loved the escape that their conversations offered her. Mia was in a bad relationship with a boyfriend, and it was a relief to forget about her own problems for a while. Admittedly, Elizabeth demanded a lot of Mia's time and energy. She would ask Mia to do favors for her all the time, like drop off milk when she was running low, pick up her dry-cleaning when she had to work late, or dog sit when she was spending the night at her boyfriend's. It could be inconvenient to help Elizabeth out so often, but it also made Mia feel important. She always had something to do—if not for her own life, than for Elizabeth's.

So when Elizabeth told Mia that she was thinking of transferring to a job in a different state, Mia didn't support the change. She started bad-mouthing the new job and saying how hard it would be for Elizabeth to be happy without having any friends in the area. Subconsciously, Mia was trying to change Elizabeth's mind because she didn't want Elizabeth to leave. Elizabeth started second-guessing whether she should change jobs. Instead of gaining support from Mia when she really needed it, she was being held back.

What was going on between Elizabeth and Mia? Elizabeth had a Type I receiving relationship with Mia, in which she demanded a lot from Mia and gave little in return. Mia was willing to engage in this dynamic because it made her feel important and it helped her escape from her own problems. At first, it sounds like a winning proposition for Elizabeth. She gets the "perfect" friend—one who will listen to her for hours, run errands for her, and even take care of her dog. On the surface, it appears that Mia is supporting Elizabeth, but when Elizabeth really needs Mia's support—when she considers a new job that could be great for her professional development—Mia withdraws her support. She will do anything to preserve the Type I receiving relationship that Elizabeth has with her because it makes Mia feel needed and it is part of her identity. If Elizabeth listens to Mia, she won't be taking her new job. A year later, she will wonder why her career isn't going anywhere. She'll have Mia to vent to on the phone, but she won't have the satisfaction of a career that fulfills her.

No matter how "great" a Type I receiving friendship appears to be to you, there is always some darker reality that makes it limiting for both of the people involved. In a sense, you are using the person, and in return he or she is using you. Neither of you has the other person's best interest at heart and so you are working at cross-purposes. You get from the other person what you need; the other person gets from you what he or she needs—but your boats get tied up together. When it's time for you to sail forward, you can't move because the other person is holding you back. When the other person tries to move forward, it is you who holds the other person back. (Note that all of the conclusions that apply to having

175

a Type I receiving friendship also apply to having a Type I receiving romantic relationship. Romantic relationships, like friendships, are meant to be Type II mutual.)

Unlike Mia, real friends will be willing to ask you for support, not just to give it. Asking for help is a sign of trust, the hallmark of a healthy relationship. Friends who truly care for you will also help you set boundaries, so you can learn to do for yourself what you've been asking them to do. This means they can save their energy to help you when something comes up that you can't handle alone. In the case of Elizabeth and Mia, Elizabeth was fully capable of running her own errands. She really didn't need a friend for this kind of support. What she needed was a friend to support her during life's big moments, like when she was considering making a career change.

Why is it that some of us form limiting Type I receiving relationships? There are a couple of reasons that tend to explain this experience. One reason that people form limiting Type I receiving friendships is because when they were young, they had parents (or caregivers) who never gave them what they needed (particularly emotionally) and always expected them to do things for them: to give much more than is healthy for children to give. In response, these children may have grown up and repeated their parents' behavior of not giving and of expecting to receive all the time. These individuals think this is a normal way to function, because of their parents' behavior; also, they are trying to fill up the part of themselves that was never filled by their parents.

The other reason people sometimes end up in unhealthy Type I receiving relationships is that their parents (or loved ones) doted on them so much during their formative years that they never learned to care for themselves—physically, psychologically, or emotionally. This treatment taught these children that it was natural for others to take care of them, even as adults, and made them feel as if they were unable to stand on their own.

If you can relate to either of the preceding cases, your

mission will be to learn about when it is appropriate to expect others to support you and when it is not. For the times that it's not appropriate, you can learn how to meet your own needs so you become self-sufficient and capable of having satisfying relationships (see the "Caring for Yourself" section later in the chapter for more information on developing self-care skills). This skill will come in very handy in life because there will inevitably be times when the people who love and care about you will be unable to be there for you, because they are busy taking care of themselves or their families.

Letting go of inappropriate support may be a challenge for you, so I recommend that you tell people in your life that you want their help in letting you do things for yourself when it's appropriate. Many people will appreciate the invitation to tell you honestly when you are asking them to do too much. If anyone resists your efforts to become more independent, you might need to spend less time with him or her until you've gotten good at taking full responsibility for the demands of your life.

Here are some of the signs that you are engaging in a limiting Type I receiving relationship.

- You feel entitled to take up your relationship partners' time and to ask your partner for favors rather than feeling gratitude when he or she offers you their time and assistance.
- You feel you are in control of the relationship.
- When you talk to your friend or partner, you don't give him or her much time to talk or respond.
- You don't ask how the other person is doing, and when you do, you have trouble listening to his or her response.
- You ask for support and favors from your friend or partner without offering support or assistance in return.
- Some friends or loved ones have mysteriously dropped out of your life; you've never understood

177

why they stopped calling you or are always busy when you want to spend time with them.

Limiting Type I receiving relationships can be hard to recognize because we get so wrapped up in our own needs that we don't even realize we are ignoring someone else's needs. They are also hard to recognize because often others will not give us feedback on the fact that we are expecting too much from them—they will simply disappear from the relationship. If someone does have the courage to tell you that you're expecting them to give you too much, try to consider this feedback as a gift, as hard as it might be to hear—an opportunity to improve and enrich your relationships.

Type II Mutual Relationships

Type II relationships are mutual relationships—those in which both people contribute equally. A Type II mutual relationship is reciprocal and balanced: each person in the relationship contributes; each person in the relationship receives.

Healthy Type II Mutual Relationships

Friendships, romantic partnerships, and marriages are examples of healthy Type II mutual relationships. Friends and romantic partners in a Type II mutual relationship will show interest in each other's lives, express caring toward each other, and listen and offer support when the other person is struggling with challenges. Each person in the relationship gives a lot, but each person also receives a lot. One relationship partner cares about the other relationship partner, so he or she wants to give. The relationship partner also receives a lot, so he or she wants to give back.

Housemates and work colleagues also do well when they have Type II mutual relationships. Housemates and colleagues will be less intimate than friends or romantic partners, but the dynamic of reciprocal giving and receiving that they participate in is the same. For housemates in a Type II mutual relationship, each will contribute to cleaning the house, paying the bills, and calling the landlord when there's a problem. For work colleagues, particularly those on the same team, each will pull their weight with job responsibilities, so that they work together to achieve company goals.

Of course, being in a marriage, friendship, or housemate situation does not automatically guarantee you will be in a Type II mutual relationship. If the dynamic in these situations is one where someone receives more than he or she gives or gives more than he or she receives, it will be a limiting Type I receiving or Type III giving relationship. Just think about the housemate who never washes the dishes, has overnight guests every weekend, and forgets to pay the bills. Or the "friend" who acts as if the other person is there to serve his or her every need. It's a sign of health when coworker and housemate situations, friendships, romantic partnerships, and marriages are Type II mutual relationships, but there's no guarantee that these relationships will be mutual. It's up to us to create that dynamic, as well as to seek partners willing to invest in that dynamic.

What does a healthy Type II mutual relationship look like in action? Is each of the people giving and receiving in equal proportion at all times? Not always. Life happens in cycles. Sometimes, you will need more from your partner than your partner will need from you. And sometimes the reverse will be true. In such times, one person might be giving more to the relationship and the other might be receiving more from it. Then, when the cycle of life continues, the dynamic will shift. The giver will become the receiver, and the receiver will become the giver. This is the beauty of Type II mutual relationships. The two people become better together than they would be on their own. When one person is feeling weak, the other person can use his or her strength to lift the other person up. This is the power of connectedness or interdependence. Here's an example of how the person who's giving versus receiving in a Type II mutual relationship fluctuates over time.

Mike and Jessica had been married for 15 years, and over that time, they had been through a lot. Jessica miscarried the couple's first child; Mike had been downsized from his company, losing his job; and each of them had lost one of their parents. Happily, the couple's relationship was strong and healthy (Type II), which helped them weather life's challenges and stay committed to each other. When one of the two was having a hard time, the other was able to offer support. The miscarriage hit Jessica particularly hard; thankfully, Mike was able to shower his love and attention on Jessica during this difficult time. Several years later, Mike lost his job. It was natural for Jessica to step in and be strong for the both of them—supporting Mike as he recovered from the shock of losing his job and considered his future job options. When life was going well for the couple, their dynamic of give and take was more balanced; when life was particularly rough for one of them, the other was able to step in and offer support.

Because Mike and Jessica were in a Type II mutual relationship, they took turns supporting each other—sometimes one gave more than the other, but the net balance of giving and receiving was equal between them over the course of their marriage. Was their marriage perfect? No. Were there times that one of them didn't notice that the other could use some extra support? Yes. But both people in the relationship *valued* being mutual partners and would usually step up to the plate and support the other person when they got a little reminder—some communications from their partner—that he or she needed some extra love and care. This is how healthy Type II mutual relationships work—each person wants to be there for the other person and is also willing to communicate when he or she needs the other person's support.

One of the most challenging times for a Type II mutual relationship occurs when both people need extra support, but neither has much energy to give. This happened for Mike and Jessica when they both lost their parents at the same time.

Mike and Jessica's parents both got sick around the start of the new year. First, Mike's mother was diagnosed with cancer; soon after, Jessica's father had a stroke. Mike and

Jessica both had close relationships with their parents, so when they got sick, it was a very sad time for each of them. Within a year, both parents passed, and Mike and Jessica's sadness deepened. The two each grieved in their own way for their own parent, not to mention the sadness they felt for the loss of their spouse's parent. The sadness they felt in their own lives made it difficult for them to support each other in the way that they might normally have during difficult times.

Because Mike and Jessica were both undergoing a lot of emotional turmoil and stress during the loss of their parents, they weren't able to engage in the typical mutual dynamic of giving and receiving with each other that they were used to. Mike needed a lot of support; Jessica needed a lot of support; and neither had enough resources to give the other the kind of support he or she needed. This was hard on their relationship; sometimes they argued, sometimes they just felt sad and distant. Happily, Mike and Jessica had the skills to draw on other resources of support—internal and external—to get them through the difficult time and allow their marriage to weather the storm.

> After the loss of their parents, Mike and Jessica had to find comfort in their larger support system, beyond their marriage, as well as within themselves, to work through the grief. Mike started attending more church events; Jessica started seeing a psychologist. Mike spent his evenings reading novels; Jessica cuddled up with a blanket and watched her favorite reality TV shows. Both of them spent more time with their sisters and brothers than they had in a long time. Slowly, they recovered from their grief, and as they did, they were able to talk more to each other about the pain they were feeling. They were able to invest back in their relationship because they had been receiving so much from the rest of their support system as well as their own inner resources.

As wonderfully supportive as Type II mutual relationships can be, most of us can't get all the support we need from a particular relationship partner. There will be times when the other person is busy, is having a bad day, or is knee-deep in struggles themselves, and they just don't have the ability to give us the support we need. We tend to know this intuitively about our friends, but we often think we can get everything we need from our romantic partners.

There's nothing wrong with expecting a lot from your partner. We all deserve to be loved, honored, appreciated, and supported. It's just that the reality of life doesn't always make this possible. Life's timing isn't always convenient— like when Mike and Jessica both lost their parents at the same time, or, on a simpler level, when two people in a relationship have both had bad days. This makes it a little bit harder for each person to give to the other.

The best way to cope with the reality that no one person can provide you with all the support you need is to (a) become good at drawing on your inner resources for support and (b) foster a diverse social network of other people in your life who you can turn to for support.

Caring for yourself. Let's look at drawing on your inner resources first. To do so means to develop the ability to rely on your own skills to calm yourself when you're feeling overwhelmed or panicked, to cheer yourself up in hard times, and to generate solutions to challenges when they arise. Having the skills of self-care are important because, as much as other people can support you and provide you with comfort and guidance in difficult times, only you can make the necessary changes in attitude and behaviors to move yourself past the difficulty.

To understand this idea that only we can help ourselves, think about the times when your loved ones are hurt or sad… when you would do anything to take away their pain. Your listening ear and smiling face might ease their pain somewhat, but you also realize that there are limits to how much you can affect your loved one's mood. Similarly, your friends' generosity and caring might brighten your day, but their care is not like a magic wand that makes everything okay. Only you can take control of your life and do things to change how you feel and act in the world. For this reason, to move forward in life you will need to cultivate your self-care skills to complement the support you will be getting from others.

How you can best take care of yourself when you are in a challenging time will depend on your personality. For some people, they benefit from going on mental vacations—heading to the movies, playing computer games, or working on their cars—anything to get their minds off what's bothering them and take breaks from their troubles for a while. Others benefit from delving into personal contemplation—spending a day hiking, listening to classical music for a few hours, or painting. The more practice you get at caring for yourself, the more familiar you will become with what kinds of things cheer you up, comfort you, and inspire you in difficult times. Once you take a break to care for yourself, you will have more energy to focus on dealing with the challenges at hand. You will be better able to support yourself (and others) and move forward.

Reaching out to others. As important as the ability to develop the skills to care for yourself is, it's even more important to learn how to reach out to others besides your romantic partner when you are in need. This is especially true when your self-care ability is just starting to grow. The old proverb that I mentioned in the book's introduction that "Two heads are better than one" is more than just a cliché; it's a profound truth about life. No matter how smart, rich, or clever we are, we can't solve all of life's problems on our own. And, as we saw in the example with Mike and Jessica, sometimes life's problems strike us at the same time as they strike our partners. When this happens, it's an opportunity to discover the value and benefit of having an extended community.

If you have developed an extended community beyond just your romantic partner, when your partner can't be there for you, as we saw with Mike and Jessica, you have other options. For example, Mike chose to spend more time at church with people from a common spiritual community, while Jessica hired a psychologist for support. And both Mike and Jessica spent more time visiting with siblings. Having these extra people in their lives helped them to cope with the simultaneous loss of their parents without making the other partner feel guilty about not providing the support that they were simply not able to give at the time. The larger your extended community, the more support you have access to; the key is reaching out to this community when you need help.

Exercise 8.1 will help you brainstorm on different activities and social arenas you can turn to in challenging times, in the same way that Mike and Jessica did, so that you don't have to rely on a single person for support and/or care in your life.

Exercise 8.1: Creating a List of Uplifting Activities

Instructions: Look at each of the following categories of activities and write down all the activities (if any) within that category that you enjoy doing. Next time you are feeling angry, tired, upset, etc., try doing one of these activities and see if it lifts your mood. Keep revising the list till you get it right; then file it away in your wallet or dresser drawer or keep it posted on a mirror to remind you of ways you can improve your mood when you are feeling down.

Arts (for example, draw, paint, sculpt, write, or dance; go to a museum; listen to music):

Entertainment (for example, go to the movies, watch TV, or rent a movie; read a magazine, the newspaper, or a book; go to a show):

Social Outings (for example, call or email a friend, meet up with a friend, hang out at a coffee shop, attend a hobby club):

Religious or Spiritual (for example, attend church, read an inspirational book, talk to a religious leader, go for a walk in nature):

Sports (for example, go for a walk, run, bike ride, or swim; go play pick-up basketball at the park; go fishing):

Other (for example, drink a cup of coffee or tea, buy a new book to read, wash your car, spend some time in your garden):

In the coming weeks, you can continue to pay attention to the kinds of activities that tend to lift you out of a bad mood and revise the list you created in Exercise 8.1. Over time, you will have a solid group of activities—small and big—that you can turn to when you need some extra support in your life.

Limiting Type II Mutual Relationships

As we've discussed, Type II mutual relationships are healthy for friendships, marriages, and other romantic relationships. Type II mutual relationships also work well for relationships between housemates, coworkers, and adult siblings. There are some times, however, when a Type II mutual relationship doesn't work very well, namely, when each person in the relationship would be served best by one person consistently giving and the other person consistently receiving. For example, when you go to a service provider—say, a doctor or a tax attorney—you want and need that person to focus completely on caring for your health or your taxes. You don't want to be called on to help the service providers solve their marital problems or health problems or tax problems. That's not your job, and you'd probably feel pretty resentful if the person you were paying for assistance expected you to help them.

Similarly, if you are in a Type III giving relationship—say, as a coach, teacher, or a counselor—you might feel uncomfortable if your student or client asks you a lot of personal questions.

185

You sense that this will shift your relationship to a mutual one, and you know that you won't be able to serve your student or client effectively if he or she starts feeling like you are friends rather than giver and receiver.

When you are in a Type II mutual relationship that would function better as a giving or a receiving relationship, I call that a *limiting* Type II mutual relationship. Here are some of the signs that you are in a limiting Type II mutual relationship.

- Your relationship started out as giving or receiving, but over time it has changed to mutual and that makes you feel uncomfortable.
- Your relationship has changed from a giving or receiving relationship to a mutual relationship, and your relationship partner has shown signs of being uncomfortable with this change (for example, made comments, cancelled appointments).
- You have a mutual relationship with someone, but your profession (medicine, psychology, teaching) indicates that it is unethical to have something other than a giving relationship with this person.

If you feel uncomfortable with a Type II mutual relationship, you have the information that you need to readjust boundaries back to a Type I giving or Type III receiving relationship or even to end the relationship. However, if you are comfortable with a Type II mutual relationship while you're relationship partner is not, it can be a lot harder to detect this. You may feel fine with the mutual dynamic without realizing that the other person does not. Your best bet to avoid this situation is to keep in mind the general principle that client–service provider relationships are usually best served by a giving–receiving dynamic rather than a mutual dynamic. Most professions teach this somewhere in their ethical codes, so as a professional you probably already know this. But as a client, it helps to remember that being in a Type II mutual relationship with a service provider can lead to conflicts of interest and breaches of trust. This isn't to say that you can't be *friendly* with your clients or service providers, just that being actual *friends* can lead to problems.

Healthy Type II mutual relationships are the kind of relationships that can last a lifetime and help sustain you as you pursue your life's goals. Because the energy flow is reciprocal, each person in the relationship is continually renewed and reinvested into the relationship. Your partner is there to offer you a stream of love and support because you offer your partner love and support in return.

Type III Giving Relationships

Type III giving relationships are those in which you are the predominant giver in the relationship. The net energy flow in these kinds of relationships is outward. To understand this relationship type, take the Type I receiving relationship and reverse it. Instead of you being the student, protégé, daughter, or son, you are now the teacher, mentor, or parent. As with Type I receiving relationships, Type III giving relationships can be positive or negative, healthy or limiting.

Healthy Type III Giving Relationships

Healthy Type III giving relationships are those in which we willingly enter the role of giver, and we do so without expecting the other person in the relationship to give back to us. School teachers, college professors, doctors, nurses, therapists, coaches, and volunteers of all kinds fit this description. Their work is based on helping others; they do not expect any help or support in return. True, many in this group do expect monetary compensation for their services, since they make their livelihoods out of giving, but they do not expect emotional support, psychological support, spiritual support, or physical support of any kind. They are the givers in the relationship, and they give happily and without hesitation.

Are there some teachers, doctors, or therapists who try to turn the Type III giving relationship into a Type I receiving or Type II mutual? Sure, there is always the possibility that some people will confuse their roles and responsibilities, overstep boundaries, and expect to receive something (other than monetary compensation) in return for their giving. But the roles of teacher, doctor, and therapist are intended to be Type III giving, and most people in these roles are interested in respecting the boundaries and maintaining the appropriate type of relationship.

Being a parent is the ultimate Type III giving relationship because the entire relationship with one's child is built around giving. It is the parent's job to provide everything for the child—physical support, emotional support, intellectual support, discipline, and even spiritual support. Some parents do better at this than others, but most parents love their children and willingly give to them.

A hallmark of healthy Type III giving relationships is that we enter into them without expecting the other people in the relationship to give something to us in return for our giving. Does this mean we don't benefit from the Type III giving relationship? Not at all. In fact, some of us gravitate toward Type III giving relationships precisely because of the rewards we receive by giving. The benefits of engaging in a Type III giving relationship can include developing a feeling of purpose in one's life, experiencing joy at seeing someone helped by our efforts, and gaining validation that we are replenishing life's river of love and care. The key here is that when we gain something by being in the Type III giving relationship, it comes out of our *giving*, not our receiving. The other person in the relationship needs to be present, but he or she doesn't have to give. *The other person's job is simply to receive.*

Imagine the feeling of being a pediatric surgeon and having a parent look you in the eye and say, "Thank you for saving my child." Think about seeing a smile pass over an elderly person's face when you show up to visit him or her at a nursing home. Or envision the excitement of your child learning to ride a bicycle because you taught him or her how to do it. What are you feeling in these situations? Probably joy and happiness. Maybe even peace and purpose. Ironically, Type III giving relationships can be some of the most rewarding relationships you'll have, in spite of the fact that you are the predominant giver in the relationship. In most healthy Type III giving relationships, you feel energized when interacting with the other person, and you are content with the role you play in the relationship—giving without receiving.

Limiting Type III Giving Relationships

Type III giving relationships provide a wonderful opportunity for you to invest back in the community, whether you get paid to teach elementary school kids or you volunteer to do gardening at a local park. Giving of yourself to others can, as was the case with my client Ron, help you develop a sense of purpose in your life and gain a sense of belonging and connectedness to your world. Nonetheless, there are some cases in which being the primary giver in a relationship can be limiting to you. A limiting Type III giving relationship occurs when you…

- unwillingly enter into the role of giver
- expect the other person to give back to you even though the initial relationship is defined by the other person receiving rather than giving
- are the predominant giver in a relationship that is meant to be mutual
- feel resentful, disappointed, or angry toward the other person in the relationship after you give to him or her
- feel the other person is in control of the relationship.

Reversed Type III giving relationship. The first kind of limiting Type III relationship is what I call a *reversed Type III giving relationship.* This occurs when what should be a Type I receiving relationship gets reversed into a Type III giving relationship, for example, when a child, because of family dynamics, is forced to fill the role of the parent. Maybe the mother is an alcoholic and the father isn't present, so the child finds him or herself stepping in to parent the other children and even the mother. The child becomes the predominant caregiver in the family, and the mother and the other children rely on the child as if he or she were a parent—if not for monetary support, then for emotional support and discipline. Does the child want this role? Did the child choose this role? No, circumstances thrust it upon the child. Being in this kind of Type III giving relationship is limiting and even harmful for the child, because it interferes with the child's natural development and personal growth. Instead of being free to be a kid, the child has to focus much of his or her energy on caring for a dysfunctional parent and often his or her younger brothers and sisters. The child is in a Type III giving relationship when he or she should be in a Type I receiving relationship.

Demanding Type III giving relationship. The second kind of limiting Type III relationship is what I call the *demanding Type III giving relationship.* This occurs when the giver expects the other person to give as well and can occur in a variety of circumstances. Maybe a therapist starts confiding her personal problems in her client or a professor tries to start a romantic relationship with a student. Suddenly, the giver is expecting the other person to give in return; he or she is confusing a Type III giving relationship for a Type II mutual relationship. But it's not the client's job to lend the therapist a listening ear, nor should a student be expected to offer companionship to a teacher. In addition, Type III giving relationships are often compromised by a change to Type II mutual relationships, so that the work of the Type III giving relationship can no longer take place.

For example, if a therapist and client start to become friends (changing their relationship from Type I receiving or Type III giving to a Type II mutual relationship), the therapeutic relationship will probably break down because of the growing personal relationship. For example, the therapist

190

might start giving advice (which is what friends do) rather than using open-ended dialogue (which is what therapist's do). The client might start feeling like she needs to support the therapist because they are friends now, which will diminish the client's ability to focus on herself in session, the goal of the therapy. If the client wants to continue therapy, he or she will have to find a new therapist.

Occasionally, Type I receiving and Type III giving relationships morph into Type II mutual relationships and both people are okay with the change. Nonetheless, when you are in a Type III giving relationship with someone—when you are the primary giver—you have a responsibility to honor the receiver's trust. The person you are serving is putting faith in you that you will make good on your implicit promise to give without the other person being expected to give. In a Type III giving relationship, you are often the person in power and control. So it is your job, and your job alone, to respect the boundaries of the relationship. If you don't respect the boundaries of the relationship, you will end up causing the other person harm. You will break his or her trust and will have abused your power.

Overly-giving Type III giving relationship. The third limiting Type III relationship, what I call the *overly-giving Type III giving relationship,* occurs when someone is the predominant giver in a relationship that is best suited for an equal balance of giving and receiving, such as a friendship or marriage. Friendships, marriages, and romantic relationships are meant to be reciprocal. When the giving and receiving is balanced, both partners feel energized and satisfied. When one person gives more than the other, however, negative emotions often develop: resentment, frustration, and disappointment on the part of the giver; guilt, anger, or indifference on the part of the receiver.

Why are you sometimes willing to give more than you

191

receive in a friendship or romantic partnership? There are many possible reasons. Perhaps you feel unworthy of being loved just as you are, so you try to compensate by serving another person to an extreme. Perhaps the other person in the relationship isn't giving enough, so you try to "jump start" his or her giving by giving a lot yourself. You carry the hope that, "If I give enough, maybe the other person will eventually want to give back." Another possibility is that you have invested a lot of time and energy in the idea that you are a giver. You believe that this is the role you are meant to play in life or the role you are *obligated* to play. This might occur if you grew up in a family where you were expected to act in a parental role or where it was the norm for you to give to your family rather than receive from your family.

Whatever the reason, when you give more than you should in a relationship, you may feel that the sacrifice of giving too much seems like a worthwhile trade-off for the reward. Maybe giving makes you feel needed, distracts you from your own life, or gives you an excuse not to care for yourself. Or maybe giving so much is part of your identity.

If you find yourself in an overly-giving Type III giving relationship, ask yourself why. What is the payoff? If you can figure out why you are giving more than is healthy for you, you can try to address this issue so you no longer want to engage in limiting Type III giving relationships. For example, if you overly give in relationships that should be mutual because you want to feel needed, try investing your giving energy in an appropriate Type III giving relationship like volunteering. If you are overly invested in giving because you feel this is the only way you can be loved by someone else, take some time to work with a therapist or life coach who can help you reconstruct your belief system so that it is more supportive to you. And so on. Try to find the root cause for giving too much in relationships that should be mutual and address them so you can achieve more balance between giving and receiving in your life and start moving forward.

If you struggle to reshape your *existing* limiting Type III giving relationships to Type II mutual relationships, you can also bring some *new* Type I receiving relationships into your life (for example, take a college class, learn a new skill, seek out a professional mentor or coach). This will give you an opportunity to practice receiving more and giving less. You can then apply this dynamic to the limiting Type III giving relationships in your life and try to reshape them into healthy Type II mutual relationships.

Although some relationships are not suited to Type III giving relationships as we have just seen, healthy Type III giving relationships can offer some of the most rewarding experiences you will have in your life. Giving to others often provides us with a fresh perspective on our own lives, instilling gratitude and appreciation for what we have. It can also connect us to our community, providing our lives with a sense of meaning and purpose. Giving your gifts—of time, support, or knowledge—to someone else can also bring you fulfillment and contentment.

Adjusting Your Relationships

Most of us begin our lives with a lot of Type I receiving relationships, and this is normal and healthy. We are surrounded by parents, grandparents, teachers, coaches, and so on—people who tend to shower us with their giving—and we don't yet have much to give in terms of money, knowledge, or experience.

Over time, we will ideally develop more Type II mutual and Type III giving relationships. We reach out to our peers and make friends, we get involved in long-term romantic relationships or marriages, and maybe we have children, nieces, or nephews. We become bosses in the workplace and leaders in our community. This is because, as we mature, we gain more of those things (money, knowledge, and experience) that we can start sharing with and giving back to others. If you realize as you reflect on your life that you are lacking certain kinds of relationships (Types I, II, or III), there are adjustments you can make to your life to attract those relationships that you are missing.

> If you find that you are overly giving or overly receiving in your relationships (out of balance) or that you are giving and receiving in the wrong situations, you can adjust your dynamic of giving and receiving to improve your relationships and move forward in life.

Questions to Ask

If you notice that you are feeling stuck in your life, take some time to assess what kind of relationships you have with others—Type I receiving, Type II mutual, or Type III giving—and to determine whether some adjustments to your life might help you strengthen your relationships and move forward in life. Here are some questions to consider.

- *Do you have some of each relationship type?*
  If the answer to this question is no, take some time to develop at least one of each relationship type. It can be helpful to have a variety of relationship types—Types I, II, and III—because we benefit from all three in different ways. In Type I receiving relationships, we often gain specialized support that we can't obtain from our Type II mutual relationships—such as education, mentorship, or healing. Also, in Type II mutual relationships, particularly those that are long-term, we experience sustained support by someone who cares deeply for us. Additionally, we get the pleasure of investing in someone else as much as he or she is investing in us. In Type III giving relationships, we learn what it means to give selflessly and enjoy the rewards of such giving—contentment, purpose, and meaning.

- *If Type I receiving or Type III giving relationships dominate in your life, what are the payoffs for you of those relationship types? What are the drawbacks?*

  o In Type I receiving relationships, the payoff may be that you've got guaranteed support and attention from others. You may choose friends who are loyal to you at all costs and surround yourself with paid professionals whose job it is to attend to you. You may bully other people into giving you their support, or they may have their own reasons for giving more than they receive. Either way, the trade-off is that you're never really sure if the people in your life are sincere about supporting you. Are they there for you because they truly care about you or because they have a personal interest in overattending to you?

  o In Type III giving relationships, the payoff may be that you have an excuse to avoid nurturing your own life. Maybe you are afraid you won't succeed with your own goals, so you pour all your attention into helping others succeed. This gives you an alibi for not getting ahead in your own life. Or, the payoff may be that you get to play the martyr. Maybe the attention you get when you complain about all that giving makes you feel loved or important. The drawback in the first case is that you are unable to focus on moving forward in your life. In the second case, the drawback is that you are never really sure if the people you are giving to sincerely care about you. It's possible that they only like you for what you do for them rather than for who you are.

- *Do you think you're in a Type II mutual relationship when you're really in a Type I receiving relationship?* When you have a Type I receiving relationship with a friend or romantic partner, it may be difficult to see that you are taking more than you are giving. It's hard to admit that the dynamic is lopsided, not only because this may be unflattering to you, but because in your mind you want the relationship to be mutual. What matters here, though, is not how you envision the relationship to be, but how the relationship really is. Once you recognize that it is a limiting Type I receiving relationship, you can make changes in the relationship to shift it to Type II mutual. With a friend, this can be as easy as asking and listening to how your friend is doing, to offering emotional support in difficult times (saying "I'm here for you"), and volunteering to be helpful when needed. These changes in behavior can shift your relationship back into the healthy zone of Type II mutual. If you struggle to make these changes, you may want to meet with a therapist or a life coach to address the deeper causes for this challenge or engage in group therapy, which will give you a wonderful chance to get regular feedback from your peers.

- *Are you expecting to receive from a Type III giving relationship?* This occurs when you are in a relationship that is designed for you to be the predominant giver (parent, coach, teacher) but you start to expect something in return from your relationship partner. If you find yourself relying on the other person for support of some kind (for example, a listening ear, reassurance, or companionship), you have begun to mistake that relationship for Type II mutual. It's time to reinstate Type III giving boundaries (you give; the other person receives) or end the relationship and work on bringing healthy Type II mutual relationships into your life (friendships, etc.).

- *Are you in a Type III giving relationship when you really want to be in a Type II mutual relationship?* If you notice that your friendships and romantic relationships tend to be Type III giving, ask yourself why? How and why are you enabling this to happen? Wouldn't you rather be in a relationship that is reciprocal? If so, you can begin to ask for more support in these relationships and draw boundaries when giving becomes too much. Communicate with your partners that you will be making these changes and explain why—so you can be a more sincere partner to them and a kinder person to yourself. If they are unwilling to accept a Type II mutual relationship, it may be time to move on and look for people who are interested in mutual connections.

- *Are you in a Type I receiving relationship when you would really benefit from a Type II mutual relationship?* Some of us are so good at surrounding ourselves with people who are willing to give to us without receiving as much in return that we've convinced ourselves that these are the kind of relationships that we want in our lives. But consider what you are sacrificing to gain a constant flow of support without you reciprocating that support. You may be giving up the opportunity to replenish life's river of love and care by giving to others, satisfaction of assisting someone else accomplish their goals, and opportunities to discover your life's purpose.

- *Are your relationship types congruent with your goals?* Our relationships can play an important role in helping us reach our goals, so it's important to reflect on how and whether our relationships are supportive of our goals. For example, if your goal is to live a life in which you help other people, are you engaging in any Type III giving relationships? If your goal is to get promoted at work, but you've been passed over a couple of times, have you considered hiring a professional coach (Type I receiving relationship) who can help you identify your obstacles to promotion? If you are struggling to reach certain goals, take time to consider what kind of relationships might help you achieve those goals.

If you find it difficult to bring certain relationship types into your life, consider the barriers shown in Table 8.2 that can make it hard to pursue one relationship type or another. This table also provides ideas on how to work through these barriers so you can bring more receiving, mutual, or giving relationships into your life as needed to achieve more balance.

Table 8.2: Obstacles to Bringing Types I, II, and III Relationships Into Your Life

Barrier	Solution	Example
Barriers to Types I and II Relationships		
Being overly independent	Work on giving up control.	When you have an important decision to make, ask a parent, mentor, or coach for his or her opinion.

Barrier	Solution	Example
Being unwilling to seek support or help, feeling that asking for help is a sign of weakness	Work on asking for help and accepting help when others offer it.	When you need to move, ask a friend to help you move boxes; when you feel sad, be willing to share your feelings with someone instead of concealing them; if there's something someone can do to be helpful to you, explain how the person can be helpful.

Barriers to Types II and III Relationships

Barrier	Solution	Example
Being overly selfish or overly self-focused	Commit to focusing more on other people.	Ask people how they are and take the time to listen to their responses; when someone is having a hard day, surprise them with a cup of coffee or flowers.
Being too focused on what you can gain from a relationship	Determine what things you are best suited to give to the relationship.	If you are good with numbers and your partner isn't, offer to help put together a budget for him or her; if you are a good cook, offer to prepare meals for your friends.
Having expectations that others are there to serve you	Try to cultivate gratitude for the things people do for you rather than expecting them to be helpful.	Say thank you and/ or do something nice for someone who has done you a favor; ask for favors rather than demand them; don't ask for help with things you are capable of doing for yourself.

It can be hard to admit to your own areas of weakness, but if you are willing to consider what barriers may be standing in the way of you achieving more balance in the kind of relationships you have in your life, the benefits will be worthwhile. You will gain valuable clues into how to adjust the ways you interact with others so that they are more able to support you and you are more able to support them. You will then be able to experience firsthand the experience that… all boats rise together!

Some Tips on Adjusting Friendships and Romantic Relationships

If you are having a challenge in a friendship, a romantic relationship, or your marriage, take some time to assess the nature of the relationship. Is it Type I receiving, Type II mutual, or Type III giving? Who's doing the giving and who's doing the receiving? Both of you? One of you? If there are hints that the dynamic of giving and receiving is out of balance, this may be the source of your relationship challenges and may be something you'll want to work on adjusting.

If you discover that your friendship, romantic relationship, or marriage is not a Type II mutual relationship, I recommend spending some time reflecting on how you can bring the giving and receiving dynamic back into balance. Once you gain some clarity on where the imbalance lies, you'll need to communicate with your partner and see if you can enlist him or her in working with you to adjust the dynamic of giving and receiving. If you are the one who is taking too much from the relationship (Type I receiving), much of the responsibility will lie with you to make behavioral changes; if you are the one who is giving too much (Type III giving), you will need to make adjustments, but your partner may also need to make some behavioral changes too.

The details of how to make adjustments in your relationships depend on the context of the situation. If you give too much to your partner because it makes you feel needed, you can make changes in your own behavior by pulling back and giving less in those areas that are inappropriate for giving. If your partner tends to demand a lot of you, your partner will also need to make some changes. In all cases, both partners are usually responsible for the dynamic that has been created between them and for making changes to it. If your partner is unwilling to change or you find it is hard to adjust a dynamic that is so natural for the two of you, it may be time to enlist the help of a therapist or even to consider ending the relationship. Ending a relationship is never a decision that's easy, but if a relationship resists positive change and limits you from moving forward, it may not be the right relationship for you.

1 + 1 = 8: How to Handle Multifaceted Relationships

An important reality you will also want to consider when looking at your relationships is the fact that they often have multiple facets to them. For example, you may work with someone and be friends with him or her at the same time. That's two relationships in one—coworker and friend. As an adult child, you may find yourself as both a caregiver to your parent and a child to your parent—again, two relationships in one. For example, if your parent is aging, you may be the caregiver looking after your parent, but you will still be your parent's son or daughter, which means some part of you still needs him or her as your mother or father.

The most multi-faceted of all relationships is with a spouse. In this case, two people usually come together because of romantic interest in each other, but over time, other facets of the relationship develop. Perhaps the two also become roommates, financial partners, and parents. This is what I call the *1 + 1 = 8* phenomenon: when two people come together and engage in multiple relationships with each other (three, four, five, six, eight relationships, etc.).

Multi-faceted relationships come with their own unique set of challenges because two people may get along very well in one facet of the relationship but not another. For example, you may get along great with your partner romantically but can't stand the way he or she wants to manage your joint money. Or maybe you have great respect for your partner as a parent but think he or she is a terrible housemate—leaving dirty clothes everywhere, splashing toothpaste on the mirror, and leaving dishes in the kitchen sink. Here's an example of how the challenges of a multi-faceted relationship can play out.

> Before I got married, I thought I was an unselfish person; but once I got married, I realized that I hated sharing my stuff! I remember coming back from my honeymoon and going into my new bathroom to unpack my toiletries. I opened the medicine cabinet to put my deodorant in it and discovered that there was no room. My wife had completely filled up the medicine cabinet with her stuff. Of course, there was plenty of room on the counter and under the sink for my toiletries, but that wasn't the point. At the time, all I could remember thinking was that my wife took up all of the space in the medicine cabinet and I had no room to put my deodorant. I was irritated!
>
> Suddenly, my wife and I were more than friends and romantic partners. We were housemates…and about to be financial partners…and eventually to be parents together. Although I had fallen in love with my wife because she was a wonderful romantic partner and friend, after we got married, I had to learn how to become housemates with her too. The only way we could have a happy, healthy marriage was if we learned to get along within all the facets of our relationship; and over time, we did.

As you work with your significant other to foster a healthy balance of giving and receiving, consider each of the different aspects of your relationship—roommate, friend, and romantic partner. In each of these realms, we usually need to focus on different issues of give and take.

If you are *housemates*, you and your significant other will want to seek harmony in your lifestyles. To do this requires each person to be sensitive to the other person's values concerning cleanliness, noise, and social activity. Rather than insisting that the other person give away all his or her rights while you keep all of yours, you will want to make sure that both of you communicate what is more important to you and work out compromises as to how to handle the less important issues. The keys when sharing physical space together are communication and compromise.

As *friends* it's about finding things you and your significant other both like to do together. This is where your preference for energizing comes into play. If you both have the same reenergizing preference, then planning joint activities together will be much easier. For example, both my wife and I are introverts, so we both enjoy staying home together on the weekends. However, if your preferences are different from your significant other's, then you will need to put some work into planning activities that will meet both of your needs. Again, you will need to be willing to do some things that may not be as enjoyable to you as they are to your partner. And hopefully your partner will be willing to do the same. By appreciating the other person's different needs and being willing to forego some of your own, you will be able to build an enduring friendship—as well as gain the bonus of being introduced to new activities (extroverted or introverted) that you might not otherwise engage in.

As *romantic partners*, you will focus on coordinating your goals, values, and priorities. Because a lot of long-term relationships involve making decisions, this is where your decision-making preferences will come into play. It is rare to find any couple whose three decision-making preferences are exactly the same as each other's. This means that you and your partner will have to be aware of your own preferences as well as understanding and accommodating of each other's preferences where they are different. Your communications preferences also come into play here. If your preferences for communication are different, take the time to learn the other partner's language so that you can effectively communicate with each other.

As you work to achieve harmony in each of the different facets of your romantic relationship, you will be making continual decisions about when to make compromises and sacrifices. In healthy Type II mutual romantic relationships, sacrifices are made for the relationship, but they are sacrifices that are reasonable and worthwhile. *Reasonable sacrifices* are those that a person can make without giving up a fundamental part of oneself or without harming oneself; *worthwhile sacrifices* are those things a person is willing to give up because the person feels he or she will gain something meaningful in return for doing so. Most long-term, romantic Type II mutual relationships involve reasonable and worthwhile sacrifices. On a small scale, this might include a husband choosing to watch less football so he can go out with his wife for an outing or a wife spending less time on the phone with friends so her husband gets more of her time and attention.

If you are used to having Type I receiving romantic relationships, you may feel compelled to end a relationship when the annoyances of a long-term situation surface. You are likely used to gaining a lot from your partner, and the idea of having to give up something in return might be hard for you. If you start to feel this way, ask yourself, is the sacrifice you're being asked to make worthwhile? Is it reasonable? It might seem easier in the moment to walk away from a relationship than to make sacrifices for it, but what do you give up by walking away? If a goal of yours is to have a healthy and fulfilling, long-term romantic relationship, you will need to learn how to engage in a Type II mutual relationship. It's the only way that lifelong romantic relationships really work. Yes, some people who are in Type I receiving or Type III giving romantic relationships stay together for a lifetime, but this doesn't mean that they are truly happy or that they have a healthy relationship.

If you are used to having Type III giving relationships, your tolerance for sacrifice in a relationship may be greater than is healthy for you. You are likely used to giving more to a relationship than you gain, so you may have a tolerance for a partner who takes advantage of your help, caring, and generosity or at least who doesn't resist it. If this is the dynamic of your relationship, you can make some adjustments. You can practice setting more boundaries for yourself—this often involves saying no—and learning how to ask for help when you need it.

For example, when your spouse asks you to mow the lawn after work but you're having a bad day, you can give yourself permission to say no. And when you come home from work exhausted, you can ask your spouse if he or she can make dinner so you can have the night off. (These are small-scale examples, but they represent times you may have trouble asking for what you want if you tend to be the giver in a relationship.) You might be surprised at your partner's willingness to support you in taking care of yourself. Then again, you might meet a struggle. It all depends on the effectiveness of your communication with your partner and his or her willingness to engage in a Type II mutual relationship. The adjustment might be difficult for both of you, but the good news is that in many cases it is possible to make changes and the rewards are well worth the efforts.

Conclusion

The goal of this chapter has been to show you the importance of being connected with people and to give you the tools you need to develop the three kinds of relationships that each of us needs in our lives.

My purpose hasn't been to simply put labels on your relationships, but really to help you notice the degree of giving and receiving you are doing in your relationships at a given time and to assess whether the balance needs to be adjusted to help you move forward in your relationships and in your life. Regardless of what labels we put on relationships—receiving, mutual, or giving—sometimes we ask too much of our relationships, and other times we give too much and ask too little.

What is your tendency? What is going on relationship-wise in your life right now? Are you too focused on what you gain from relationships or do you instead give too much, too often? Would you benefit from bringing more support into your life (Type I receiving and Type II mutual relationships) or perhaps you would grow by engaging in more relationships that are based around the giving of yourself (Type III giving relationships). The prescription for each of us is different, depending on our personality types, goals, and the context of our lives. Once we reflect on our unique needs, we can begin to make small adjustments to our relationships that will eventually add up and help us form the island chains—and communities—that are so vital to us moving forward in life.

Part II—Executing Your Life Plan

9

Building a Vision

Before we jump into Part II of the book, let's pause for a moment—and take some time to reflect on the significant work you've done while reading Part I. As you've worked your way through the chapters, you have likely made some real discoveries about yourself. You've gained insight into how you reenergize, how you make decisions, and how you communicate with others. You probably also have a better understanding of the dynamics of giving and receiving that exist in the world and a sense of where you fall on the continuum of giving and receiving within your own relationships. You've learned about the importance of sharing your strengths with others and of asking others for support.

From the work you've done in Part I, you've hopefully also gained a new model for understanding your whole person. You know to examine your behaviors, your beliefs, and your belongings (your three identity Bs) when trying to understand who you are and how you operate. And when you encounter challenges, you now know to ask yourself, am I behaving, believing, and belonging in-sync with my true self? Do I need to realign my three identity Bs with my personality preferences? Or do I need to intentionally mask my personality a little more often to achieve my goals?

It's not always easy or comfortable to take an honest look at who you are and how you are behaving, believing, and belonging in the world. And it takes a lot of energy, as well as courage, to examine the ways you interact with others and the reasons why. Hopefully, you are discovering that the journey is worthwhile. Congratulations on each and every step you are taking!

The reason we spent so much time in Part I of the book focusing on your personality preferences is because I believe that the key to finding success in your life—to achieving your life vision—is to build a life that is in-sync with your true self. I call this *nurturing your nature*, which means that

209

you design your life to honor (nurture) your inborn traits and temperaments (nature). In Part I of the book, we spent a lot of time gaining a clearer understanding of the preferences of your unique personality (or nature). Now, we will spend Part II of the book focusing on how to nurture that nature: by creating a life plan that is in-sync with your personality, developing a strong support group in your life, cultivating meaningful group memberships, learning how to give back to the community that supports you, and more.

Part II of this book also offers a means of putting your new understanding of yourself and others into action. It's about taking the wisdom you've gained in Part I and transforming it into a life that satisfies, fulfills, and uplifts you. We begin this journey of action here in chapter 9, by focusing on developing a life plan that is in-sync with your personality. This life plan will be the starting point for a life of meaning and fulfillment. You will learn in the remaining chapters how to nurture that plan—and your nature—through the relationships and connection you maintain with others.

Finally, when others see you living an authentic life, they may be inspired to do the same. So, in a way, you will also be learning how to uplift others in Part II. By living your best life, you will be showing others how they too can live a meaningful life—you will be making a positive contribution to the communities in which you live.

Now that you have a better understanding of who you are in the world, how you act, how you communicate, and where you belong—now that you have a clearer sense of your personality and your identity—you are ready to create a life plan that is right for you and to work toward achieving that plan. You are ready to turn your dreams into your reality.

Bigger Than Your Dreams

The first step in living a satisfying and fulfilling life is to create a vision of what you want your life to look like. Just as successful entrepreneurs start out with a clear business plan and just as winning political candidates follow a smart campaign strategy, each of us needs to develop a personalized *life plan* or *life vision* before we can achieve the life of our dreams. No matter how blessed we are in our lives—no matter how much we want to achieve fulfillment—a life of contentment will not happen to us accidentally. The only way to achieve your goals and dreams is to define what those goals and dreams look like. You can't hit a target, after all, unless you know what you're aiming for.

One of the first things I do with my clients when they show up in my office is to help them figure out what their life visions are. This creates the framework for all of the coaching that happens between us—the big picture of who a client wants to be and where he or she wants to go in life. In other words, this gives both the client and me a picture of the target that the client is aiming for. We can then put that target on a "map," and sketch out what work needs to be done to hit that target.

So what exactly is a life vision? A life vision is a picture of the kind of person you want to be in the world and of the life you want to lead. A life vision is more than a dream. A dream is usually just the picture of what you want, without any of the supporting plan or details on how you are going to achieve that dream. *A life vision, as I define it, is a picture of what you'd like to achieve in life, supported by a detailed plan of how to turn that dream into a reality.*

> Dream + Plan = Life Vision.

Because of the structure involved in a life vision, I also refer to a life vision as a *life plan*. Here is an example of the difference between a dream and a life vision.

Dream: *I want to write a book one day.*
Life Vision: *I want to write a book in the next two years. To achieve this goal, I will come up with a topic for a book, write every day, read books on getting published, network with other writers, and hire an editor to help me polish the book.*

Dream: *I want to play basketball for the NBA.*
Life Vision: *I want to play basketball for the NBA when I*

graduate from college. So I will get good grades in high school and apply to the top NCAA ranked schools. I will practice and train every day to keep my skills sharp. I will work with my coach to set up meetings with scouts and recruiters. I will play my best at every game.

So a life vision is different from a dream in that it is more than a picture of what you want; it is a picture of what you want *plus* a plan for how to achieve what you want.

Let's look at one more concept that is similar to a life vision but that has a significant difference: a fantasy. *A fantasy is a dream or a vision that is unlikely to come true.* On the basis of your own limitations or the world's limitations, a fantasy will never be transformed into a reality. For example, if I am terrible at playing basketball, my dream or life vision of playing in the NBA is a fantasy. It is not grounded in what is possible or real, so no matter what plan I follow to achieve it, it is highly unlikely to come true.

One of my clients was (and still is) not very tall, but he loved the sport of basketball. He could tell me every stat about every team and player and their histories. He was a decent player, but not extraordinary. In our first meeting, he told me that he wanted to work on a plan for becoming an NBA player. He said that he was willing to practice as much time as it took and travel to wherever it was needed for him to get the opportunity to play for a professional basketball team. I asked him if he really thought that becoming an NBA player was a realistic goal for him. He said, "Probably not, but this has been a dream of mine for so long, I don't want to let go of it now." I told him that sometimes dreams don't come true, but realistic visions do. I gave him a homework assignment and asked him to think about and write down other things that he could do with his basketball knowledge and athletic skills that did not involve playing for the NBA.

When we met at our next session, my client had a list of four things: team coach, private coach, sports writer, and sports broadcaster. I congratulated him on coming up with realistic alternatives and asked him which of these appealed to him the most. He said team coach, because he really liked helping people (during his personality assessment we discovered that he had a preference for feeling). I asked him if he knew of any coaching opportunities that he could try out to see if he really liked team coaching. He replied that his former high school coach had been trying to get him to help coach the boys JV team at his old high school for a long time but that he hadn't responded because he was busy pursuing his dream of becoming an NBA player. I suggested that he contact his former coach and see if the opportunity to help out with the boys JV team was still open. It turns out that it was, and my client found out that he loved coaching. His knowledge of basketball is making him a great coach. Plus, he gets to share his passion for the game with the boys on his team. He has achieved a realistic vision for his life. A few months ago, I asked him if he regretted not chasing the NBA player dream anymore and he replied, "No. Truth is, I would probably still be chasing it and would have missed out on all the wonderful opportunities I have had to do something real."

So while it might be hard to admit to yourself when you're holding on to a fantasy or an unrealistic dream, you can see from my client's experience that a fantasy can be tweaked and adjusted into an achievable vision. I often work with my clients to help them differentiate between life visions and fantasies and then to remake their fantasies into realistic, achievable life visions. Here's another example.

One of my clients, who is famous and was recently pictured on the cover of *People* magazine, told me that what he really wanted most was for his daughter to be able to lead a "normal" life. He didn't want her to be treated differently than other children and he wanted her to grow up "just like the other kids in her school." I asked him, how many of the other children's parents were on the cover of *People* magazine last week? He smiled and said, "None." This admission opened the door for us to have a good discussion on fantasy versus reality. The reality is that my client is an international celebrity, which means that his daughter is not going to have a "regular" childhood—so that vision would be totally unachievable; it is in fact, a fantasy. I did a little probing and found out that my client was afraid that his daughter would become like so many of the other celebrity children that he had met or read about—spoiled, selfish, rude, and maybe even addicted to drugs or alcohol. This concerned him, because he didn't want his daughter to turn out like that. Now we had something realistic to work with.

So over the next couple of coaching sessions, I helped my client create a vision for his daughter that would give her the tools and incentives to become kind, considerate, generous, and grounded. It soon became apparent that if this was his vision for his daughter, there would be some changes that he would have to make to his life. So he cut back on some of his concert dates, so that he could spend some more time with his daughter. He scheduled trips with his daughter back to where he grew up, so that she could appreciate what she was growing up with compared to what he had as a child. He spent more time meeting his daughter's friends and made himself available to be home, so that she and her friends could spend their free time at his house instead of somewhere else. These were things that he could do, that he had control over. Instead of trying to do the impossible, my client was able to create a life vision that was very possible and achievable.

Although this particular client was a celebrity, the same issues can apply to those of us who aren't celebrities. For example, you may want your child to have a certain kind of upbringing but because you travel all the time for your job or work a lot of hours as an executive, you are having trouble providing your child the kind of upbringing you say you want him or her to have. Once you recognize that your dream for your child is unrealistic under the current circumstances, you will have the opportunity to change your work circumstances so your dream is achievable after all. Maybe you decide to cut back hours at work, or you work from home more often. Maybe you change jobs or switch to a position that involves less travel. Once you recognize that a dream is unrealistic, you have the power to adjust your dream—or to change your life—to make the dream more achievable.

So, building a life vision, rather than a fantasy, allows you to root your expectations for your life within a framework of reality. As we have just discussed, part of this process involves considering your limitations. Another important part of the process—the flip side of your limitations, in fact—involves looking at your *opportunities*. Many of us have trouble focusing on our opportunities, and, instead, we see only our limitations. We get stuck focusing on what we don't have or can't get.

To help my clients get over this kind of tendency, I often ask, "What opportunities do your circumstances provide you that others do not have?" In the case of my celebrity client whom I described previously, I asked him, "What are the benefits for your family of your fame? How can you use those benefits to your family's advantage? If you weren't famous, what are the opportunities your children might miss out on?" If you find yourself focusing on your limitations rather than your opportunities, you may want to ask yourself a similar question: What current life circumstances, personal gifts, and personal strengths provide you with opportunities that you may want to incorporate into your life vision?

Now that you have an understanding of what a life vision is,

Dream + Plan = Life Vision,

you can begin to contemplate what your unique life vision is. Do you have a life vision right now? Or are you flying blind? Maybe you have a dream but no plans for how to turn that dream into a reality. Or maybe you have lots of plans but they don't support a particular dream.

If you are reading this book, chances are you already have a dream—probably lots of dreams. After all, if you are feeling stuck in some area of your life (one of the reasons you may have picked up this book), this implies that you have a destination you are trying to get to. This implies you have some sort of picture in your mind of what you want to achieve. This is the dream part of the vision equation, and a good start.

Of course, it's also possible that you *think* you have a dream when what you really have is a *plan* or part of a plan to achieve that dream. For example, I had a client who came to me saying he wanted to pass his next oral interview at work so he could be promoted to police sergeant. As my client framed it, getting promoted to sergeant represented his dream. After we talked things through a little further, though, it became clear that my client's real dream was to be a leader in his organization. Being promoted to sergeant was actually just one of the things he needed to do (part of the plan) to become a leader within his organization.

Once we were able to identify my client's real dream, it became clear that my client needed to do more than pass his next oral exam to achieve his dream of becoming a leader. He also needed to start reading leadership books, learn how to adopt certain behaviors that promote strong leadership, and begin communicating his desires to the existing leaders in the department so that they could help with his leadership development. So you can see the importance of defining your dreams accurately: You won't be able to develop an effective plan for achieving your dreams unless you are clear on what your dreams are. Like my client, you don't want to confuse part of the plan for the dream itself.

It All Starts With a Dream

What are your dreams right now? Maybe you are aspiring to get promoted within your career field, maybe you want to find a romantic partner to share the rest of your life with. Maybe you hope to be a billionaire by age 40, maybe you want to change the world. No matter what your dreams, dreams tend to involve a picture of one of the following three things:

1. what you want to *have* in your life (not necessarily material)
2. what you want to *achieve* in your life

3. the *quality* of person you want to be in the world.

What you want to have in your life. What would you like to have in your life tomorrow that you don't have today? A new car? A new house? A million dollars? A thinner body? A job that you love? A family that you enjoy spending time with? Friends who support and listen to you? Some of the things we dream of having in our lives are material, some of them are not. Take some time to consider what it is that you'd like to bring into your life that you do not already have. Also remember that sometimes to gain something, you may have to get rid of something else. For example, if you want to have peace in your apartment at night, but you live next to loud neighbors, you may have to give up your apartment and move to a quieter place. If you want to be able to afford to travel more often, you may need to trade down to a less expensive car to free up money in your monthly budget.

What you want to achieve in your life. The second type of dream we tend to have involves the things we want to *achieve* in our lives, for example, run a marathon, write a book, be elected to political office, record an album, run your own company, improve the government, raise children, and so on. This type of dream doesn't involve adding something new to our lives like the first type does. Instead, this type of dream involves accomplishing something that is worthwhile or that you are interested in. It can be as simple as graduating from school or as complex as finding a cure for Parkinson's disease.

The quality of the person you want to be in the world. The third type of dream we tend to have involves the kind of person we want to *be* in the world. As we know from Part I of the book, you can't actually change your personality (your true self), so I'm not suggesting that you can change that aspect of who you are (you can mask it, but you can't actually change it). What I am referring to here is creating a dream for the *quality*

217

of person you'd like to be in the world, for example, being kind, generous, thoughtful, sensitive, easy to talk to, down-to-earth, friendly, approachable, respected, considerate, or available. When I say *quality*, I am referring to your character. Without being morbid, think of what you would want people to say about you at your funeral or what you would hope they would inscribe on your tombstone ("A man who spent his life teaching others...", "A woman who always protected children...").

Note that all of the visions we will discuss in this chapter will involve attaining, achieving, or being something *in the future*. In truth, our visions are not just limited to acquiring, achieving, or being something new; they can also include *maintaining* something we already have in our lives, like a loving marriage or a fulfilling career that you already possess. As most of us know, healthy relationships need attention and energy, and successful careers take work. So your life vision should also include the things in your life that you want to keep—the things in your life that you currently have, the things you are currently achieving, and the qualities you currently embody that you want to hold on to—so you can develop a plan to maintain these things.

Finally, as you identify your dreams, you will also want to bear in mind what your personality preferences are. Designing your dreams to be in-sync with your personality preferences will increase your chances of being successful at achieving your dreams and will also increase the likelihood that your dreams will fulfill you when you achieve them. It will also make the process of pursuing your dreams more fluid because you will be working toward something that flows naturally from your true self. This can be something as "simple" as planning your dream vacation or as "difficult" as finding your dream job.

For example, I have a client who was very frustrated with his life at the time we met. He told me that his job of working as a supervisor in a clothing warehouse was unfulfilling and his life seemed to lack purpose and direction. This was causing him to feel bitter and depressed. I gave him an assessment to help him discover his preferences. As a result of the assessment and the subsequent conversation that we had, my client determined that he had preferences for extroversion, intuition, feeling, judging, and direct communication— ENFJD.

Based on what I know about the needs and aspirations of people with the ENFJD preference combination, I suggested a few career possibilities for my client to consider. All of the career possibilities that I suggested involved a few key themes: personal involvement with others, ability to be creative, and continued personal growth and development. The funny thing is that one of the career possibilities—graphics designer—was something that my client had always enjoyed doing, but he didn't feel that it was practical enough for him to pursue. It appeared that he had developed this belief to please his father (who I would characterize, on the basis of my client's description, as an ESTJD—very traditional and down-to-earth). So my client was pursuing a career that was satisfying to his belongings (his dad) but that was not in-sync with his personality. The coaching process gave my client *permission* to walk down a different road and he hasn't looked back. He went back to school to improve his graphic design skills, started working at a company that lets him use those graphic design skills, and plans on starting his own company one day, designing great logos and artwork for himself and other clients. He is extremely happy and excited about his life now because he is living in-sync with his true self.

The Different Domains of Life Fulfillment

There is another way of understanding the different kinds of dreams we may have for our lives. We can look at the different life domains—professional, personal, community, and spiritual—and consider the dreams we hold for fulfilling these different domains. That is, we can develop dreams for what we want to have, what we want to achieve, and the qualities we want to display at work, at home, in the community, and in our spiritual world. We are not always good about tending to each of these domains, but if we want to lead fulfilling lives, it's important to create a vision for each of these areas.

The *professional domain* is the part of your life that involves work, career, or what might be called *vocation*, regardless of whether you are being compensated for that vocation. We will talk about vocation more in depth in chapter 14 on pursuing your passion in life.

Can You Be a Professional If Your Work Is Unpaid?

You have to have a paid job to have a professional life, right? Actually, the answer to this question isn't that simple. If you have work in your life that you approach in a serious and professional manner, then you have a professional life, regardless of whether you are financially compensated for that work.

Let's look at examples of a couple of people who consider themselves to be professionals at what they do, even though they are not paid for it. First there is John, a volunteer firefighter. He works once a week at the local engine company and is considered by the paid firefighters as another member of the team. John keeps up-to-date on the latest trends in fire service by subscribing to and reading journals and books on the field of emergency management and by attending company training sessions when offered. Although he works for free, he takes pride in the fact that the citizens can't tell the difference between him and the full-time crew members.

Next let's look at Katrina, a stay-at-home mom. Katrina used to be a high school teacher before she had children, so she takes the same energy and enthusiasm that she used to bring to her classroom and uses it when raising her own kids. She plans out the month with activities and lessons that she plans on teaching her son and two daughters. She reads up on child development topics and is continually improving her knowledge about parenting. She considers herself to be a professional parent, even though she isn't being financially compensated for it.

As you can see from John and Katrina, being a professional is not about whether you are compensated for your work but instead relates to how you approach your work. Although John and Katrina don't receive pay for their work, they treat their work professionally and thus feel fulfilled in the professional domains of their lives.

The *personal* part of your life is made up of your home, your hobbies, and your leisure activities. This is the part of your life that involves rest, relaxation, and recreation.

Your *community life* is made up of family, friends, and other organizations that you belong to. This is the domain where you discover the different types of relationships that you are involved in.

Your *spiritual life* is made up of the people and practices that involve your religious or spiritual beliefs.

A complete life vision will touch on all the domains in your life, and a compete life vision will help you lead a life that is fulfilling on all levels. To assess how much attention you are currently giving to each domain of your life, you can complete Exercise 9.1, the Calendar Exercise. Sometimes, life goes by so fast that we don't realize where we are spending our time. If that sounds like your experience, the Calendar Exercise is a great way to help you determine how much time you are devoting to the main domains of your life.

Exercise 9.1: The Calendar Exercise

Instructions: Complete steps 1-3.

Step 1: Print out a calendar for the month that just ended. (If you don't have a printed calendar, then just make up a table with five rows and seven columns, print the dates in the corresponding boxes, and now you have a calendar.)

Step 2: Determine how much time you have been spending in each domain. In each day, there are 24 hours; figure that 8 of those are used for sleeping, and 4 of those for other things like eating, showering, getting dressed, etc. That leaves 12 hours per day that you want to track. For each day, list how many hours you spent in the professional domain, the personal domain, the community domain, and the spiritual domain. (There may be some overlap between the domains—that's okay, just split the time evenly between the overlapping domains, being careful not to count the time twice.) Now add up all the time that you spent in each of the domains and you will see where you are spending your time. If you have trouble remembering how you spent your time during the past month, you can track how you spend each day for the coming month. Each morning when you wake up or each night before bed, record how you spent the previous day.

Step 3: Create a pie chart for your time allocations. Take some time to review the following pie charts (Figures 9.1–9.3). Which one most closely represents how much time you spend in each domain? Take out a pen and paper and draw a pie chart that is reflective of your current life.

Figure 9.1: Balanced Time Allocation

Figure 9.2: Normal Time Allocation #1

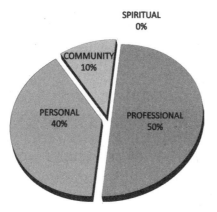

Figure 9.3: Normal Time Allocation #2

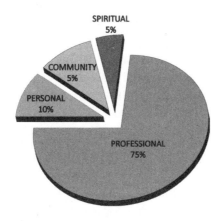

What have you discovered by selecting a pie chart that represents the way you spend your time? Have you found that you maintain a desirable balance in your life, in which you participate fairly equally in all of your life domains? Or do you find that you neglect certain areas of your life or give more time and energy to one domain than you'd like to? Remember, time is fixed, so if you are going to make changes, then you are going to have to adjust the time that you spend in one or more of the other domains. For example, if your desire is to spend more time in the spiritual domain, then to do that you will have to spend less time in the professional, personal, or community domains. The Calendar Exercise is a great way for you to determine how you are actually spending your time, not just how you think you are spending your time.

There are many different breakdowns (pie charts) of how people spend their time and in which domains. And there is no set prescription for the perfect breakdown; only you can sense which breakdown would be right for you. Do you want to spend more time with your family and less time at work? Would you like have more time to pursue your hobbies or do you feel you've been neglecting your religious or spiritual life? Reflecting on the current breakdown of your time and how you feel about that breakdown will help you determine what kind of dreams you may want to add to your life plan.

Will Your Dreams Fulfill You?

When you start to examine your dreams, you'll most likely find it useful to spend some time asking yourself whether your dreams really do have the potential to bring you satisfaction and fulfillment in life. Sometimes, the things we think we want to acquire or achieve won't actually bring us happiness when we attain them. For example, if you want to enter a career that is completely out-of-sync with your personality preferences, you may find that once you attain that career, you are as restless or unhappy as ever. Perhaps you are a feeler who studies to be a doctor, only to realize you'd rather be a social worker. All of your work toward realizing your dream of becoming a doctor will have been for nothing, because that dream does not fulfill you when you finally achieve it. If you can detect that a dream is unable to fulfill you *before* you strive to achieve it, you will of course save yourself a lot of time, energy, and resources. Instead of expending your resources on fruitless tasks, you can make sure you are focusing your time and effort in the places that will yield true fulfillment in your life.

One of the biggest pitfalls of formulating dreams that won't really fulfill you occurs within dreams that involve acquiring material things. So many people think that if they have more money, more expensive clothes, a bigger house, or a better car, they will finally feel happy—they will finally feel satisfied with their lives. But material things, in and of themselves, cannot provide happiness.

Money, for example, certainly has the potential to help you lead a more comfortable and stress-free life, but it is no cure for discontentment. Discontentment usually comes from living a life that is out-of-sync with your preferences (your true self) and out of touch with a nurturing community. No matter how much money you have, if you are living out-of-sync with your true self, you will feel discontentment in your life. No matter how many material possessions you acquire, if you are not linked into a nurturing community, you will feel some dissatisfaction in your life. Think about all the wealthy people out there in the world. Do you get a sense that they are all happy? Probably not. Think about all the wealthy celebrities we see getting divorces, checking themselves into rehab centers, and confessing about the terrible relationships they have with their families. Wealth does not guarantee happiness.

Neither does celebrity. Just like money, fame in and of itself cannot bring happiness. Being famous, as an actor or musician, say, can provide more opportunities to perform and to do what a person loves—acting or singing. Being famous may provide people with ample money to provide for their families. And being famous can provide celebrities with a platform for fighting for issues that they believe in—

like working to protect the environment or to feed hungry children. But it's the *advantages* of fame—engaging in pleasing professions, providing well for one's own family, working to help others, and so forth—that can bring people happiness, not celebrity itself.

The same is true for achieving a different body—thinner, stronger, taller, shorter, tanner, wrinkle-free, or whatever ideal image you hold. Let's look at weight loss for a moment, since it is a goal of so many people. What can weight loss do for you? If you are an actor, having a thinner body might help you get more roles; if you are a personal trainer, being thinner may help you win more clients. Being thinner might also give you more confidence with which to conduct yourself at your job; it also might help you live a longer life. But achieving outward physical beauty is no replacement for realigning your life with your preferences. Only when you make improvements to your "inside" can you enjoy the benefits of making improvements to your outside.

Unfortunately, many people lose weight only to discover that they still feel unhappy or unworthy inside. True, there are many benefits to taking care of your outside self and there is nothing wrong with striving to lose weight (or refreshing your wardrobe, getting a makeover, and so on), but it's important to recognize that these things can only provide you with confidence, not contentment. Contentment comes from living an authentic life—one that honors your true self.

Those of us who think that material things will bring us happiness are relying on a faulty equation. We neglect to see the "does not equal" sign in the following equation:

$$\text{Dream of Material Things + Plan to Achieve Those Things} \neq \text{Happiness.}$$

Sometimes, we think the preceding equation is true, especially while we are chasing our dreams of material things. Once we attain those material things, though, we are likely to realize that we are still generally the same people we once were, with the same level of contentment or discontentment in our lives.

If you think or feel that material things will bring you happiness, then you will want to reformulate the preceding equation to look more like this:

Dream of What I Expect Material Things to Bring Me
+ Plan to Achieve That Dream
=
Fulfillment in Some Area of My Life.

What has changed in the new equation? A couple of things. First, instead of your dream focusing on the material things themselves (for example, money), it focuses on the *benefits* you hope to derive from those material things (for example, less stress, more freedom to pursue your hobbies, opportunity to give more money to charity). In this way, you will be able to aim for the right target: the *benefit* you feel might be provided by the material thing rather than the material thing itself.

Second, we see that by achieving our dreams, we will achieve fulfillment in *some area of our lives* but may not achieve happiness in all areas. We are multi-dimensional human beings; as such, no one dream alone can satisfy all levels of who we are. As we discussed earlier, we need to formulate dreams to support all areas of our lives: professional, personal, community, and spiritual.

Let's look at some examples of how you can reformulate your material dreams to focus on the *benefits* of material things rather than material things themselves.

Material dream: *I would like to have a new house.*
Dream reformulated to focus on desired benefits of material object: *I would like to have more room to entertain so I can have friends over more often. (Variants: I would like to have more storage space so my living area isn't so cluttered. I would like to have a home office so I can comfortably work from home more often.)*

227

Material dream: *I would like to be millionaire.*
Dream reformulated to focus on desired benefits of material object: *I would like to live in a neighborhood with a better school system, be able to go on more vacations, save for my kids' education, and save for my own retirement. (Variant: I would like to be in a career that commands respect from my peers.)*

Material dream: *I would like to have a thinner body.*
Dream reformulated to focus on desired benefits of material object: *I would like to feel better about my appearance.*

All of the preceding dreams started out with an end goal of achieving something material or superficial (a house, a certain income, a particular body type). But with some contemplation and refocusing, we can see that what the person with the dream really wants is a *benefit* of that material thing more than the thing itself. Do you really want more money or do you want the peer respect that you assume more money can bring you? Do you really need a new house or can you simply reorganize your current house or build an addition to achieve your goals of entertaining more or working from home more often?

Reformulating your material dreams to focus on the larger benefits you seek will allow you to create a targeted plan for achieving what you *really* want—freedom to entertain, more respect from peers, confidence, and so forth—and increase the number of ways you can achieve these benefits. Now instead of being limited to money or a thinner body as the pathway to your dreams, you can consider other options as well. Perhaps a bigger income *is* what you need to be able to go on more vacations, but there are other options too: getting a job that enables free travel or the accumulation of frequent flyer miles, becoming more savvy on finding travel discounts, visiting destinations where friends live to avoid hotel costs, selling some possessions and putting the proceeds in a travel fund, or cutting spending elsewhere in your budget and routing the extra money toward your travel budget. Suddenly, instead of having only one option to achieve your goal—a bigger income—you have several options. That's empowerment!

If you find yourself formulating dreams that focus on material things, I recommend taking some time to ask yourself what the anticipated benefits of these material things are (see Exercise 9.2). Then work to reformulate your dreams to achieve those benefits rather than the material things themselves. When you are ready to develop a plan, you will have many options for achieving those benefits.

Exercise 9.2: Reformulating Material Dreams

Instructions: Answer the following questions here or on a separate sheet of paper.

What are the dreams that I have that involve material things? (include in these money, possessions, physical appearance, and fame)

Material Dream 1: _____
Material Dream 2: _____
Material Dream 3: _____

What are the benefits I anticipate gaining by attaining this material dream?

Benefits of Material Dream 1: _____
Benefits of Material Dream 2: _____
Benefits of Material Dream 3: _____

How can I reformulate my dream to focus on the benefit I hope to attain rather than the material thing itself?

Reformulated Dream 1: _____
Reformulated Dream 2: _____
Reformulated Dream 3: _____

What are all the ways I might be able to achieve my reformulated dream?

Possible ways to achieve Dream 1: _____
Possible ways to achieve Dream 2: _____
Possible ways to achieve Dream 3: _____

Hopefully, by doing this exercise, you will discover that there are many ways to achieve your dreams—ways that go beyond acquiring material things. This exercise should also help you realize that material things don't actually make up your dreams but instead can serve as part of the plan for achieving your dreams.

Plans Transform Dreams Into Visions—and Then Reality

Now that you have an idea of what a dream is, let's talk about the second piece of your life vision: formulating a plan to achieve your dreams. To develop a plan for achieving one of your dreams, you will want to ask yourself, "What are the tangible steps I need to take to make this dream come true?" Here is an example of a plan that could be used to support a person's dream of having a career that focuses on improving others' lives. As you will see, the dream and the plan together make up the person's life vision.

> **DREAM**: *Help others through my life's work*
>
> +
>
> **PLAN:**
> - *Read books and talk to a career counselor to help identify careers in which I can serve others*
> - *Take a career preference assessment test to determine which careers might satisfy me*
> - *Arrange informational interviews with people in those professions to learn more about them*
> - *Volunteer in one of these career fields to see if I like it*
> - *Attain necessary training to be in this career field*
> - *Network with others to develop contacts in the career field*
> - *Apply for jobs in this career field*
>
> *= LIFE VISION*

As you can see from the preceding example, a plan involves many steps toward achieving the dream or larger goal. I call these smaller steps your *point goals* and the larger dream your *process goal*.

When you put your process goals together with your point goals, you are likely to achieve your overall vision:

> Process Goal + Point Goals = Achievement.

Do you remember my client who wanted to pass his oral interview and get promoted to sergeant? When we first started working together, my client thought that the promotion to sergeant was his process goal. But it turns out that this was actually one of many *point* goals he had to set for himself to achieve his larger *process* goal of being a leader in his organization.

While your process goal can be somewhat general or abstract (for example, make the world a better place, find a satisfying career, marry a loving spouse), your point goals need to be concrete and tangible. In this way, you will have a clear plan to follow to achieve your process goal.

Two other important characteristics of your point goals are that they need to be integrated and comprehensive. That is, your point goals should work together (be integrated) to help you achieve your process goal, while nonetheless covering different angles (be comprehensive). As you can see, in the preceding life-vision example, the point goals cover a variety of angles (are comprehensive)—self-assessment, practical experience, training, and networking—that are all related to (or integrated with) the larger process goal. You will be much more likely to achieve your process goal if your point goals are comprehensive.

For example if you get special training for your desired career field, but you don't bother to network with others in the field, when you apply for jobs in that field, you may find it quite difficult to get hired. Similarly, your point goals need to be integrated. You want them to support each other rather than have you running off in unrelated directions that dissipate your energy and make it hard for you to accomplish anything real. For example, you will notice that all of the point goals in the previous example have something to do with finding a meaningful career. How out of place would it be for the person to have written, "Learn calculus" as one of his or her point goals? That would not have made any sense and would have been unrelated to the overarching process goal. Instead of being supportive to the person's process goal, that point goal would have been distracting and wasteful of the person's resources.

Looking to Others for Support

Dreams are very personal. No one can know but us which dreams will bring us fulfillment in our lives. Nonetheless, talking about our dreams with others can be very helpful when we are in the process of considering whether these dreams will really fulfill us once they are achieved. When we talk to those who are good listeners and to those who encourage us to live in-sync with our personalities rather than our identities, we can gain a lot, such as perspective on ourselves and insight into our lives.

If you are an extrovert, you may find it helpful to talk to others early in the process when you are first brainstorming about your dreams because talking is a way for you to think out loud and sort through what you want. If you are an introvert, you may feel more comfortable waiting to talk to others until after you have been able to reflect internally on what your dreams are. But eventually, you will want to share your ideas with one or more trusted people. If you trust your friend's objectivity, consider your friend's insight into whether your dreams sound well-suited to your personality.

Hopefully, you will gain valuable feedback from the other person, but, more importantly, you will gain feedback from yourself. As you begin to speak about (extroverts) or internally process (introverts) your dreams when engaging with someone else, pay attention to what is happening—do you sound ready to proceed or do you sound reluctant? Do you get an excited feeling or a sick feeling as you talk about or reflect on your dream? What kind of thoughts are you having? Look for feedback from yourself on whether your dream is in-sync with your true self and whether it has the potential to fulfill you.

Similar to when you are identifying your dreams, you will also benefit from turning to others for support when you begin formulating a plan for achieving your dreams. When you are trying to achieve a goal, you probably won't know everything you need to know to achieve that goal—and you can't know what you don't know, so it can be helpful to call on others to supplement your own ability to create an effective plan. When it comes time to develop a viable plan, you can call on acquaintances, friends, colleagues, experts, and trained helping professionals for support and guidance.

So don't be shy about calling on others who know something about the process goal or life vision you are pursuing; people are often thrilled to share information about what they know and to offer help. Ask people questions; talk to them about your plan; and ask for specific feedback. You can integrate people into the process of achieving your point goals as well. As you can see from the previous example plan, the point goals of this person's life plan involved talking to a career counselor, conducting informational interviews with people in a certain field, engaging in volunteer opportunities, and networking—all activities that involve other people and the community.

Remember, we need other people to achieve success. We can't do it alone!

Building Your Life Vision

Now that you have a good understanding of the process that is involved in creating a life vision—identifying your dreams and creating a plan to achieve those dreams—you are ready to begin building your own unique life vision.

Step 1: Identify Your Dreams

Take some time to consider what kind of dreams you have for each of the domains of your life—professional, personal, community, and spiritual—and answer the following questions. You may want to look at all of these domains right now or you may choose to focus on one particular domain—perhaps the domain that first got you interested in this book. If the latter, you can then come back to the other domains at a later time. Take some time to think the following questions over and write down your answers on a sheet of paper. Note that some of these questions involve considering your personality preferences. If you need a review of the personality preferences, return to chapters 3–7. Reading the tables in these preference chapters can offer a quick review.

Professional:
- What would your dream job be?
- What would you like to have in your professional life that you don't have right now?
- How in-sync is your professional life with your true self and personality preferences?
- What would you like to achieve in your

professional life?
- What have others told you that you are capable of achieving in your professional life?
- What kind of person would you like to be in your professional life?
- What situations, achievements, and personal qualities in your current professional life would you like to maintain?

Personal:
- If your life was perfect, what activities and relationships would make up your personal life?
- What would you like to have in your personal life that you don't have right now?
- How in-sync is your personal life with your true self and personality preferences?
- What have others told you is missing in your personal life?
- What would you like to achieve in your personal life?
- What kind of person would you like to be in your personal life?
- What situations, achievements, and personal qualities in your current personal life would you like to maintain?

Community:
- If you could belong to any groups or organizations in the world, what would they be?
- What would you like to have in your community life that you don't have right now?
- How in-sync is your community life with your true self and personality preferences?
- What would you like to achieve in your community?
- What kind of person would you like to be in your community?

- What situations, achievements, and personal qualities in your current community life would you like to maintain?

Spiritual:
- Why do you think you are here? What activities and belongings would you like to add to your life to support this life purpose?
- What would you like to have in your spiritual life that you don't have right now?
- How in-sync is your spiritual life with your true self and personality preferences?
- What would you like to achieve in your spiritual life?
- What kind of person would you like to be in your spiritual life?
- What situations, achievements, and personal qualities in your current spiritual life would you like to maintain?

At this point, don't worry too much about distinguishing between dreams (the achievable) and fantasies (not likely to be achieved). The following process will help you sort those out. But for right now, just put down all of the dreams that you can think of, especially ones that you haven't thought about in a long time. In other words, don't limit yourself or give in to any inner voice that judges your dreams. Give yourself the freedom to write down all the dreams that excite and appeal to you.

If you note that any of your dreams involve acquiring material things, I recommend that you complete Exercise 9.2 so that you can reformulate these dreams to focus on the benefits of material things rather than the material things themselves. This will increase the chances that achieving a particular dream will bring you the fulfillment you seek.

Step 2: Prioritize Your Dreams

Some of us are great at multitasking and pursuing lots of ventures at once. Others of us do best when we focus on a single venture at a time. Even those of us who are great "multitaskers," however, can't typically pursue all of our dreams at once. So, it's important, in step 2, to take some time to reflect on which dreams are most important to you and which are most pressing.

How would you like to prioritize your dreams? Which dreams do you want or feel you need to accomplish first; which dreams do you hope to accomplish at a later point in time? Answering the priority question will help you decide where to direct your energy right now so it is most effective. Remember, a plan for achieving a single dream has many parts to it, so it can be hard to go after all of your dreams at once. Instead, to be most effective, you want to be focused about what you are trying to achieve. When prioritizing your dreams, consider the following questions. Again, consider writing your answers on a sheet of paper.

- Which dreams are of greatest interest to you?
- Which dreams can you realistically accomplish at this point in your life?
- Which dreams are time-sensitive (in other words, which dreams have to be accomplished sooner rather than later)?
- Which dreams require the assistance or cooperation of others? Is that assistance available to you right now?
- Which dreams can you financially afford to pursue right now?
- Which dreams are related to each other and need to occur before your other dreams can be attempted?

As you try to prioritize your dreams, it may become clear which dreams you need or want to pursue first. Alternately, you may struggle to figure out which dream to pursue first. If you're an introvert, this would be a good time to write in your journal, go for a run or a drive, or do whatever it is that allows you quiet reflection time. If you're an extrovert, this would be a good time to reach out to others: talk through your concerns and your considerations with friends and see if you can start to get a sense of which dream you'd like to pursue first. Introverts and extroverts alike can also benefit from talking to a life coach or therapist to sort through which dreams they want to pursue first.

Step 3: Make Plans

Once you've decided on which dream you'd like to pursue first, you are ready to make a plan to support that dream. You are ready to turn your dream into a life vision. So sit down with a piece of paper and brainstorm on all the things you think you need to do to accomplish your dream. You can do this in solitude, or you can brainstorm with a friend. If you find yourself cramping up at this stage—focusing on all the reasons why you might not accomplish your dream or coming up with reasons why you can't accomplish the steps on the plan—set the plan aside and come back to it on a different day. You need to be in a creative and open-minded mood when you create your plan. If you are in a negative or fearful mood, you're not going to be able to come up with a very effective plan. If you continue to have difficulty developing a plan each time you try to draw one up, you may want to meet with a professional life coach or therapist who can help you work through the fears and concerns that are impeding you.

After you've come up with your initial plan, work on filling it in and making sure it's a good plan. Do research, talk to others, and take some time to contemplate the feasibility of your plan. Ask yourself these questions:

- Is your life vision realistic and achievable given your strengths and the reality of the world around you?
- Does your plan include all the steps needed to

achieve your life vision or are you leaving some steps out?

- Do the steps in your plan work together or do they work at cross-purposes?
- Does your plan involve reaching out to others for support? (Remember, we need others to move forward!)
- Do you need to make any adjustments to your beliefs for your plan to be a success?
- Is this the life vision you want to be pursuing right now?

When answering these questions, look within yourself for answers as well as to others for insight. By looking within, you will gain valuable wisdom from your true self on what dreams excite you and work well with your strengths. Supportive others can help you detect steps in your plan that you've forgotten to include and also may be able to help you see beyond your own limitations (letting you see that a dream is within reason). (Unsupportive others may try to tell you that you can't do something, when you can...so you'll want to disengage from people you suspect don't fully understand your true self.)

Step 4: Commit to Your Plan and Follow Through

Once you've created a plan to achieve your life vision, you will have a road map to follow in your pursuit of life fulfillment. Congratulations if you've made it this far! You now have a realistic and viable vision for a fulfilling life. Now it's time to commit to your plan and to follow through with it.

One way to commit to your plan is to tell others about it and ask them to check in with you on your progress. This helps you stay accountable. You should also add the steps of your plan to your daily calendar as appointments. This will help you allocate the appropriate time to the tasks that need to be accomplished. In addition, you can write in your journal on a regular basis about how your plan is coming along. This is another way of staying accountable and remaining focused on achieving your vision. Finally, working with a life coach is another great way to stay accountable and build support into your life.

As you try to enact your plan, you may encounter certain obstacles. It's helpful to consider these obstacles so you can be prepared to handle them when they arise. Here are some of the possible challenges you may face.

- **"I don't have enough time to accomplish my plan."** This is one of the most common things I hear from clients. The truth is that no one has enough time to do everything that he or she wants to do. But if you prioritize your dreams, decide which dream to focus on first, and then create a plan for achieving that dream that involves manageable steps, you will be able to accomplish one dream at a time, step by step. This may also involve giving up some things in your life to make room for accomplishing your plan. The nice thing is that once you accomplish your plan, you can resume doing those things you gave up. (See Exercise 9.1 - The Calendar Exercise for another way to address to this challenge.)

- **"I don't have enough resources** (for example, money, education, social contacts) **to accomplish my plan."** This is the second most common thing that I hear from clients. The keys to overcoming lack of resources are creativity, courage, and patience. First, you can be creative in finding alternate ways of funding your plan (for example, bartering, selling some of the things you no longer use on eBay, volunteering to gain skills rather than paying for a class). Second, you will need to confront your fear of asking for help and boldly go out and start talking to people—letting them know what you need and accepting their help when offered. Finally, it may take you three years instead of one to accomplish your plan because you have to do it in smaller increments that you can financially afford. That's okay, it doesn't matter how quickly you accomplish your plan, only that you do accomplish your plan. (See Exercise 9.3 - The Checkbook Exercise, which follows, for another way to address this challenge.)

- **"I'm afraid that I am going to fail to accomplish my plan like I have failed to accomplish my plans in the past."** This is an easy barrier to overcome. Take a look at yourself now compared to yourself in the past. What has changed? Well, the biggest thing is the book that you are reading. You now have some tools and insights that you didn't have in the past, which will help you be successful in accomplishing your future goals. You also now know about the importance of relying on other people in your life to help you move forward.

- **"Someone in my life is interfering with my ability to enact my plan."** This is probably the most difficult barrier to overcome, but it is possible to do it. I have devoted a good part of chapter 11 to dealing with this issue in detail (see the "Handling Challenging Relationships" section), but for now all you need to know is that it's going to come down to a choice between accomplishing your plan and maintaining the current status of your problematic relationship. If your plan is worthwhile and in-sync with your true self, then the significant people in your life should be supporting you in accomplishing it. If they are not, then you may have to change the nature of the relationship.

- **"I am older and most of the people doing this will be younger; I am embarrassed."** There are two things that you need to remember to help you overcome this barrier—there is no clock running on achieving goals, and experience counts. First of all, there is no guide book or instruction manual out there that says that you should have accomplished your specific plan by a certain date. You are not delinquent or behind, you are right where you need to be, primed and poised for action. Second, all of your life experiences to this date are invaluable aids in assisting you with accomplishing your plans. You can't put a price tag on experience, but you can use that experience to help move you along faster and to avoid some of the pitfalls that people with less experience may encounter.

Exercise 9.3: The Checkbook Exercise

Instructions: Sometimes, we can find money to put toward achieving our life visions by rearranging our budgets. I sometimes ask my clients to bring in their checkbook register (or a printout of it if they use Quicken or MS Money, etc.). We then look at the things that they are spending money on and tie them into the things that they have said are most important to them. Oftentimes I find a disconnect between the two. This leads to a discussion on budgeting and redirecting one's material resources to support one's life vision. Take a look at your checkbook or past several months' bank statements. What do you find you are spending your money on? Are these the things that will further your life vision? Can some of this money be redirected in the future to go toward pursuing your life vision?

Conclusion

Each of us has a unique life vision, and it's up to us to uncover the right life plan for our lives. The answer is not always easy or obvious, but with some time and effort, you can find your path to fulfillment.

As you've begun to discover from this chapter, you will need to take some significant time contemplating the kinds of things you hope to achieve in your life and the kinds of belongings, beliefs, and behaviors that you expect will bring you meaning and fulfillment. You will need to reach out to others for insight, support, feedback, and accountability. You will also benefit from looking within and assessing the needs and passions of your true self.

As you engage in self-reflection and as you connect to others, you will begin to uncover the dreams that will fulfill you; as you draw up a plan to support that dream—turning that dream into a vision—you will be laying the foundation for a life that will uplift and energize you.

10

Running to Win

Unless you're a third-grade teacher or the parent of small children, it's probably been a long time since you've seen a hamster. Do you remember the wheel that comes with most hamster cages—the one the hamster can run on for hours without actually going anywhere? It's a perfect toy for a hamster that's stuck in a cage, but not such a good device for a hamster who actually wants to get somewhere.

A lot of times we humans are just like hamsters running on a hamster wheel. We put forth a lot of energy, desperate to achieve our goals, but we never seem to get very far. We're exhausted from trying, but we don't have much to show for our efforts. This book is all about gaining the tools you need to step off the hamster wheel and start moving toward your goals.

So far, we've covered a lot of the tools you will need to move forward in your life. You've gained a better understanding of your personality, so you know what you need to do to make good decisions, reenergize, and communicate effectively with others. And you've spent a good deal of time contemplating your life vision and learning how to turn it into a viable action plan, an essential aspect of moving forward. All of the elements we have explored so far are like the supplies you'll need to get started on your journey—like comfortable shoes, a water bottle, and a map. This chapter (and the rest of Part II, actually) will focus on the tools you need, not just to get started, but to make it to the finish line of any given goal or to complete your life plan as a whole. In particular, this chapter will focus on the need for commitment (and related behaviors like patience and discipline) to reach the finish line of your goals and plans.

The kind of commitment you'll need to fulfill your life vision is long-term, like the commitment of a marathon runner to finish a race. To understand this concept better, let's look at the difference between a sprinter and a marathoner.

A sprinter is good at short bursts of speed but will then fade out over the long haul, while a marathoner has the capacity to run a steady pace over many miles.

To achieve your goals, there will be times when you need to sprint, but, for sustained success, you will also need to learn how to commit to the longer race. For example, while you might need to sprint to get a paper written for graduate school or to pass a test for a professional licensing exam, there are some goals that sprinting won't help you meet.

Losing weight is a good example of a goal where you need to be able to stay committed for the long-term. When it comes to losing weight, most of us are good at sprinting but struggle to run the marathon. We get really gung-ho about losing some pounds and are able to stay on a diet for a few weeks; then life throws us a challenge, we lose our motivation to diet, and we "fall off the horse." In other words, we are able to follow good habits for a period of time (like sprinters), but we struggle to maintain these good habits long-term (as marathoners would do).

Successful dieters don't sprint and then fade out; they commit to the marathon. The same is true of people who achieve their life goals and to fulfill their life plans—they commit to their life plans for the long-term.

Some people love the challenge of a marathon. They hear the word and they get excited about the prospect of training hard, running hard, and proving to themselves and the world that they can do anything they put their minds to. Other people hear the word "marathon" and run the other direction (or maybe they just walk)! This is understandable. The idea of running 26 miles can seem overwhelming. Most of us wouldn't even be willing to get in the car and drive 26 miles to get to the grocery store, let alone run 26 miles just for the heck of it.

So if you grumbled a little when I compared the journey of achieving your life vision to a marathon, I understand why you might be a little put off. But my goal here isn't to scare you out of running the race; instead, it's to prepare you. If your expectations of the journey are realistic, you'll be more likely to stick with your plan. If you know that challenges will arise, you'll be more prepared to handle them.

Although the idea of running a marathon can seem daunting at the start, once you've begun the journey toward achieving your life plan, you may actually find it comforting in challenging times to remember that your journey is about the long-term time frame. Unlike a sprinter, you don't have to go at supersonic speeds to meet your goals. In fact, if you get tired, you can walk; you can even stop and rest—because achieving your life vision is about staying on course, not about achieving your goals quickly. In other words, to achieve your life vision, you don't have to race toward it; you just need to be committed to keep moving forward over the long-term.

Are You Committed to the Journey?

Imagine I came and knocked on your door one morning before sunrise and told you that you *had* to join the Marine Corps and that boot camp was starting the same day. How well do you think you'd do at running several miles, doing countless push-ups, and navigating an obstacle course where your opponents were shooting blanks at you? Unless you are an Olympic athlete or a former military member who kept in shape, you'd probably struggle. Some of your struggle might be from lack of fitness, but you'd probably also experience a mental struggle as well. Boot camp is hard enough if you *want* to join the military—imagine how hard it would be if you had absolutely no desire to reach the end goal. The reality is that it's hard to accomplish something when you're heart isn't in it.

When I work with my clients, I always try to get a sense of whether they are really interested in achieving what they say they want to achieve. For example, if I sense a lack of passion on my clients' part or if I hear contradictions in what they are saying, I usually dig a little deeper to help them figure out whether they are really committed to whatever it is that they say they want to attain or achieve—because they can only achieve their goals if they are *committed* to them. The same will be true for you. You can only achieve your goals if you are committed to them. And you can only *commit* to your goals if you are *sincerely interested* in achieving them.

So before you go any further on your journey, take some time to look at your life plan and imagine what life will be like after you have achieved your various goals. Do you feel joy and excitement when you envision this new life? Or do you feel dread and disappointment? Do you feel fulfillment and pride when you imagine the outcome of your life plan or do you feel emptiness or resentment?

If you've based your goals on the framework of your true self (your personality and its preferences), you will probably feel excitement at the prospect of achieving your goals. If, on the other hand, you've based your goals on the framework of an identity that's out-of-sync with your personality, you may have some unpleasant or conflicting thoughts or feelings about achieving your goals. If the latter is the case, all of these unpleasant thoughts and feelings will serve as static (or resistance) that will make it hard for you to achieve your goals. Before you will be able to follow through on your goals without any static, one of the first things you will need to do is examine whether or not those goals are in-sync with your personality. (If they are not, they still may be worth pursuing, but you will need to realize up-front that because they are out-of-sync with your personality, they may take more time and energy to achieve because you will need to overcome the internal resistance you will experience.)

As a life coach, one way that I know clients might not be committed to the process of change is that they miss appointments. Another way that I detect a lack of commitment is if clients don't follow through on assignments that we've agreed they'll complete in between appointments or on things they have stated they are interested in accomplishing. If you find yourself canceling plans that relate to accomplishing your goals or you simply never find the time to work on the tasks that will help you accomplish your goals, you may want to reflect on why this is occurring. Here are two major reasons

248

we struggle to follow through on working toward goals:

1. we aren't ready (in the short-term) to give things up to achieve the goal (in the long-term) OR
2. we aren't sincerely interested in achieving that goal (it is out-of-sync with our true self).

If it's the first case—that you're not interested in making sacrifices in the short-term—you probably have developed a life plan that is in-sync with your true self, but you aren't yet willing to give up certain things to achieve those goals. In other words, in the long-term, you really want to achieve your life plan, but you are not ready in the short-term to make the necessary changes to pursue that plan. It's not until things get more uncomfortable or less satisfying to you in your life that you will have the motivation to make the necessary changes to achieve your life vision.

Here's an example. One of my clients hired me to help her develop a plan for obtaining her undergraduate degree. She had entered the workforce right after high school and didn't go to college. Although she thought she had done pretty well at her company, she was starting to feel like she wouldn't be able to get promoted any further until she obtained an undergraduate degree. We met and discussed what it would take to achieve her objective of getting a degree. We developed a plan that included taking classes at the school she was interested in attending, studying, and writing papers. My client agreed that she would apply to the school and then begin to execute the plan.

The next week, though, my client didn't call in for her scheduled coaching session. The same thing happened the following week. On the third week, I called my client and went straight to voicemail. I left her a message and did not hear back from her until *nine months* later. In the interim, it seems that my client had decided that she really wasn't ready to make those short-term changes in her life that would help her achieve her long-term goal. She had decided that she would learn to be content with her current role and position in the company and not be so concerned about moving ahead. But her contentment only lasted for a little while and soon she found herself wanting to earn her degree so that she could have more options.

When my client came back to work with me the second time, she had already enrolled at the university and was scheduled to begin her first class in less than three weeks. I am happy to say that after two and a half years of hard work and commitment, she earned her degree. She is now considering a graduate degree.

> *Note*: Lack of follow-through toward your goals doesn't always indicate a lack of interest in your goals or an unwillingness to make sacrifices; sometimes it points to other things, like fearing making changes in your life, lacking a supportive community, or not having enough free time. If you lack a supportive community, you can work on ending toxic relationships, building your fan club, and joining supportive groups (see chapters 11 and 12 for more information). If you fear making changes in your life, this is an excellent topic for discussion with a life coach or therapist. If you don't have enough free time, you can follow the suggestions shown in Table 10.1.

So it's possible that after you create your life plan, you will find yourself, like my client, taking some time off before you begin following through with your plan. That's okay since this is a marathon you're running, not a sprint. You can start (or resume) the journey when you're ready. Just remember that although you don't have to run *fast* to reach your goals, you do need eventually to run toward them. The only way you will cross the finish line *tomorrow* is if *today* you start moving your legs in the right direction.

Now let's look at the second preceding point: a situation in which you don't follow through on your life plan because you're not really interested in achieving the goals you've set out for yourself—because your life plan is out-of-sync with your true self. If your life plan and true self are out-of-sync, no matter how hard you try to accomplish your life plan, static will get in the way. You will procrastinate. You will spend your resources in other places. You will spend a lot of time planning and very little time doing. This is your true self's way of telling you, "I don't want to do this plan!" And your true self will try to throw up bigger and bigger road blocks until you hopefully get the point.

Let's say you have gone back to school so you can get your master's degree in school administration. You're a teacher right now, which you love, but everyone keeps telling you what a great school principal you'd make. Plus, the principal at your current school is set to retire in a year and is willing to recommend you for the position. You also know you'd make more money as a school principal than as a teacher and, as the primary bread winner in your family, you feel a little pressured to apply for the job. When you start your degree program, though, you find yourself falling asleep in a lot of the classes. Then, a few months into the program, you start getting chronic headaches. Right around exam time, you come down with a case of mono and have to stay in bed for three weeks, missing all of your final tests.

What's happening here? Your true self is trying to tell you that you really don't want to become a school principal. Despite the fact that other people are telling you that you should become a principal, deep down, you really don't want to do this.

Whenever there is a conflict inside ourselves (psychologists call this *cognitive dissonance*), the result is stress, which manifests itself as headaches, a weakened immune system, an inability to concentrate, sleeplessness at night, sleepiness during the day, and a host of other possible symptoms. Although consciously you are pursuing an objective that seems right, your true self, through your body, is sending you signals that you are headed down the wrong path.

If you are showing physical signs or symptoms of not being committed to your goals, then instead of trying to make the symptoms go away by taking medication (for example, for sleeplessness or headaches) or by engaging in "vices" (watching too much TV, overeating, drinking alcohol), I suggest that you seek out the root of the symptoms—the larger problem. You can do this by taking some time to reflect on your goals and see if they are truly in-sync with your true self. (Of course, sometimes you need medicine to get back on your feet, but if this is the case, try to simultaneously seek out the larger cause for your symptoms so you can resolve the larger problem and achieve true relief).

In summary, there are multiple reasons why you may struggle to follow through on working toward your life plan. The two key reasons we've covered here are (1) a resistance to making sacrifices in the short-term and (2) a life plan that is out-of-sync with your true self. Other reasons you might have trouble following through, as shown in the previous text box, include fear, an unsupportive community, and lack of free time. Table 10.1 provides an overview of the possible challenges to following through on your life plan and offers possible solutions for working through these challenges.

If you discover an inability to follow through on completing the steps of your life plan—a lack of commitment—take out a pen and paper and circle which challenges and solutions apply to you. You can then make adjustments to your life to address these challenges.

Table 10.1: Working Through the Challenges to Following Through on Your Life Plan

Challenge	Indicator(s)	Solution(s)
Unwillingness to make sacrifices	When I think about my life plan, I feel overwhelmed with all that it's going to require.	Review the "Will Your Dreams Fulfill You?" section in chapter 9 and determine whether or not you have the right target. Perhaps if you change your target, you'll be more willing to sacrifice a few short-term things to achieve it.
Out-of-sync life plan	When I think about my life plan, I feel constrained, sick, unhappy, resentful, or angry.	Go back to the preference chapters (3–7) and review what kinds of behaviors and belongings match up with your preference. Compare these to your life plan. If they do not sync up, see what kind of changes you can make to your life plan.

Challenge	Indicator(s)	Solution(s)
		Work with a life coach or career counselor who is familiar with personality preferences (Myers-Briggs) who can help you adjust your life plan.
		If you are trying to please others, work with a life coach or therapist to process your concerns about pursuing an in-sync life plan.
Fear	I'm afraid to do the things in my life plan.	Write down the worst possible things that can happen when you pursue your life plan. Can you deal with these things? Probably!
		Commit to doing one thing that causes you fear and see how you feel afterward. You might discover it's not so bad after all.
		Work through your fears by talking to a life coach or therapist.

Challenge	Indicator(s)	Solution(s)
Unsupportive community	The people in my life discourage me from pursuing my life plan.	Spend less time with people who discourage you from pursuing your life plan.
	The people in my life encourage me to follow a life plan that is out-of-sync with my true self.	Explain to people who encourage you to pursue an out-of-sync life plan what your real life plan is and why this will be supportive to you.
		Ask people to refrain from making unsupportive comments about your life plan.
Time	I don't have time to follow the steps in my life plan.	Adjust your schedule or life style to make the pursuit of your life plan more feasible (ask for help at home, hire a babysitter, reduce your work hours, change jobs).

The challenges in Table 10.1 are not necessarily easy challenges to address, so spend some time with them. Write in your journal, talk to a friend, or work with a life coach to process them. Until you address the issues that stop you from committing to your life plan, you will struggle to move forward in your life.

Note: Even if the life plan you create today is in-sync with your true self, over time as you grow and change, it's possible that you will need to adjust your life plan to reflect the new reality of who you are. In addition, you may learn over time that the goals you thought you wanted to achieve don't end up delivering what you hoped they would, so you will want to readjust your life plan. If you ever find yourself getting stuck on the journey of pursuing your life plan, check in to see if you've lost your commitment to the process. If you have, this is an opportunity to recommit to your vision by working through the issues that are holding you back or to readjust your life plan so you naturally feel more committed to it.

Do You Have What It Takes to Finish the Race?

As we have just seen, the follow-through to complete your life plan can only occur when you have things like the following: a willingness to give some things up in the short-term for long-term gains, an in-sync plan, adequate time, and a supportive community. To run the marathon—to reach the finish line of your life plan—there are some other things you will need as well:

- courage
- patience
- discipline
- deliberacy.

Although we tend to think of courage, patience, discipline, and deliberacy as natural *traits* that we are either born with or without, in fact, these things are actually *behaviors*. That is, we *behave* courageously, patiently, with discipline, and deliberately. If you don't feel like you have one or more of these behaviors in your life, that's okay. With some practice, courage, patience, discipline, and deliberacy can all become part of your daily routine. Using these skills on a regular basis will enable you to achieve your life goals and cross the finish line of your life plan.

Courage

When you are walking or running along the path to pursuing your life plan, you may at some point encounter a fear that makes it hard for you to complete one of the steps on your plan. You might feel fear for any number of reasons. Maybe you feel afraid of trying something new because you don't know what to expect the process or outcome to be like. Maybe you are afraid of failing at something. Or maybe you fear the way that people in your life (your belongings) will judge you for doing something in particular.

Regardless of the fear that holds you back, courage will help you move past the fear and keep on walking toward your life vision. Remember, courage is not a trait that you either have or you don't—courage is a *behavior*. Courage is about choosing to do something even if it scares you. In other words, you don't have to be unafraid to be courageous, you just have to be willing to do something in spite of your fear.

Imagine that you discover that there is buried treasure on an island and this treasure contains the key to every happiness you've ever wanted for yourself. If you are willing to hire a pilot and parachute from a plane onto the island, you can get to the remote spot where the treasure is buried. But you are afraid of heights and the thought of skydiving is terrifying to you. The only thing that stands between you and an amazing life is your fear of jumping from an airplane. If you jump, you will have the life of your dreams. Will you jump?

This is where courage comes in. If you want the life of your dreams, sometimes you're going to have to be willing to jump from what feels like thousands of feet above the earth. For example, if you want to start your own business, you may need to quit a lucrative job and take some risks. If you want to have a loving family to grow old with, you may need to get past your fear of giving up your freedom and independence and jump in and have kids or adopt. If you want to be promoted through the ranks of your company, you may need to learn how to stand in front of a crowd and speak publicly even though it makes you get major butterflies in your stomach.

> Speaking of public speaking, a good friend of mine was terrified of it. One-on-one he was calm, confident, and even inspirational. But put him in front of a crowd and he went into mental and physical vapor lock—my charismatic friend became a living zombie. So he asked for my help. One of the first things we did was videotape him while he was practicing a speech. He would start out fine, but as soon as he noticed the camera was on—vapor lock. We kept at it for several weeks until at last he was comfortable speaking in front of the camera. Then we sent him out into the real world. I recommended that he join Toastmasters and he did. Week by week he had to conquer his fear and give short speeches that increased in length over time. Little by little he became better and better at speaking in public. Today, he is still afraid of speaking in public, but he has mastered that fear and speaks regularly and confidently in front of hundreds of people.

Courage is like a muscle that grows with practice. So the more you use your courage to do things that you fear, the easier it will be to do these things in the future. You won't need courage all of the time, but you will need it some of the time. Here are some tips to remember when you encounter a fear or a challenge that will require you to draw on your courage.

- You don't need to be without fear to overcome your challenges; you just need to be willing to go forward in spite of your fear.
- When you're afraid of something, the first step forward is often the hardest. Things tend to get easier as you go.
- The more often you do something that you're afraid of, the better you'll get at doing it and the less scary it will seem.
- When doing something that you are afraid of doing, it helps a lot to have members of your fan club around for support. (See chapter 11 to learn more about building a supportive fan club.)
- Remember that you are not the only one who has faced the fear that you are facing. Thousands, maybe millions of people, have walked in your shoes and moved past the fear to achieve their goals. Take courage from their collective examples.

So you don't have to be a tight rope walker or a fighter pilot to have courage, and you don't need to be one of some lucky few who are born with courage. We all have courage inside of us: the ability to do something even though we feel fearful about it. Courage comes down to a choice—the choice to withstand some discomfort for a temporary period of time so you can gain the life of your dreams…the choice to take that first step from 3,000 feet above the earth in an airplane and trust that your parachute will open and you'll eventually land. With courage, you can accomplish your life plan, overcoming all the obstacles that test your commitment.

Patience

Because the journey of achieving your life goals will take

time, you will probably need patience along the way. For example, if you want to become a doctor, it's going to take you several years (and a lot of patience) to achieve your career goal. First, you will need to pass difficult premed courses; next, you will need to get accepted into medical school (an incredibly competitive process); finally, you will need to get picked up for a residency somewhere (also a very competitive process)—not to mention all of the smaller milestones you will need to complete along the way. If you don't have the patience to make your way through all of these different tasks and challenges, then you will not be able to achieve your goal of becoming a doctor.

So when you are setting goals for yourself, you'll want to consider how long it will take you to achieve these goals. Do you want something badly enough that you're going to be willing to work through the long process of achieving it? If you suspect you don't have the patience to make it through such a long process, consider what your other options are. Are there other avenues for achieving the same goal? Or could you pursue a different goal—that takes less time to achieve—that might be equally satisfying to you? Alternately, can you set up a plan to provide you with the support you'll need to make it through the long journey of achieving your goals?

Celebrating the small achievements you accomplish while you pursue your larger life vision is a great way to provide yourself with a sense of movement and accomplishment. So don't just celebrate getting into medical school; for example, celebrate finishing writing all of your applications. Don't just celebrate completing your first residency, celebrate your first day working at the hospital for your residency. Each and every step forward is worth honoring.

These small celebrations will give you a chance to pause, rest, and appreciate everything you've accomplished so far. Whether you go out to dinner with friends, call your family to update them on your success, or give yourself a mental pat on the shoulder, fill your life with moments of celebrating what you have accomplished. This will help you enjoy the journey as well as cross the finish line of your goals.

If you are struggling to find patience, here are some things to remember.

- Anything worth achieving usually takes time; it doesn't matter how fast you move, just that you keep making progress.
- Even the longest journeys are made one step at a time; don't focus on how many steps you have to take, just keep moving forward step-by-step.
- Celebrating small successes will help you appreciate the progress you are making.

Discipline

If you've ever run a marathon or similar long distance race, you know it takes discipline to succeed—discipline to train and discipline to keep on running during race day. On the other hand, if you've never run a marathon, one of the things that may have stopped you from trying was the idea that you lacked the discipline to train on a regular basis.

No one can successfully run a marathon without training for months in advance and without training several days a week. Similarly, achieving your life plan will involve discipline, as was the case in the earlier example of becoming a doctor. That is, you can only become a doctor if you have the discipline to complete a lot of applications, go to school for a long time, study a lot, and work long hours and difficult schedules (night shifts and holidays). Let's look at another example. If you want to own your own business one day, you need to write out a detailed business plan, save enough to capitalize it or fill out a loan application or persuade an investor, market your products and/or services, and deliver your products or services to your customers everyday that you are open. This means early mornings and late nights, but that's what it takes to succeed: discipline.

Discipline is the ability to do something regularly, even if it's hard, oftentimes in the absence of external support. Exercise takes discipline. Going to school takes discipline.

Working takes discipline. Saving money takes discipline. Writing takes discipline. And the list goes on and on. Most things that offer a positive benefit take discipline.

Discipline comes more naturally to some of us than others—but all of us have the ability to be disciplined. Being disciplined is all about practice. People who are good at being disciplined usually have had a lot of practice at it. They know from previous experience that if they show up for something again and again and again (exercise, school, work), their consistency and effort will pay off. Because these people are aware of the rewards of discipline, they are more able to put in the effort up front.

If you are struggling to be disciplined, here are some things to remember.

- If you get out of the habit of doing something, don't criticize yourself or call yourself undisciplined. Just "get back on the horse" and start doing your work again. The more you do something, the easier it gets to do.
- Remember, it takes at least 21 days for an activity to become a habit. Don't be discouraged if it takes you a while to get started; just don't give up.
- Showing up regularly and doing something hard has its rewards. Not only will you receive end-benefits from your discipline, but you might actually enjoy the process (of exercising, learning, etc.).
- We all have the ability to be disciplined, even if we haven't been disciplined in the past. Discipline is all about scheduling the work you need to do and showing up to follow through on that work. You don't have to enjoy the work, you just need to show up for it and do it.
- Discipline is 1% physical and 99% mental. Believe that you can do a thing and you will eventually be able to do it. Disbelieve that you can do a thing

and you will never be able to do it.

Discipline is related to commitment. That is, when you are mentally committed to achieving a goal, you will find it easier to be disciplined about working toward that goal. Your commitment—your motivation to accomplish something—will give you the energy you need to be disciplined about working for something. Some days, your discipline might wane—not because you don't want to achieve your long-term goal, but because you feel tired or distracted or unfocused. In these moments, it will be tempting to stray from the disciplined work you need to do to achieve your life plan. But remember that you don't have to enjoy showing up for every task related to achieving your life plan, you just need to show up and power through a task. Once you're engaged, you might even find that you enjoy the process.

> Take writing this book for example. There were several days when I would rather have been doing *anything* other than working on the manuscript. But I knew that it had to be done, and so I put my head down and did it. It wasn't always easy, enjoyable, or fun, but because I used discipline, I was able to complete the book. And now I have reached one of my professional goals and created a useful guide that would not exist if I had not finished this project.

Deliberacy

When you see a film star, best-selling author, champion athlete, or any other person at the top of his or her game—at an awards show, at a book signing, on a TV interview, and so on—it's easy to envy what the person has achieved and to think, "Isn't he lucky?" "Isn't she lucky?" When you haven't seen all the hard work that goes on behind the scenes to lead to someone's success, it can be easy to think that a person simply has a lot of luck. But success doesn't happen accidentally; it always happens as a result of deliberate intention, deliberate planning, and deliberate action. Does life sometimes throw little gifts of opportunity our way? Absolutely. Yet, only if we are on the lookout for those opportunities and only if we are prepared to take advantage of those opportunities can they be converted into tangible achievements. That's why it's important to create a life plan as you did in the previous chapter: so you have an intentional scheme for achieving your goals.

Creating a life plan is a way of declaring your intentions and then creating a tangible plan for how you hope to realize those intentions. If you don't create this plan, you'll be like a cave explorer walking through a cave without a flash light. If you find the natural wonders of the cave that you are seeking, it will only be because you accidentally stumble into those places where there is natural light. Sadly there will be hundreds of treasures and opportunities that you'll miss, simply because you are not able to see them. With a life plan, however, you will have a guiding light to not only direct you on the path that is right for you, but to also reveal to you opportunities for discovery and achievement along the way. When you start achieving things on your life plan, others looking on might think you are simply "lucky," but you'll know that it was only through deliberate intentions and hard work that you have *created* a meaningful and fulfilling life.

To understand the power of intentions, imagine that you decided to run a marathon because a coworker who you were romantically interested in was running a marathon and he or she offered to train with you. But when your coworker decides to step the training up to 10-mile runs, you find yourself really dragging. You start coming up with excuses to skip workouts, and you eventually decide to drop out of the race. Your coworker doesn't understand why you've changed your mind when you seemed so excited about training for the marathon in the beginning; you may not understand what changed either. Yet, if you examine your intentions, you will realize that you never really wanted to run a marathon in the first place, you just wanted to spend more time with your coworker.

Once you become conscious of your intentions, you can

design a much better and more effective plan—one that helps you spend more time with your coworker, your real goal in the situation. For example, you can offer to help your coworker train without going the full distance yourself. You can promise to cheer your coworker on the day of the race. And so on. This way, you don't have to waste energy pretending to be interested in something you're not. Even better, you'll be more likely to achieve your intention of developing a good relationship with your coworker. He or she might be attracted to your enthusiasm and might be appreciative of your support. And your coworker will probably respect you more if you're honest up front about the fact that you don't want to run the marathon. So there is real value in being clear on your intentions and in being deliberate about your pursuit of your life plan. The clearer you are on your intentions, the more focused your actions to bring about those intentions can be.

Since we tend to gravitate in the direction that our intentions (even unconscious ones) are set, you want to be sure that your intentions are aligned with your life plan. Otherwise, you'll find it hard to follow that life plan, because your intentions will point your actions in a different direction. If you find that you get stuck on your trajectory to achieving your life plan, take some time to consider your intentions. Table 10.2 provides a list of different challenges that can occur with intentions and ideas on how to address these challenges.

Table 10.2: Problematic Intentions and Ways to Address Them

Pitfall	Description	Solution
Competing intentions	These occur when you have two intentions that are the opposite of each other (part of you wants a job promotion because of the pay raise, but the other part does not because of the added responsibility of the new position and the longer hours).	• Figure out which intention is most important to you right now and/or most in-sync with your personality preferences and pursue this intention while letting the other intention go. • If you have trouble letting the out-of-sync intention go, process this with a life coach or therapist.
Unfocused intentions	This challenge occurs when you set vague intentions rather than specific ones (your intention might be to have a career in which you use your creativity, but you don't have any specific intentions regarding what kind of work you will do and how you will achieve that career).	General intentions are a good place to start, but eventually you need to get more specific. Create a detailed life plan with specific intentions and a plan for turning those intentions into a reality (for example, take graphic design classes, talk to graphic designers to learn about the field).

Pitfall	Description	Solution
Someone else's intentions, not your own	This occurs when you incorporate someone else's intentions for you (or your perceptions of someone else's intentions for you) into your life plan (you believe that your spouse wants you to be a dual-income earner for your family so you stay at your job, but you really want to stay home and raise your children full-time).	• Spend some time examining whether your intention is your own. • If it's not, determine what your real intention or desire is and adjust your life plan to pursue it. • Consider talking to the person you were trying to please with your former intention. Maybe the person will be supportive of you adopting an in-sync intention. • If the person is not supportive, explain why the intention is important to you. If the person still cannot support you, set up new boundaries (don't talk about certain things) or reduce the time you spend with the person.

Pitfall	Description	Solution
Intentions to fail	These happen when you have expectations that you will fail because you were raised to believe it would be hard for you to succeed (your father told you that you were the "slow" one in the family, so as an adult you avoid all mental challenges because you believe you are slow).	<ul><li>Do what you can to clear your mind of failure-based intentions.</li><li>Pay attention to your thoughts and notice or write down when you have thoughts that tell you that you are going to fail in some way.</li><li>Think of or write down a positive thought to counteract the negative thought.</li><li>Next time the negative thought comes up, counter it by telling yourself your new positive thought and intention.</li></ul>

Depending on your particular personality preferences, you may find it more difficult to address some problematic intentions more than others.

Sensing judgers, you may find it difficult to drop an opposing intention or an intention that is someone else's simply because you are unwilling to give up your plan for how things in your life are supposed to go. Be sure to step back from time to time and take a look at the bigger picture of your life. As you grow and change, your intentions and actions should be changing over time because you are growing and changing over time. Be willing to revise your plans and make modifications to the things you are doing.

Perceivers, you may struggle to revise unfocused intentions to be more specific because doing so may make you feel constrained or tied down. You will be giving up the sense of allure and freedom that comes with more general intentions. Don't worry, though; remember instead that you can always shift your focus once you have completed a given action. But you will need to start with one intention for each given action.

Feelers, you may find it hard to reject someone else's intentions in favor or your own because other people's opinions matter very much to you. While its okay to seek the input of others, take the time to examine the intentions that you are pursuing to make sure that they are indeed your own and not someone else's expectation of you.

Judgers, you may find it challenging to get rid of failure-based intentions because you often measure yourself by looking at the percentage of things you got wrong instead of the percentage of things you got right. For example, if you take a hundred-question test, you are likely to focus on the fact that you answered ten questions incorrectly rather than being excited about the fact that you answered ninety questions correctly. You will want to make sure that you don't focus on the negative aspects of progress when developing your intentions. An intention should be something that is based on success, not failure or mistake-avoidance.

So check in from time to time with your intentions, especially if you start to feel stuck or unhappy in your life. Ask yourself, what are your intentions right now in whichever area of your life you are feeling stuck? Are your actions (and your life plan) in-sync with these intentions? If not, what adjustments can you make to align your actions and your intentions? Also, are your intentions and actions aligned with your true self? As soon as your intentions and your actions sync up with your true self, you will find yourself moving forward again. In other words,

Deliberate Intentions + In-Sync Actions = Forward Movement.

Conclusion

Before you continue with the rest of the chapters in this book, I encourage you to spend some time contemplating whether you are ready for the process of change—because moving forward can be difficult, and change can be uncomfortable. As a result of this reality, we sometimes choose to stay with the known "evils" in our lives rather than pursue the unknown rewards promised by our life plans. This approach keeps us stuck, however.

If you find that you have fallen into a pattern of resistance against your life goals, this doesn't mean you have to remain stuck in that pattern forever. It's really an opportunity to pause and reflect on what's going on for you. Ask yourself, what does your resistance signify? That you're not willing yet to give up what you have for what you would like to have? That you need more tools to help you change? That you need to take a refresher course in all the things that will help you move forward (for example, reread parts of this book or start meeting with a life coach)? That you need to bring more supportive people in your life and stop spending time with toxic friends? That you need to take a break for a while and come back to your life plan in a few months or a year's time?

Rather than judge yourself negatively for resisting, try to understand yourself. Rather than giving up on yourself, try to come up with a new plan that will help you get moving again. And if you decide to take a break from working toward your life vision, try to make it a conscious one. It's okay to take breaks—we all need them—and sometimes life circumstances force us to take them, but try not to let breaks turn into road blocks or detours. Schedule time on your calendar in a few months to come back to your life plan and get started again or start working with a coach or therapist who can help you process whatever challenges are keeping you stuck.

With commitment, courage, patience, discipline, and deliberacy, you will have the tools you need to run the marathon and to make it to the finish line of your life plan. Taking time to celebrate your small successes along the way will help you stay motivated and enjoy each stage of the journey. Happy running!

11

Surrounding Yourself With Support
by Starting a Fan Club

Two heads are better than one. All boats rise together. Rain doesn't fall on one roof alone. These are the mantras sprinkled throughout this book because this is an *others-help* book, which is to say that this book will teach you how to help yourself by reaching out to others for support and by honoring the value of community. This book is built on the premise that your belongings—or relationships with others—are absolutely essential to your ability to achieve your life vision. I would also argue that your belongings are instrumental to your happiness and fulfillment in life.

I can't say this enough: *we need to be connected to other people* to feel fulfilled in our lives and to move forward toward our life vision. This is because there are simply some things that other people can do for us that we can't do for ourselves. For example...

- Other people can validate our self-worth by showing their care, love, and concern for us.
- Other people can offer us support when we are feeling overwhelmed, tired, sick, or sad.
- Other people can offer us clarity when we have lost perspective.
- Other people can teach us information or skills we need to achieve our goals.
- Other people can challenge us and can help us grow stronger and wiser as well as more caring and considerate.

The bottom line is that each one of us needs to be involved with other people in groups and relationships to lead lives of meaning and to experience success in the pursuit of our life visions.

Human beings are social creatures. This means we need

each other to survive—whether that be for the food that comes to our local grocery stores from farmers, for the care that our families receive from doctors, or for the safety we experience on the roads because construction crews work through the night to maintain highways. We are also social creatures because of all the invisible ways that we need each other for love and support. A smile from someone else can brighten our day; a hug or a long conversation can give us the encouragement to go on when things feel like they are falling down all around us.

If you find yourself feeling some resistance to this idea that we need other people, then you will probably find it helpful to explore this resistance as you read this and the other four chapters in Part II that focus on belongings (chapters 12, 13, 15, and 16). On your own, in your journal, or maybe even with a professional helper, I would recommend that you process your resistance to being connected with others. Although we are all born as social creatures, sometimes our environments cause us to develop in such a way that blocks us from seeking—or finding—healthy connections with other people. If you can unblock this tendency toward connection and transform it into a desire to form meaningful relationships in your life, you will eventually find yourself living a life of not only progress but also personal fulfillment.

> ### *Learning to Nurture Your Belongings and Part II*
>
> Because of the important role that connecting to other people plays in helping you create a meaningful and fulfilling life, we will be looking in Part II at how you can develop a group of close supporters who will help you nurture your nature and achieve your life plan (the present chapter). We will also look (in chapter 12) at widening your circle of support to include communities or group organizations that you can join, to support you in your pursuit of happiness and fulfillment. Chapter 13 will focus on the kind of impression you make on others and will help you learn how to make that impression a positive one. If you can learn how to convey your true nature to others while seeking an authentic life vision, you will find that others will be willing to help you move forward and achieve that vision. In chapter 15, you'll learn how to get along with the people from your early life (often your family)—who helped you formulate your identity and possibly mask your personality. The goal will be to honor these individuals and keep them in your life while staying true to your personality rather than masking it. Finally, chapter 16 will explore the joys of giving back to others and will help you increase the number of Type III giving relationships in your life.

Why will we spend so much time and energy on connection to others in the remainder of Part II? Because if you learn how to nurture your belongings, everything else in your life will fall into place. Surround yourself with supportive friends and communities, and you will find it easier to live in-sync with your true self. Learn how to convey a positive impression to others, and you will find that others will engage in helping you achieve your life vision. Begin to invest yourself in your community through volunteer work and generosity and you will find that your community provides for you in ways that you could never have provided for yourself. *The key to moving forward in life is your belongings.* So let's get started learning how to bring nurturing belongings into your world.

What Is a Fan Club?

One of the secrets to successfully achieving your life vision will be having a group of people in your life that supports you on your journey: friends, loved ones, mentors, and even professionals who will cheer you on and help you stay connected to your vision for yourself. Remember how I've been saying throughout the book that community is essential to your fulfillment and progress in life? This chapter is going to give you some of the tools you need to bring a supportive community into your own world so you can enjoy that fulfillment and progress.

I call this supportive community your *fan club*, because it is made up of people who are totally dedicated to your success. If you had a mailing list of the people who admire you, respect you, believe in you, cheer for you, and want the best for you, the people in your fan club would be on this list. If you had a Web site showing your life's successes, failures, challenges, and opportunities, the people in your fan club would be the first ones to check for updates and to post messages of encouragement. Your fan club is made up of all the people who appreciate who you are and what you want to accomplish in your life; they care for you unconditionally, support you unfailingly, and are sincerely happy for you when you achieve your goals.

> Your fan club is made up of those people in your life who want you to succeed and who are able to support your true self.

You probably have already started to think of at least a couple people in your life who fall into the category of fan club, though I suspect you've never described these people as "fans" before. In this chapter, I'm going to encourage you to start thinking of people in your life as members of your fan club and to look into expanding that fan club to support you fully in achieving your life vision. This means that you won't be relying on good fortune to provide you with a strong fan club; you'll be actively selecting the members of your fan club and then inviting your fans to commit to supporting you. You will be turning your trusted friends and select family members into a formal resource that you incorporate into the achievement of your life plan.

We will also spend a good portion of this chapter looking at how to eliminate relationships from your life that hold you back. For your fan club to have its maximum positive effect in your life, you need to be sure that you have cleared away those relationships in your life that are unsupportive, limiting, or negative. This chapter will give you the tools to do so.

Why Do You Need a Fan Club?

There are a lot of things you can do on your own to work toward achieving your life vision: for example, you can design a plan, work toward the point goals on that plan, and measure your progress. Nonetheless, there are some things you just can't do all by yourself—this is where your fan club comes in. Here are some of the many benefits of having a fan club. Your fans can...

- provide you with validation
- offer you partnership in reaching shared goals
- serve as a safety net when you need physical or emotional support
- act as a sounding board, to help you sort through your thoughts
- help you stay true to your personality
- help you stay accountable to your life vision
- offer you a fresh perspective
- celebrate your accomplishments with you
- support you while you work through life's disappointments and challenges.

As you can see, your fans can offer you support in a variety of ways. Interestingly, some fans are better at offering certain kinds of support than others. For example, some fans are great at listening without saying a word; others are great at being direct with you—coming right out and telling you when you seem to be straying from the course of your life plan. Some fans are good at reminding you of things you've said in the past and holding you accountable to those ideas, while others are great visionaries, who can help you think creatively to solve challenging dilemmas. The more fans you have in the club, the wider the range of support you will have to draw from when working toward your life vision.

What Kind of Fans Are Out There?

Friends

The first kind of fan is friends. When you think about the people you call your friends, can they also be described as your fans? If the answer to that question is no, than the people you've been calling your friends might not really be your friends after all—because it's impossible to be a true friend without being someone's fan. If someone you call a friend has trouble listening to you, never seems to get excited for you, sabotages your plans to work toward your life vision, or generally is unsupportive of you, he or she is not a fan (or a true friend) of yours. It can be hard to admit that someone isn't truly your friend, but it's important to come to terms with this reality. If you want to achieve your goals in life, then you need to surround yourself with friends who are fans.

Now that we know what a friend isn't, let's look at what a friend *is*. This poem provides an excellent definition of friendship.

What is a friend? I will tell you.
It is a person with whom you dare to be yourself. Your soul can be naked with him. He seems to ask of you to put on nothing, only to be what you are. He does not want you to be better or worse. When you are with him you feel as a prisoner feels who has been declared innocent. You do not have to be on your guard. You can say what you think, so long as it is genuinely you. He understands those contradictions in your nature that lead others to misjudge you. With him you breathe freely. You can avow your little vanities and envies and hates and vicious sparks, your meannesses and absurdities and, in opening them up to him, they are lost, dissolved

on the white ocean of his loyalty. He understands. You do not have to be careful. You can abuse him, neglect him, tolerate him. Best of all, you can keep still with him. It makes no matter. He likes you—he is like the fire that purges to the bone. He understands, he understands. You can weep with him, sin with him, laugh with him, pray with him. Through it all—and underneath—he sees, knows, and loves you. A friend? What is a friend? Just one, I repeat, with whom you dare to be yourself.

C Raymond Beran

In other words, friends are those people who see you as you are, like you as you are, and appreciate you as you are but who also see you as you can't see yourself because they have a kind of distance from you that you can't have from yourself. As a result, friends help you to see, appreciate, and inhabit those aspects of yourself that you have trouble seeing. Friends validate the parts of yourself that you are familiar with and love, while helping you face and even embrace the parts of yourself that you don't recognize. Finally, friends let you be yourself, even if who you become is different than who they think you should become. In other words, friends don't have an agenda for you; they support you in pursuing your own life vision. As such, your friends make up an essential part of your fan club.

Family

What about family? Can they be part of your fan club too? Absolutely. If your family members are supportive of your true self and your life vision, then they fall into the category of fans too. Being a family member doesn't automatically make someone a fan, but plenty of family members are their loved ones' biggest fans. The same applies to significant others. There is no guarantee that someone you are dating, living with, or married to will be a fan of yours, but the goal and hope, of course, is that they will. Again, it all depends on whether your significant other is supportive of your true self and your life vision. If your significant other is, you can count him or her among your fans.

Allies

The next category of fans is what I call *allies*. Allies are all the fans in your life who fall outside of the categories of friends or family. If you hire a professional in your life to help you advance your goals, that person will probably join the ranks of your fan club (assuming, of course, that he or she follows through on the promise to support you). Here are some examples of hired professionals who can be your fans: life coaches, mental health counselors, private educational tutors, and personal trainers, to name a few. Another group of fans that I call allies are those who are involved in teaching, training, or supporting you but who you haven't directly hired to support you—religious leaders, school teachers and college professors, community sports coaches, and motivational speakers. If you have a supportive boss at work, he or she may also be one of your allies.

The ultimate criteria for being a fan is that a person values your true self and supports you in achieving your goals.

Allies Versus an Entourage

Do you know the difference between allies and an entourage? Or the difference between friends and an entourage? Unfortunately, we can't assume that everyone around us is a friend or an ally. Sometimes, people are part of an entourage that has formed around us, rather than really being our friends or allies. There are two kinds of members in an entourage—those who choose to hang around us to get something in return from us (what I call *clingers*) and those who are paid to be involved in our lives who don't have a sincere interest or ability to support our true selves and life visions (what I call *ringers*).

Let's look at the first group—clingers. Clingers have chosen to be in your life because of something they feel they can gain from being around you—fame, power, material things, social respect, drama, attention, career advancement, wealth, and so on. Because clingers' main focus is to gain something from you, they are unable to be real friends, allies, or fans to you. They put their own interests above yours and therefore you can't rely on them to offer you support or an objective perspective.

Compare them to ringers, who physically show up for the work you've hired them to do, but they lack either the ability to support your true self and life vision or they lack sincere interest in supporting you. As a result, ringers cannot be counted among your fans. Of course, every person you employ in your life doesn't have to be a fan (for example, your house cleaner), but you want to be sure that the people you have hired to support your true self and your life vision (for example, life coach, personal trainer) are people who can follow through on that commitment. If the hired professionals in your life cannot or will not support you, having these people in your life will likely do more harm than good.

This is also true for the people you've hired to support your children (babysitters, nannies, tutors). If these professionals are unable to support the life vision you've created for how you want to raise and nurture your children, they will be holding you and your family back rather than helping you move forward. I'm not saying that you want these people to mimic your philosophy like robots but that you want people in your children's lives who are naturally supportive of your life vision for your family (and your children's true selves as well). For example, if your life vision is to help your children discover the joy of playing music, but you notice that their music teacher is focused on entering competitions, this particular music teacher will be out–of–sync with the goals you have for your children and you will probably want to find a new teacher.

Building Your Fan Club

Now that you have a sense of what it means for a person to be your fan, look around your present world. Who in your life right now can you count among your fans? Which of your friends are also your fans? Hopefully all of them, but if not, take notice. Are there any people among your list of friends who are poor at listening to you? Who seem to discourage you from pursuing your life vision? Who impede you from aligning your behaviors, beliefs, or belongings with your true self? Who are all-around negative? If so, it's probably time to recognize that these people are not your fans. Now look at those in your life who you've hired to support you. Do you feel comfortable being your true self around these people? Do you feel they are sincerely interested in you advancing your life goals or do you just get the feeling that they are there only because you pay them? It's perfectly appropriate for people you hire to have boundaries (for example, to work with you only during scheduled times and to expect compensation for all of your work together), but people you've hired should still show genuine interest in your progression toward your life goals. It's this sincerity and interest in your advancement that you will want to gauge when assessing whether someone you've hired is really a fan of yours.

If someone is your fan, he or she will do the following:

- support your true self and your life vision
- respect you
- care for you unconditionally
- listen to you
- challenge you to stay true to yourself and your vision
- have time for you.

A fan is also someone who won't take you too seriously. This is important because there are times in our lives when, if we are honest, we get too full of ourselves. We have moments when we think that everything we do or say is perfect and wonderful, when the truth is, it really isn't.

A variation of this is when we get too focused on ourselves and lose perspective on the fact that there is a bigger world out there beyond our own problems. Yes, our challenges are important, but if we can remember that we are not the only ones struggling in the world, it can help us keep things in perspective and manage our own challenges with more ease.

When we take ourselves too seriously, clingers won't tell us the truth, because they fear losing their position around us if we get angry at them for disagreeing with us. Ringers won't tell us the truth, because they don't think its their job. Fans, however, will tell us the truth, because they want us to be the best that we can be. They will risk hurting our feelings to keep us on the right road.

Now that you've gotten a sense of your current fan club, how is it looking? Is your fan club as big or diverse as you'd like it to be? Are all the people in your life that you'd want to be your fans (for example, spouse, housemates, teachers), really your fans? Is there anyone in your life who isn't a fan that you realize it's time to stop spending time with? These are big questions and they may take some time to answer.

As you spend time with people in the coming month, pay attention to whether the people in your life display the traits of a fan. Over time, you will find the answer to these questions and you will know how you need to proceed to strengthen your fan club. You may need to add more people to your fan club, and you may need to remove certain people from your life—stop spending time with an unsupportive friend, end a romantic relationship, or hire a different professional. As you begin to make such changes, you will find that achieving your life vision will start to seem more achievable. Why? Because all of the people in your life will be offering you guidance and support. They will be encouraging you to live in-sync with your true self, and when you do, it will be more natural and possible to achieve your life vision.

Once you've identified people in your life who are your fans, I recommend you formally invite them to be in your fan club. While it's already natural for these people to support you, it can be even more beneficial to let them know you are hoping to draw on them for tangible support as you pursue your life vision. Formalizing this process will strengthen the bond between you and your fan because it will let your fan know how much you appreciate and depend on his or her involvement in your life. It will also allow you to ask for specific kinds of support from your fan that he or she might not otherwise know you need.

Here's how you might proceed in bringing someone into your fan club.

- Take each fan to coffee or write each fan a letter or a card.
- Explain to the person what a fan club is.*
- Tell the person why you would like him or her to be in your fan club.
- Tell the person what you would expect from him or her as a fan (for example, "Here are my preferences, here are my core needs, and here is where I will need help embracing my personality rather than my identity; here are some new things I will be trying to do where I will need support and encouragement.").
- Tell the person what they can expect from you (for example, honesty, gratitude, communication, receptivity to feedback).
- Ask the person if he or she is willing to become a member of your fan club.
- If you have defined your life vision at this point, share it with the other person; if not, make sure to share your life vision with him or her at a later time.

In this way, you will be actively enlisting people in supporting you in achieving your goals. Your fans will now know how to be most supportive to you and will feel encouraged to keep supporting you because you have let them know you appreciate their roles in your life. In turn, as you build your official fan club—one member at a time—you will know who you can turn to for support and guidance in

* You can use any term you like if "fan club" doesn't fit your style (for example, board of directors or advisory council).

pursuing your life vision.

As time progresses, you will want to regularly interact with your fans and ask for feedback on how you appear to be doing in light of the life vision you have expressed to them. You may even want to start a personal newsletter or blog to your fan club, updating them on how you are doing in meeting your life goals. This will help you stay accountable to your life vision, provide you with opportunities to reflect on how you're doing in your pursuit of that vision, and give your fans the information they need to continue supporting you.

Challenging Relationships

Just as you will be formally inviting people into your fan club, you may also need to end, curtail, or suspend certain relationships so you are surrounded by supportive people in your life as much as possible. Even one or two people who are unsupportive of you can have a negative impact on your ability to pursue and achieve your life vision, so it's important to be on the lookout for this kind of relationship.

For example, one of my clients, an actor originally from Minnesota, but now living in the Los Angeles area, had a workout buddy who is extremely negative about everything. When I started coaching sessions with my client, I began to notice a pattern. In our coaching sessions, he would excitedly agree with new strategies that he would seek to implement to become a better father to his young daughter, but when we had our follow-up conversations, he seemed to have changed his mind.

After I realized what was happening, I shared my observations with him. He admitted that after our coaching sessions, he would go and talk to his negative workout buddy, who would convince him that the things we talked about in the coaching session would never work. I asked him if he was willing to try a different approach—instead of talking to his negative workout buddy about our coaching sessions, talk to someone who was interested in seeing his relationship with his daughter develop and improve. He told me that his uncle

285

still living in Minnesota fit into that category. So, I asked him if he would be willing to talk to his uncle instead of his negative workout buddy. He agreed.

The next time we met, my client had implemented one of the new strategies that we had talked about and his attitude was greatly improved. By limiting his exposure to the negative thoughts and feelings of his workout buddy and increasing his time with his positive fan (his uncle), my client was able to improve his relationship with his daughter, which was a key part of his life plan.

Challenging Friends and Acquaintances

When a relationship has a negative impact on your ability to pursue your life vision and remain true to your personality, I call that relationship *challenging*. Here are some signs that you are in a challenging relationship.

- My stomach sinks when I see this person's caller ID on my phone.
- Whenever I am going to spend time with this person, I get into a bad mood.
- I feel bad about myself after being with this person.
- After leaving a get-together with this person, I tell myself that I am never going to do that again (but I do). I feel drained rather than reenergized, angry rather than excited, or sad rather than happy.
- When I am with this person, I feel like an outsider or that I have to prove myself.
- I notice that I am defensive when talking with this person.
- When I'm with this person, I feel like I have to take care of him or her all the time. It rarely feels like he or she ever takes care of me.
- I need to remain in a relationship with this person because he or she needs me or doesn't have any other friends.
- This person loves to be listened to but has no

interest in or ability to listen to me.
- I am only in a relationship with this person because I don't know how to end the relationship without hurting the person's feelings.

When you read the statements regarding challenging relationships, do any of them ring true for some of the relationships in your life? If so, for which acquaintance, friend, significant other, or family member do they resonate? Challenging relationships can occur in any area of your life—at home, at work, with friends, acquaintances, and family. And it's possible that you may have more than one challenging relationship, so you'll want to take some time to reflect on all of the relationships in your life when assessing for negativity.

Note that some relationships are not challenging in their entirety, but they do have *limiting aspects*. In other words, you may relate to someone and get along well with the person on one level, but on another level or in another area, you are incompatible with the person. He or she does not know how to be supportive to you when you try to connect on that particular level or in that area. To get a clearer idea of how challenging relationships can vary in degree, let's examine the examples of Melissa and Eric, who have different kinds of challenging relationships with their friends.

Melissa's relationship with her friend, Carmen, is challenging in all of its aspects. Carmen puts Melissa down on a regular basis, in subtle but powerful ways. She is also terrible at listening to Melissa when Melissa wants to share but will spend hours talking to Melissa about her personal problems. Carmen has no interest in supporting Melissa; she is only interested in what Melissa has to offer her. Melissa stays in the friendship because she has known Carmen since they were very young and Carmen is a family friend. But there is nothing in their relationship that supports or benefits Melissa. She always feels bad about herself after she's spent an afternoon with Carmen or spoken to Carmen.

And Carmen calls Melissa all the time, so Melissa feels the negative impact of the relationship on a consistent basis.

Eric had a decent relationship with his friend, Ben. They loved watching football together and talking sports. And whenever Eric needed advice on women, Ben was really helpful. He had been in a great relationship with someone for the past five years and seemed to really know how to have a successful partnership. But when it came to talking about Eric's career aspirations, there were limits to Eric's relationship with Ben. Ben could not relate to Eric's interest in working with kids and always seemed to talk down about Eric's interest in becoming a teacher. He just couldn't see how this kind of work would justify Eric's intelligence, as he put it. So even though Ben could support Eric when it came to developing a healthy relationship with a woman and he was a fun person to relax with, Eric had to learn to avoid talking about his career with Ben. It served no useful purpose.

As you can see, Melissa and Eric both have challenging relationships with their friends, but these challenges vary in degree. Melissa's relationship with Carmen has so much negative impact on her life that it is outright toxic. There is no benefit to her continuing her relationship with Carmen, and in fact, this relationship holds her back. On the other hand, Eric benefits in a lot of ways from being friends with Ben, but he needs to learn to protect himself from Ben's challenges to Eric's career aspirations. Eric doesn't need to end his friendship with Ben, unless Ben's lack of support for Eric's career aspirations becomes pervasive. Instead, Eric can learn to set boundaries with Ben, choosing not to discuss his career aspirations with Ben and even asking Ben to refrain from making unsupportive comments. If Ben can manage this change, then Eric can maintain this relationship and still enjoy its other supportive elements.

Finally, challenging relationships can even occur within acquaintances. Even if you don't know someone very well, coming in contact with a person may still drain you of your energy or make you feel bad about your (true) self. Challenging acquaintances can take a variety of forms: college dorm mate, hair stylist, work colleague, sales person, neighbor, doctor, or any of the paid professionals we've talked about earlier. Sometimes, when you have a challenging acquaintance, you can learn how to block out his or her negative effect on you when interacting; other times, a good option will be to end the acquaintance and move on.

Challenging Family Members

Not surprisingly, challenging relationships can occur not only with friends but also with family. Here are some signs that you are in a challenging relationship with a family member.

- Whenever I am going to spend time with my family member, I start feeling anxious, stressed, or sick.
- When I am with my family, I feel like an outsider or that I have to prove myself.
- I notice that I am defensive when talking with my family members.
- I feel bad about myself after being with my family.
- After leaving a family meeting, I tell myself that I am never going to do that again (but I do).
- My parents are physically or verbally abusive.
- My siblings are overly competitive and I always seem to lose.
- My parents hold up the successes of my siblings to highlight my failures.
- My parents demean or ridicule my choices and decisions.
- My parents refuse to accept me as an adult and treat me like a child.

Another hallmark of a challenging family relationship is that you don't feel comfortable showing your true self around your family. There are a number of reasons why you may have

289

trouble showing your true self. Perhaps you don't know how to act in-sync with your true self around your family because they are the ones, when you were young, who encouraged you to develop an identity that unintentionally masked your personality. Maybe they are capable of understanding and supporting your true self now that you are an adult, but you don't realize this or you simply don't know how to show it. Maybe you always end up falling back into unhealthy patterns around your family because this is how you are used to interacting with them. You do have a choice about how you act, but you may not feel like you do.

Alternately, the challenge in staying true to your personality around your family may come from the fact that your family continues to treat you as if you were a child and has not adjusted to the new reality that you are an adult, with the freedom and independence to make your own decisions. Or, the unfortunate fact may be that someone in your family has an agenda for you, because of his or her own unresolved issues, in which this family member clearly pushes you to act (as well as belong and believe) in-sync with his or her personality and discourages you from acting (believing and belonging) in-sync with your true self.

Handling Challenging Relationships

If you have a challenging relationship, it's important to make some adjustments to eliminate the negative effects that this relationship has on your life and your ability to move forward. You may need to put some boundaries into place that limit the negative effects or you may even need to end the relationship.

Ending Challenging Friendships

Let's talk first about dealing with friendships that are entirely toxic, with no redeeming elements. Usually, the smartest bet with this kind of friendships is to end the relationship altogether. Unlike family, which we don't get to choose, we do get to choose our friends. So why choose friends that bring us down or make us feel bad about who we really are? The hardest part here is the act of ending a friendship. In society, it's acceptable to end a romantic relationship, but you never hear much about ending friendships. You might hear, "I just broke up with my boyfriend," but you don't usually hear, "I just broke up with a friend." That doesn't mean it doesn't happen, just that our culture doesn't teach us much about how to end a friendship.

When I am teaching my clients how to end challenging friendships, I usually begin by sharing with them the lyrics from a song by the country group, Rascal Flatts. The song is called, "I'm Moving On", and here are the lyrics that relate to this difficult activity.

I've lived in this place and I know all the faces
Each one is different but they're always the same
They mean me no harm but it's time that I face it
They'll never allow me to change
But I never dreamed home would end up where I don't belong
I'm movin' on

The reason that I love to use this song is that there are three key elements to ending challenging relationships and all three of them appear in this song.

Element #1: The negative effect that the person has on me is not personal, so I shouldn't overreact. This is represented by the line in the song that says, "They mean me no harm but it's time that I face it." Most challenging friends aren't being challenging intentionally. They are just being themselves, and their toxicity comes from a slew of personal issues that they face. Although their toxicity affects you, it is usually not about you, so don't take it personally. When someone is challenging, it's easy to feel like you've done something wrong. Of course, relationships are two-way streets, but that doesn't mean it's your fault if someone is abusive or disrespectful in how they treat you. So don't take it personally when you find that a relationship is challenging. Just identify what you need to do to protect yourself from its negative effects and move on.

Element #2: The relationship and its negative effects are not going to get better if I don't do anything differently. This is represented by the line in the song that says, "But it's time that I face it, they'll never allow me to change." As much as you'd probably like to, you can't just wish challenging friends away; you are going to have to take deliberate action to end the relationship.

Element #3: It's not going to be easy to end the relationship, but if I want to move forward in life, it is necessary. This is represented by the last line in the song that says, "But I never dreamed home would end up where I don't belong, I'm movin' on." Let's face it, even though the friendship may be challenging, in most cases, you have some history with the person. And the longer that you have known the person, the more history you have. And the more history that you have, the harder it will be to end the friendship. Like the song says, the person may even represent "home" to you. But, if you are going to move forward in life, then you have to end your challenging friendships and find a more authentic home, with new belongings who will support you.

Here are some guidelines on how to end a challenging relationship.

Step 1: Depending on your level of comfort with the other person, decide if you are going to do this in person, over the phone, or by written communication (letter or email). All of these options are reasonable and valid options for ending challenging friendships. Remember, your goal is to limit your exposure to these kinds of people. I often advise my clients to end challenging relationships using written communication. Written communication has the benefits of giving you time to compose your thoughts and feelings, allowing you to say what you want without being interrupted and preventing you from being ridiculed or made to feel guilty about your decision.

Step 2: Deliver your message. No matter which delivery method you choose (in-person, telephone, or written), at some point you need to deliver your message. Your message should be short and to the point and say something like this: "Recently, I have been discovering some new things about myself and making some important decisions about my future. During this process I've had to honestly evaluate the relationships in my life. As a result of this evaluation, I don't think (or I don't feel) that we are traveling down the same paths anymore. So I wanted to let you know that I will probably be spending less time with you in the future. I know that this may be hard for you to understand and accept, but I would ask you to honor my choice. One day, I hope to be able to explain it to you. In the meantime, I want to thank you for your friendship over these past few years." Now you can modify that message to suit your particular circumstances, but make sure that you let the person know that you are "movin' on."

Step 3: Prepare for an emotional reaction from your challenging friend. No matter how well you craft your message and how sincerely you deliver it, most likely your challenging friend will react in anger. More than likely, your challenging friend will neither understand nor accept your decision. Instead, he or she will probably try to make you feel bad or guilty or try to hurt you emotionally. If you expect this to happen, when it does happen, you won't be surprised by it and you'll be better prepared to handle the reaction.

Step 4: Stick to your guns. After experiencing the emotional response from your challenging friend, you will inevitably feel like maybe you were wrong and your friend is right, and you will be tempted to change your mind. DON'T! Challenging people are extremely good at manipulation. Remember that you are not ending this relationship because you have anything personal against the challenging friend, but because you need to move forward in your life. So, don't let your former challenging friend talk you into getting back into a relationship with him or her. (That's why I recommend the written form of delivery—it puts some space between you and the challenging person.) You made the right decision to end the challenging relationship, so resist the pressure to change your mind.

Step 5: Continue to expand your fan club. Now that you will be spending less time with your former challenging friends, you can start spending more time with your fan club members and even finding new members. Remember that the key to moving forward in life is to surround yourself with people who will honestly support you on your journey.

Dealing With Challenging Family Relationships

What happens when our family relationships are challenging to us or impeding our growth? We can end relationships with our friends, but not usually with our family. Admittedly, some people have family members who are so challenging to them that they have to end the relationship completely, but most of us need or want to maintain some form of relationship with our family members, even if there are some limiting aspects of our relationship with that family member. In this case, you can put some boundaries into place that will help protect you from the damaging effects of a challenging family relationship.

First of all, give yourself *permission* to create some space between yourself and a challenging family member. Doing so is part of any person's healthy development, and often the only way you will learn to reclaim your true self is by disengaging (symbolically or literally) or taking time away from your family, since it is our families who most often have taught us to unintentionally mask our personalities in the first place. It's easy to feel guilty about putting distance between yourself and a family member, but sometimes it's the healthiest thing to do. It's okay to take some time away or do what's right for you. Roger is an example of someone who had to give himself permission to break away from his father.

Roger's parents divorced when he was a senior in college. Roger's mom moved to California and Roger's dad stayed in Oklahoma. Because Roger was going to college in California, he saw his mother more than he did his father. Since Roger was spending a lot of time with his mother, Roger's father, who was an alcoholic, wanted Roger to come to Oklahoma during Christmas. Roger agreed. During the time that Roger was home visiting his father, though, Roger's father was drunk most of the time. During this time, Roger's father would say a lot of mean and unkind things about Roger's mother. And Roger's father would seem to get angry with Roger when Roger didn't agree with him. At that point, Roger decided that he couldn't spend any more Christmases with his father.

Roger graduated college and moved to Northern California near his mother and found a job at a local newspaper there. Roger's father wanted Roger to move back to Oklahoma to be near him, but Roger had politely declined his father's request. Pretty soon Christmastime rolled around and Roger's father asked him to come to Oklahoma for Christmas. Roger asked his father bluntly, "Are you still drinking?" Roger's father replied, "Why is that any of your business?" Roger responded, "Because if you are still drinking, I'm not coming to Oklahoma for Christmas." Roger's father pleaded with Roger to come home, "I'm lonely son. I miss you. It's not fair that you spend so much time with your mother and not any time with me." But Roger knew that going home while his father was still drinking would not be good for Roger, so he politely declined his father's requests.

Roger *wanted* to have a positive relationship with his father, but he could not control his father's drinking or verbal abuse, so it just wasn't *possible* right now to have a healthy relationship with his father. Roger could, however, control his own behavior, so he gave himself permission to stop visiting his dad at Christmas to protect himself from his father's hurtful comments. He made a decision and changed his behavior to minimize the negative effects of his challenging relationship with his father.

By doing so, Roger was also engaging in the next step of managing a challenging family relationship: *setting boundaries* with your challenging family member(s), so you can give yourself the room you need to reclaim your true self or to develop a life that is minimally affected by the negative energy of that family member. Like Roger, you may choose to spend less time with the family member. Or you may talk less often on the phone, talk or visit for shorter periods of time, or adjust family visits to a new locale (at your home instead of the family member's or at a neutral place like a restaurant or coffee shop).

Finally, you will need to decide which topics of conversation you are willing to have with a family member and which you want to keep off limits (for example, your finances, love life, career track). This is another form of boundary setting. The first time one of these topics comes up, you will want to explain to your family member that you'd prefer not to discuss it. Most times, they will probably want to know why. Rather than feeling like you have to explain why, you can simply say, "I understand your need to know why, but please honor my request to not discuss this topic right now." In the future, if the family member tries to discuss this topic you can patiently remind him or her, "Remember, this isn't a topic I want to talk about." If the family member keeps pushing, keep a patient tone and simply repeat yourself, "This isn't a topic I want to talk about." So first you will set conversation boundaries with your family; then you will follow through on keeping these boundaries intact. Here's how Roger set up conversation boundaries with his father.

Roger had developed a fan club of supportive friends, including a professional life coach. Christmastime was getting close and so he asked his coach what he should do about visiting his father this year. His coach advised him to consider whether or not Roger felt strong enough to spend time with his father and still maintain his true self. Roger felt that because of his new fan club and the new skills he had learned through coaching, he probably was strong enough. Roger's coach encouraged him to go visit his dad but reminded him to maintain the boundaries.

Roger went to Oklahoma for Christmas. The first night he was there, his father asked him about Roger's mother. Roger said, "I am not comfortable talking about mom. If you want to know how she is doing, you should just call her." The next night, after having a few beers, Roger's father asked him if Roger's mother missed him. Roger patiently responded, "Like I told you last night, I am not comfortable talking about mom. If you want to talk to her, give her a call yourself." Roger's dad then got angry and started saying mean things about Roger and Rogers' mother. Roger calmly went into his room, packed his bag, and called the airline to see about changing his flight. He changed his flight and then called a cab. While he waited for the cab to arrive, he called one of his fan club members and told him what was happening. The fan club member reassured Roger that he was making the right decision. When the cab arrived, Roger said good-bye to his father, wished him a Merry Christmas, and then started his journey back home to California.

The situation wasn't ideal—Roger wished his father had respected the boundaries he set for conversation—but at least Roger felt proud of himself for trying to connect to his father without sacrificing his true self. It's possible that over time, Roger's father will learn to adjust to Roger's new boundaries. If he doesn't, then Roger still has the skills he needs to stay true to himself and not be held back by his challenging relationship with his father.

The last piece of the puzzle in getting along with challenging family members is for you to *adjust your expectations of your family*. If you have tried to communicate to your family what you need from them and what you'd like to keep private in your life, they may or may not respect that. If you work on staying aligned with your true self when with your family, it is still possible that your family will not understand, appreciate, or support your true self—in part or in full. While this isn't preferable, it is okay: because it's not a requirement for your family to understand you for you to be happy in life or successful in realizing your life vision. Realizing this truth may help you avoid disappointment when your family doesn't act the way you'd like them to. It may also set yourself and your parents free from unrealistic expectations. No matter how much your family loves you, they may not know how to support your true self. Happily, you are developing a fan club to play that role in your life.

By creating boundaries with your challenging family members, you will give yourself space to reconnect with your true self and to diminish the negative effects of a challenging family relationship on your ability to move forward in life. Ideally, after you have had some time practicing leading your life in-sync with your true self, you will be able to reengage in that family relationship and work on staying true to your personality while in that relationship. Assuming your family isn't verbally or physically abusive, this can be a very rewarding growth experience for you and them. If your family is abusive to you, it will most likely be healthiest for you to limit contact with abusive family members on a permanent basis.

There may be no such thing as *complete* freedom from family dynamics and challenges (these are hard to shake!), but you can still make substantial changes that will allow you to be more content in your life and, more important, more connected to your true self.

In summary, here are the steps that you should take to deal with challenging family relationships:

1. give yourself permission to create space between you and a challenging family member
2. set boundaries with your challenging family member
3. adjust your expectations of your family.

Redefining Family

If you are ending or redefining a family relationship and you are worried about being alone, remember that you can redefine your family to include all of the people in your life who see and appreciate you for who you are. Do you have a wonderful friend in your life who you can count on to be there if you are ever in need of a helping hand? Someone you can count on like a brother or sister? It's true that we can't choose our biological family, but we can choose the people who we count among our closest loved ones—why not consider these people to be part of your family?

Reintroducing Yourself

There are some relationships in our lives that we will pull back from for a period of time but then will return to once we have strengthened our ability to behave, believe, and belong in-sync with our true selves. Our family relationships are often the kind of relationships we will return to after a period of growth: most of us want to maintain relationships with our family members, regardless of the challenges we face within those relationships. So while we may set some new boundaries or reduce the time we spend with family, most of us will want to learn how to develop healthy relationships with our families rather than ending family relationships altogether.

When you take time off from a relationship or pull back from it, I recommend that you use that time to strengthen your ability to behave, believe, and belong in-sync with your true self (see the "Developing an In-Sync Identity" sections of chapters 3–7 in Part I). You may also use that time to identify your life vision and set up a plan to pursue it. Finally, you might use that time to practice many of the techniques suggested in this book.

At some point in the process of aligning your behaviors, beliefs, and belongings with your true self, you will gain a strong enough sense of your personality and you will have gained enough of the skills needed to live in-sync with your true self that you will be ready to spend more time in some of the challenging relationships you have taken time off from. If you're interested in reengaging these people, you will be in a better position to do so because you will have a whole new set of skills for remaining true to your personality in the face of challenges to it.

A lot of times, family relationships will be the ones you return to. Since you can't choose who your family is, it will be helpful to learn how to get along with your family. As for friendships, you may or may not choose to return to some of them. You can choose new friendships—and you already will have if you've followed the recommendations in this book—but you may also be interested in spending time with friends from whom you've taken a break. Once you've matured, learned more about yourself, and practiced living in-sync with your true self, you might find it possible to return to previous friendships and enjoy them. In chapter 15, we will focus on how you can successfully reengage challenging relationships from your past. For now, it's enough to work on building a supportive fan club and reducing the negative effects of challenging relationships on your life.

Conclusion

To create an environment of support in your life, you will want to do two things: surround yourself with fans and diminish or eliminate challenging relationships from your life. Remember what I said at the beginning of the chapter—more than any other B, your belongings will have the greatest influence on your ability to achieve your life vision. That's why surrounding yourself with fans and diminishing challenging relationships is critical. Doing these two things is like weeding your life's garden and adding fertilizer to the soil so you can grow and thrive.

If you bring true fans into your club and remove or limit challenging relationships, your belongings will become the rich, nutrient-filled soil that nurture your nature. When you are surrounded by supportive fans, you will gain the confidence, strength, and knowledge you need to remain true to your real self no matter how challenging your other relationships become. And when this happens you will be well on your way toward achieving your life vision.

12

Getting Connected to the Community

There's something special about groups. A group of students can raise thousands of dollars for charity. A group of volunteers can build a home for a low-income family. A group of doctors can go to an area hit by a natural disaster and save hundreds of lives. People can accomplish in groups what they might never be able to accomplish alone.

But groups are special not only for what they can yield externally; they are special for the gifts they offer directly to their members. When you are part of a group, you have the sense of belonging somewhere, maybe even of having a home. When you are part of a group that is healthy, you will also receive support from other group members or insight or knowledge. Groups can provide you with a place to regroup and relax; to learn something new; or to fulfill a part of you by taking on a certain project, responsibility, or role. Groups provide us with opportunities that we cannot experience when we're alone.

In this chapter, we will talk about the different kinds of groups in existence and which kinds of groups you are most likely to enjoy and benefit from, given your particular personality preferences. We will also consider what you have to give up to be in a group, and we'll weigh that against all the benefits of being in a group. By the end of the chapter, I hope you'll be convinced that it's worth it to join one or more groups—because belonging to the right groups can be critical to moving forward in life.

Your Outer Support Circle

The fan club you started to build in the previous chapter represents your inner circle of top supporters, but you will also want to have an outer circle of people in your life to help you move forward. This outer circle is made up of all the groups, organizations, and associations you belong to. Interestingly, for some of us, we have to join a group first, before we build or expand our fan club, because that's where

303

we will find some of the people who will make up our inner circle of supporters.

While your inner circle is made up of your fan club—the core group of people you've invited to support you in achieving your life vision and who have committed to supporting you—your outer support circle is made up of the people in the groups that you belong to.

Figure 12.1: The Circles of Support

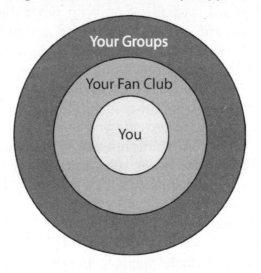

Figure 12.1 provides a visual portrayal of the supportive entities in your life. First, there's you—your number one supporter if you're living in-sync with your true self. Then, there's your fan club, made up of all the people who support your true self and your life vision—loved ones, friends, teachers, mentors, coaches (see chapter 11 for a full discussion of developing a fan club). Finally, there are all of the groups you belong to. Your group memberships are not automatically supportive of you, but if they are in-sync with your preferences and are made up of the right kind of people (for example, healthy rather than destructive, optimistic rather than pessimistic, supportive rather than challenging), they will serve as an essential means of moving forward in your life.

Whereas your fan club makes up your inner circle of support (see previous chapter), the groups and communities to which you belong will make up your outer circle of support.

There are as many kinds of groups in the world as there are people. This means there is a group out there for you, probably several groups. If you already belong to a number of organizations or groups and they are the right fit for you, you are probably well aware of the benefits and pleasures of belonging to a group. If, on the other hand, you tend to keep to yourself and don't currently belong to many groups, you may have your doubts. My hope is that you will see by the end of this chapter that there are groups you can not only benefit from belonging to but that you will also enjoy being a part of. Here are some of the many types of groups that exist out there:

- hobby clubs or associations
- sports teams
- philanthropic and volunteer organizations
- community and civic associations
- religious organizations
- educational organizations
- social groups
- career-related associations and networking groups.

Let's take a more in-depth look at each kind of group. We'll start with groups built around a common hobby. *Clubs based on hobbies* are some of the most fun to belong to because they are based on an activity that you enjoy. Membership in a hobby club enables you to set aside time each week or month to enjoy your hobby and to meet people who enjoy your hobby as well. Outdoors clubs, book clubs, gourmet groups, gardening associations, computer gaming clubs, wood-working clubs, photography groups, writers' groups, knitting circles, and scrapbooking clubs all represent examples of hobby-related groups. Chances are, if you have a hobby, there is a group that meets to enjoy and learn more about that hobby. Collectors associations are another kind of hobby club. Whether you like to collect stamps, coins, comic books, model airplanes, teapots, or Beanie Babies, there are likely other collectors out there meeting to trade and sell your favorite items and to learn about the newest collectibles coming on the market.

If you enjoy playing sports, you'll probably be able to choose from a number of *athletic groups* in your community. Regardless of the size of your town, most cities have a variety of athletic groups to choose from. Adult sports leagues usually run the gamut from runners' clubs to early morning swim clubs to basketball teams to coed softball teams to ultimate Frisbee clubs. There are usually groups that match up with any athletic level too—some groups are highly competitive, while others meet just for fun and exercise. So even if you're not a Division I athlete, there's probably a sports group out there for you.

Volunteer groups are another enjoyable kind of group to belong to. On the face of it, volunteer groups may sound like too much unreciprocated hard work, but anyone who has volunteered for the right cause knows that working to help other people returns a special kind of joy that you can't get from more self-focused activities. Some of you might be in doubt, but if you find the right kind of volunteer group for you, it can be both enjoyable and rewarding. The trick is finding the right group for you. There are many volunteer opportunities out there: teaching adults to read or speak English, building houses for low-income community members, coaching a kids' sports team, mentoring a child, painting city murals, maintaining a community garden, planning expensive fundraising galas, and more.

Civic and community associations are one more kind of group to consider joining. These organizations work to oversee or improve some aspect of the local community—anything from parent–teacher organizations focused on supporting the local school system, to neighborhood associations who advocate for homeowners interested in managing local development, to crime-watch groups. Membership in a civic group enables you to contribute to the success of your local community while meeting your neighbors.

Religious organizations include not just churches, synagogues, temples, and mosques but also any of the classes and subgroups offered within a particular religious organization—Bible study, youth groups, volunteer groups, art classes, travel clubs, language classes, and so on. The number of activities offered within any one religious organization is usually amazingly large and varied. If you follow a particular religion, belonging to a religious organization (and maybe one of its subgroups) will be a logical community membership for you.

Educational groups include community classes, degree programs, and alumni associations. If you enjoy learning new skills, taking a class can be a fun way to meet new people and bring a new group into your life. Alternately, alumni associations usually offer a wide range of activities to choose from, so you're likely to be able to find an activity that interests you—from watching your alma mater's football team each Saturday with fellow graduates to attending presentations with guest speakers or meeting for cocktail hours. Sometimes, alumni associations also offer activities to different age groups—recent alums, alums with children, and alums in their retirement years. Alumni groups can be a great way to connect to people because you already have something in common—your former school—a common bond that can create a natural sense of trust on which friendships can be built. Alumni associations are usually flexible organizations too, which often means you can start a new group within the association for alums with a similar interest to you (for example, hiking, wine-tasting, cooking). This can be a good way to meet people with the same interests as you.

Social groups include book clubs, movie clubs, concert or theatre associations, and even online groups and forums.

These groups are a fun way to meet and spend time with other people because they usually don't involve much of an obligation beyond attending an enjoyable social activity. You can find out about social groups through library and community newsletters, the local newspaper, bulletin boards in cafes and fitness clubs, and word of mouth. If you have an aversion to joining groups because they sound like too much hard work, try a social group first. If you pick a social activity you enjoy, you're more likely to enjoy being a member of the group.

Finally, there are *career-related organizations*. These include networking clubs and professional associations, as well as organizations designed to improve your professional development. Toastmasters—a group that enables you to practice giving speeches—is an example of a club that can support your professional development if you do a lot of speaking at work. Many associations that offer membership to people in a specific field or profession also offer professional development classes and training courses. Other benefits of clubs in this category are opportunities to network with others in your field, stay up to date on developments in your field, support advocacy for your profession, and gain access and discounts into career-related products like professional insurance, journals, and software.

More and more, groups of any kind are available in an online setting. For nearly every interest and hobby out there, there is now an online forum—for those who enjoy fixing cars to those who are trying to lose weight to those who are classic movie aficionados.* Online groups are great because they are flexible—you can sit down and connect to one according to your own schedule—in the morning, on your lunch break, or late at night. Online groups shouldn't be the only kind of group you join—because they lack in-person contact with others, which has unique benefits—but these groups can still offer surprising opportunities to connect with people: many friendships and even romantic relationships have developed from relationships that began in an online setting.

So you can see that not only are there a number of *kinds* of organizations—hobby and sports clubs, volunteer groups, civic associations, religious organizations, and career-related associations—but within each organization type, there is a wide range of groups to choose from: a sport for someone of any interest or level, a hobby club for anything from stamp-collecting to dollhouse making, and clubs with a religious affiliation that help you get closer to God, the community, or the natural world.

* *I have created an online community for readers of this book. You can visit it by following this link: http://www.lifechangingcoaching.com/ discussionboard.php*

Why Join a Group?

Admittedly, you give some things up to be in a group: some privacy, some control, some of your individuality, and some of your personal reputation (that is, you become aligned with the group's reputation and lose some of your own). You also give up some of your time—to attend group functions and to follow through on your responsibilities and commitments to the group. Groups sometimes involve membership fees or dues, so you may also need to expend some money to be part of a group. But as with most things in life, the commitment of your time, effort, and resources to group membership will yield benefits.

Different groups provide different benefits, and most groups provide multiple benefits. By joining a group, you will gain things like support, camaraderie, enjoyment, energy, specific information, access to people, feedback about yourself, and some reputation (that is, you become aligned with the group's reputation and gain some of its reputation).

The benefits of group membership aren't just extra bonuses in your life; they are actually essential to your success in achieving your life vision. Why is being in the right group essential to moving forward in life?

- People in the group can provide you with

309

information that you'd otherwise not have.

- People in the group can provide you with opportunities that you'd otherwise not have access to.
- People in the group can provide you with a fresh perspective.
- People in the group may be interested in joining your fan club or actively helping your promote your life vision.
- Belonging to the right group will help you recharge socially (even if you are an introvert, there is a unique boost that you get from social connection—it allows you to feel accepted, known, understood, and worthy).
- Participating in group activities can give you a constructive break from pursuing your life vision so you can return to it with energy and new ideas.
- People in the group may lend a hand when you get into a challenging situation.

So you can see that there are all kinds of benefits and advantages to belonging to a group (or groups). Without access to the people in groups, you might miss out on information or opportunities essential to achieving your life vision. You might not gain a much-needed perspective on how to deal with a challenge you face, or you might run out of energy to keep pursuing your life vision. By meeting others in a group setting and choosing the right group, you increase the opportunities for meeting people who are well suited to supporting your life vision and to helping you grow in areas that interest you.

Groups can provide you with information, insight, opportunities, and support that you may not have access to on your own.

What Kind of Group Is Right for You?

A key aspect of enjoying your membership in a group is finding a group that is right for you. There are different factors that will play into whether you enjoy being in a particular group—your interests, your preferences, your present goals, and even your age (depending on what stage of life you're in, different groups may hold interest for you). A good gauge of whether a particular group might be right for you is if you find yourself getting excited at the thought of joining that group. This is likely to happen if you find a group that matches your interests or that promises to make your life better in some way. You might still have reservations about joining the group—reservations that relate to some of the things you have to give up to join a group—but you will still feel some excitement or interest in joining a group when it's the right fit for you.

Figuring out which groups you are likely to enjoy often involves a process of trial and error. In other words, you often need to experiment until you find the right group or groups for you. Whenever you join a new group, you should plan to take some time determining whether it's the right fit for you. For those of you who don't like new situations or who are shy about making new relationships, it may take several weeks before you feel comfortable in a new group. Only then can you tell if it's the right group for you.

At this point, I want to let you know that you should not feel obliged to join a group just because you attend one meeting. Too often people feel that if they go once, they have to keep going…forever, even if the group is not right for them. Don't let yourself fall into that trap. Remember that joining a group is a big deal, because these people can either help you to achieve or prevent you from fulfilling your life vision. So take all the time that you need to find a group that is the right fit for you and don't be afraid to pass on joining a group when you sense that it will not support your life plan.

You will also find that some groups are right for the short-term, whereas other groups may be well suited to support you for the long-term. In addition, there will be times in your life when you will benefit from belonging to several groups and other times in your life when you will find yourself needing to scale back. As you grow, change, enter new stages, and set new goals, you will want to consider changing, expanding, or reducing your group memberships to meet the current needs and goals of your life.

Understanding what kinds of groups tend to match up with your preferences can make the trial-and-error process of finding groups that are right for you a little easier. Let's look at what kind of groups each preference type tends to enjoy.

- *Sensing perceivers (xSxPx in your life code)* are experimenting people who value groups where they can learn and perfect a skill. If you are a sensing perceiver, you might enjoy joining an art class, forming or joining a band, participating in an exercise class, taking martial arts lessons, becoming an expert hiker, or joining a drama or improv group.

- *Sensing judgers (xSxJx in your life code)* are structured people who enjoy groups that run like clockwork and have a purpose for meeting and goals to accomplish. If you are a sensing judger, consider joining a community group like Rotary, Kiwanis, or your child's parent–teacher's association. Depending on your life goals, you might also enjoy joining a group like Weight Watchers or taking a computer skills class.

- *Intuitive thinkers (xNTxx in your life code)* are idea people who like to be in groups that value thinking and that challenge their intellects. If you are an intuitive thinker, you might enjoy belonging to a think tank, getting your master's or doctoral degree, or joining a book club.

- *Intuitive feelers (xNFxx in your life code)* are "people people" who like to be in groups that are highly social and involve helping others. If you are an intuitive feeler, you might be interested in joining a group that feeds the homeless, an organization that mentors children, or a group that teaches adults how to read.

Your preference for introversion versus extroversion will also have an effect on what kind of groups you will enjoy belonging to. For example, if you are an intuitive feeler with a preference for introversion (life code of INFxx), you might enjoy the one-on-one experience of mentoring a child or teaching an adult to read. If you are, on the other hand, an intuitive feeler with an extroverted preference (life code of ENFxx), you might prefer to teach English to a whole class of adults or to volunteer at a soup kitchen where you will work alongside multiple volunteers and serve meals to many different individuals. If you are an introverted sensing perceiver (life code of ISPxx), you might prefer to be part of a musical group or an exercise class where you don't have to do a lot of talking. As an extroverted sensing perceiver (life code of ESPxx), you might prefer taking an improv class, in which you get to expend lots of outward energy performing in front of a group.

When you are seeking a new group to join, consider your personality preferences and see if you can find a group that matches up with these (for a review of personality preferences, see chapters 3–7). Here's an example of how this might be done. I'm an intuitive thinker and one of the things that I enjoyed most about being an officer in the Marines was the intellectual challenge I faced in analyzing the capabilities of the men I was leading, evaluating the tactical options of the mission I was given, coming up with a plan that took into consideration all of these things (including any lessons learned from historical battles), and then executing the plan in a dynamic and uncontrollable environment. When I left the military, I soon discovered that civilian life did not have a lot of these elements in it. So, I looked for a group to join that would allow me to start using some of those intuitive–thinking skills again.

As a result of this search, I chose to become a reserve deputy sheriff with the Orange County Sheriffs Department, which means that I am a part-time peace officer. Being in law enforcement is a lot like being in the military. Whenever I put on the uniform or act in the capacity of a peace officer, I am usually faced with several intellectual challenges. What is the best way to accomplish my mission, using the limited resources that I have, considering the prior experiences of the person or group of people that I am dealing with? What approaches have worked or not worked in the past? I love drawing on my intuitive–thinking skills in my role as a volunteer deputy sheriff. If I did not volunteer for the Sheriffs Department, I would be missing a key opportunity in my life to nurture my true self.

The previous descriptions of the kind of groups that different preference types might enjoy is only meant to serve as a starting point for your own process of discovery— because, interestingly, people with different preferences can actually enjoy belonging to the same kind of group but for different reasons. So there is no exact prescription for what kind of group you'll enjoy—especially because, as I mentioned earlier, multiple factors will play into which groups you enjoy: interests, preferences, present goals, and age.

Here's an example of how the same group can bring enjoyment to those with different preferences. For me, an intuitive thinker, being a peace officer is about matching *wits* with the bad guys and *outsmarting* them. For my friends who are intuitive feelers, being a peace officer is about *helping people* in need and making the community a better place. For my sensing–perceiving friends, being a peace officer is enjoyable because every day promises to be different and they have *different options* available to them for enforcing laws. And for my sensing–judging friends, being a peace officer is about *preserving society* by enforcing its laws and helping people do the right thing.

When you are trying to assess whether a group is right for you, you will also want to consider what it is you'll be giving up to join that group. Can you sustain what you'll be giving up? Is the sacrifice worth what you'll be gaining? If you choose the right group, your answer will probably be yes.

For example, to join the Orange County Sheriffs Department, I have had to give up some control of my time. I have a minimum commitment of hours that I must work, and I am expected to be available during emergencies or disasters. I have also had to give up some of my decision-making ability: what I can and can't do is first prescribed by statutory law and then further restricted by departmental policy. In some cases, I do not have a choice in what actions I may or may not take. I have had to give up some of my personal reputation. When I put on the uniform, I cease to be Paul Edward—husband, father, life coach, professor, writer, etc.—and I become just another peace officer. But the enjoyment and personal satisfaction I receive from being a volunteer deputy sheriff—the mental stimulation, my sense of doing something good in the world, and the camaraderie I enjoy by being around other law enforcement officers—make it worth it to me to give up these things.

You will want to figure out if what you gain by being in a group is worth what you have to give up. If you find a group that is a good fit for you, chances are, you will be willing to make some small sacrifices to be a member.

Are You Connected?

Now that you've had a refresher course on the different kind of groups out there, take some time to consider whether you currently belong to any groups. If so, what kind of groups? Are they the right groups for you? Do they bring you satisfaction and enjoyment? Do they support your true self? Are they working to support you and your life vision? Are the sacrifices for the group worth the benefits?

Complete Exercise 12.1 to learn more about your current

group memberships.

Exercise 12.1: Assessing Your Current Group Memberships

Instructions: Write a list of all the groups you currently belong to. (A group is defined as being two or more people. But don't count relationships with friends and family unless you have a formal relationship with that person that focuses on doing something beyond being friends and family, for example, losing weight or volunteering together.)

Hobby groups: _____

Sports groups: _____

Volunteer groups: _____

Civic groups: _____

Religious groups: _____

Educational groups: _____

Social groups: _____

Career groups: _____

What do you gain from your current group memberships? What do you have to give up for your current group memberships? Is the trade-off worth it to you? Are you comfortable in these groups; are they the right fit for you? Complete Table 12.1 to answer these questions (you may need to use an additional sheet of paper.) You want to be able to answer "yes" to the last of these two questions. If you can't, it might be time to find a new group.

Table 12.1: Group Evaluation Exercise

Group	Gains	Drawbacks	Worthwhile Trade-Off?	Good Fit?

If you are finding that the groups you are in right now are worth whatever they involve giving up and that you feel comfortable in these groups, congratulations! You already have a valuable resource in your life for moving forward: healthy group connections. If, on the other hand, some of your current group memberships aren't the right fit for you or you are finding that the trade-offs aren't worthwhile to you, don't worry. You can learn how to adjust your group memberships to make them more satisfying and supportive to you. We'll also talk about joining new groups, for those of you who are finding you could use more or new group memberships.

Adjusting Your Group Memberships

If you are dissatisfied with a current group membership, you have two options: you can adjust how you interact with that group or you can leave the group and replace it with a new one. Let's start by looking at the first option.

If you are discontent with a group membership, ask yourself why? Do you dislike some of the people in the group? Has the group fallen short of your expectations? Is there some part of your preference type that is not being satisfied by the group? Regardless of which of these issues is at stake, you may be able to make some adjustments to how you interact with the group that will increase your satisfaction with the group.

Readjust Your Expectations or Readjust the Group

If the group has not met your expectations, working through your disappointments and focusing on what you *do* gain from the group—making a mental adjustment of sorts—might allow you to enjoy what the group does have to offer you. Alternately, if you think others would be interested in making changes to the group that would help align it more with your interests, look for an appropriate forum to express your interest in changing the group and express your suggestions in a diplomatic way since you want to be careful not to insult or alienate other group members. Coming up with specific recommendations for change will also help the group assess what you are asking for and whether it is right for the group. You still want to be flexible and open-minded during the process, though, because the group might have other ideas for adjustments that can be made to meet your interests in a way that you haven't considered yet.

Reinvent Your Role

If your preference type is not being satisfied by the group, is it possible that you can volunteer for new responsibilities or engage in different aspects of the group that will help you enjoy it more? For example, if you feel it's important to support your child's school's parent–teacher association, but you find the meetings boring, can you volunteer to be the Webmaster or the newsletter editor? Meetings might not seem so boring if you are engaged in gathering information for the association Web site or newsletter. If you haven't been enjoying your church experience lately, what else can you do at church to enjoy it more—join the choir? Sign up to teach Sunday school? Volunteer to direct the Christmas pageant? If you're creative and you keep your personal preferences in mind, you may be able to come up with a way to increase your satisfaction with a current group by taking on a new role or activity.

Shield Yourself From Toxic People

Sometimes, a few people can really ruin the group experience for the rest of us. Before you leave a group because you don't care for or get along with a few of the group members, though, ask yourself if there's some way to lessen your contact with these particular people so you can still enjoy the other people in the group and what they have to offer you. Maybe you can take care to sit next to those members you enjoy most or even drive to the meeting with a favorite person so you get a little extra time with someone whose company you enjoy. Maybe you can learn to keep your communications brief with someone in the group who tends to be toxic. Using brief, close-ended responses can be one way to do this (for example, saying "no thank you" rather than "what do you think"?). If you are willing to be even more proactive, perhaps you can work with the group to create guidelines for group interaction that will help reduce negativity by members.

Admittedly some people are so toxic that they manage to bring down the energy of a whole group. If you can't find a good way to reduce this toxic energy or keep it from ruining your group experience, it may be time to find a new group— perhaps one with a similar mission or common interest, but with different members.

Finding New Groups

The benefit of making adjustments to your current group memberships is that you can build on the energy and time you've already invested in these groups. But there's no reason to stay in a group if it's truly not the right fit for you. In that case, there are so many groups out there to choose from and so many groups with the potential to support you in achieving your life vision that you might as well redirect your energy and efforts to these groups instead. Here are some of the reasons you might want to trade a current group for a new one.

- You find yourself not wanting to go to group meetings.
- You feel pressured to act out-of-sync with your true self when with this group.
- You feel bad about yourself when in the company of the present group.
- You feel drained at the end of group meetings rather than reenergized.
- You don't feel like you are making a contribution to the group or getting anything from the group.

If you find that a group is lowering your energy level, consistently raising negative feelings in you, or discouraging you from acting in-sync with your true self, it is probably time to look for a new group. It may also be helpful to reflect on what it is about the group experience that is raising those

319

negative feelings or making it hard for you to embrace your true self. The challenges you face when in a group can provide you a lot of insight into yourself. You might even find areas of yourself that you'd like to improve.

When you are looking for new groups, try to find ones…

- that match up with your preferences
- that have members and/or a mission that encourage you to live in-sync with your true self
- that have members that are energizing to you rather than toxic
- where the members interact with each other in respectful and healthy ways.

When it's time to find a new group, you will probably need to do some research. If you already know of a group you want to join, you'll only need to do some logistical research to find out when and where the group meets and if there are any fees to join or any paperwork that needs to be submitted. If you don't have a new group in mind, you will need to brainstorm on what kind of group you'd like to join next and then do some research to find a group that matches your interests and preferences. Exercise 12.2 can help you get organized to join a new group. But first, let's look at the different ways you can learn about groups.

You can learn about the groups in your community in a variety of ways. Check out bulletin boards at local coffee shops, where flyers are often posted for anything from exercise classes to parents' groups to book clubs. Libraries, YMCAs, and other community centers also often have bulletin boards that may have flyers advertising local groups. Many communities have newspapers and newsletters that will report on the activities of local groups as well as include advertisements for neighborhood groups.

The Internet is another good place to track down groups. If you want to find a group with a particular interest, look for a Web site for a national association that focuses on your interest. National organizations often provide links to local chapters, so you can search for a group in your area. Or simply type in some search words that relate to your interest and your location and see what you find: for example, "Santa Monica book clubs," "Manhattan mothers," "Orlando softball," or "Des Plaines writers."

Word of mouth is another good way to find out about groups. Ask everyone you know if they have any favorite groups they'd recommend. If you know what your interest is, ask others if they know of any good clubs that match your interest.

When you are ready to get serious about joining a new group, take some time to complete Exercise 12.2, which will help you get organized and focused.

Exercise 12.2: Getting Organized and Joining a New Group

Instructions: Complete steps 1-6.

Step 1: Brainstorm on all the different kinds of groups you might be interested in joining and write them down next to the appropriate category. Include those that you think will provide you with enjoyment as well as those that may help you advance your life vision. For now, don't worry about any of the limitations you may face in joining the group. Just write down any ideas that come to mind. Later, you can consider any challenges or obstacles you might encounter. If you need some inspiration, consult Appendix A for a list of the different organizations in existence in many communities and towns.

Hobby groups: _____
Sports groups: _____
Volunteer groups: _____
Civic groups: _____
Religious groups: _____
Educational groups: _____
Social groups: _____
Career groups: _____

Step 2: Look at the list you've generated in step 1 and circle the three groups that you get most excited about joining. Do some research on these groups to find out what options you have in your local community to join these groups (Internet research, newspaper classifieds, flyers posted in the local community, word of mouth). During your research, try to answer the following questions.

- How often does the group meet? Where? What time?
- What costs are associated with joining this group?
- How might the group align with your preferences? (See the preference chapters, 3–7, for a review.)
- What will you have to give up to be in this group?
- What do you hope to gain?

Step 3: Given your answers to the preceding questions, are you still interested in joining any of your top three groups? If so, prioritize which group you'd like to try first and keep the others in mind for the future.

Step 4: If you decide, based on your research, that you don't want to join any of your top three groups, look at the other options and start over again with three more groups. If you continue to have trouble finding a group, ask yourself why you are having so much trouble. Is there a personal issue that needs addressing before you are comfortable joining a group? Contemplate these issues in your journal or meet with a life coach or therapist to identify and work through them.

Step 5: Identify the challenges you might face in participating in a particular group that interests you (for example, expensive membership fees, long commute to the meeting place, big time commitment) and develop a plan to deal with these challenges (rearrange your budget so you have the money you need to join the group, arrange for babysitting, find someone to carpool with, ask for help at home so you have the time to attend your group each week). If the challenges are ones you're not willing to address, then look for a new group. But keep in mind that all groups involve some time commitment, so this will be a common challenge you will need to address no matter what group you choose.

Step 6: Now, make a plan to join your top group. Schedule out when you will sign up for the group, do any necessary preparation, and attend your first meeting. Then follow through. If you are shy about joining a group, see if you can find a friend who's interested in joining with you. Or call the group president and have a conversation so you will feel like you know someone when you attend the first group. You can even ask to speak to other group members to learn more about the group before you attend your first meeting. *Lastly, remember—just because you attend one meeting, that doesn't mean that you have to join that group. The process may take time!*

I suggest that you join one new group at a time so you can focus your energy on making that group experience a success. You can always join more groups later, after you've found a rhythm with your current group. I also generally recommend that you join a new group before leaving an old group. In this way, you won't have a period of your life where you lack group camaraderie. Also, having a new group might make it easier for you to leave the old group. And while you're still getting adjusted to the new group, the old group will provide you with a sense of familiarity and community since you are known by those in this group. Of course, if you find that your old group is toxic rather than just not being the right fit for you, it may be more constructive to leave the group as soon as you can, even before you've replaced it with a new group. You will need to weigh the pros and cons when deciding when to leave an old group. This would be a great topic for you to discuss with your coach or a member of your fan club.

Overcoming Blocks Against Joining Groups

As you've started to brainstorm on potential groups you'd like to join, are you finding yourself getting excited? Are there any old hobbies you're ready to pick up? A guitar that needs to be dusted off or some paint brushes that need to be unearthed from the basement? Or maybe you're ready to get back in shape and you've discovered a local sports group to join. If you're feeling excited and you've done your research—or you have a plan for getting going—good for you. You're on your way to enjoying the benefits that come with belonging to a group. On the other hand, if you are still feeling wary about joining a group, you're not alone. Some of us—whether we're introverts or extroverts, shy or outgoing, optimists or skeptics—find it a little more difficult to commit to a group than others. If you find yourself in this camp, take some time to read this section and see if you can work through the challenges that might be impeding you from joining a group.

You Feel Shy About Joining a Group With All New People

A lot of us feel shy about joining a new group. And for good reason—it can be hard to put yourself in a new situation where you don't know what to expect. This can particularly be the case for those with a judging preference—people who like routine and certainty. Introverts may feel some resistance to joining groups too, since they prefer small-group interaction to large groups.

To deal with shyness in joining a group, I recommend that you start by reducing uncertainty regarding the group. Do some research about the group in advance and try to have phone conversations or exchange emails with members before attending a meeting. Phone conversations and email exchanges will have dual benefits—you can learn about the group as well as make members' acquaintances before showing up at the first meeting. You might also see if you can get a friend to go with you for your first meeting of the group.

Another option is to join a group in which all of the members are new—like a language class or an exercise class. There might be some regulars who are returning, but there will likely be a group of new members too. And it can be easier to make acquaintances with others when they are new because everyone is in the same boat—new and open to making friendships.

Another technique for dealing with shyness is to pick a group that involves an activity rather than just conversation. That way, you will have a project to focus your energy on at the first couple of group meetings, which will give you time to get comfortable with the other group members without feeling like you have to make conversation.

If you're shyness is really more about introversion—that you prefer to spend your time in one-on-one interactions—then you can work on fostering group connections that are actually based in one-on-one relationships: for example, mentoring a student, visiting a patient in a nursing home, or conducting a research assignment for a nonprofit charity.

You can work on changing your beliefs to deal with shyness too. When you feel nervous about attending a new group, ask yourself—what's the worst thing that can happen? You won't like the group? People won't be friendly to you? You'll be at a loss for how to make conversation? Then ask yourself, can I handle these negative situations if they come up? The answer will probably be yes, which can go a long way to reducing anxiety. And when you stand in a room full of strangers and feel overwhelmed, just remember, all of the people you are friends with now were once strangers to you. If you are shy or anxious about joining a group, this is another excellent area of discovery for your work with a coach or fan club member.

You Have Trouble Getting Along With Groups or Other People

If you hold the belief that you don't enjoy spending time with people or if you have gotten feedback from others that they don't enjoy spending time with you, you may hesitate to join groups. You may not believe you will do well in a group, or you may believe you won't enjoy your time in the group. Rather than using these beliefs as a reason to skip groups altogether, though, try to work through these issues so you can benefit from the value of group connection in your life.

Interestingly, some kinds of personal development can only take place within groups. In fact, group dynamics will bring up certain issues for all of us that won't come up in one-on-one interactions (this is one of the reasons why group membership is important for all of us). Also, group members can provide you with valuable feedback about yourself that you can't come across through friends or on your own. The value of group membership to help people achieve their goals is apparent in the countless recovery groups in existence in this country—Alcoholics Anonymous, Smoking Cessation, Weight Watcher's, and so on.

If you find it hard to get along with others or you receive feedback from others that they have trouble getting along with you, don't despair. Use your group membership as an opportunity to learn more about yourself and to resolve issues that may be holding you back from achieving your life goals. Write in a journal to keep track of what you are discovering about yourself as you interact with other group members; better yet, work with a life coach or a therapist who can help you process your group experience and learn from it.

Letting other group members know you are interested in their feedback and asking them how they'd recommend you adjust your behavior can also be very helpful. Doing this takes humility, but there's no better way to become good at getting along with others than to get feedback from them and then practice acting on that feedback—right in the group. If you are open-minded and willing to practice new behaviors, you are likely to find that people begin to respond to you in positive ways. If people are too set in old interactional dynamics with you, you can join a new group where others don't have a preconceived idea of who you are and try your new behaviors there.

You're Too Busy

Are you too busy to join a new group? The busy excuse is sometimes just a cover for one of the earlier issues—shyness, an aversion to groups, or trouble getting along with others. So if you say you are too busy to join a group, start by asking yourself whether there is some other reason, besides being busy, that is holding you back from joining a group. If you discover that there is, try to address this issue. If, after some reflection, you really do feel like you are too busy to join a group—which many people do—try to start with a small group commitment.

Look for groups that don't take up a lot of your time. This can take the shape of infrequent meetings or groups that don't involve any work outside of the group's meeting time. For example, book clubs usually only meet once a month and sports groups don't usually involve any time outside of group matches. You can also look for groups that don't have strict attendance policies, so if you have to miss a meeting from time to time, it will be okay. This is often the case for community association meetings and hobby groups.

If you're still not coming up with any groups that fit your schedule, it may be time to make an adjustment to your daily or weekly calendar. Think about what you can do to free up some of your time. Go into work an hour earlier so you can leave an hour earlier and make a sports outing? Get a babysitter on Wednesday nights so you can join a writer's group? Or record a TV show instead of watching it live so that you can go to a night class. If your time constraints remain strict, what creative solutions can you come up with to get around these? Maybe you can take an online class, which works well for people with busy schedules and parents who can only do activities for themselves late at night or during kids' naps. (Internet communities lack some of the benefits of face-to-face communities, but they still can provide information, learning, and some degree of community.) Another creative option would be to start your own group and set a meeting place and time that works for you.

Whatever your challenges to joining a group—shyness, trouble getting along with others, or a busy schedule—these issues can generally be worked through, whether on your own using the preceding tips or with the help of a life coach, therapist, or fan club member. Stick with the process and you will be able to find a group that you enjoy.

Conclusion

The benefits of belonging to a group can be subtle, yet life-changing. Without even realizing it, your connection to a group may provide you with a little extra confidence, which you in turn will naturally filter into your pursuit of your life vision. Your group connections may keep you feeling reenergized, so that when it's time to engage in the hard work of achieving your life vision—step by step—you have the fuel you need to move forward. Your group involvement may provide you with access to opportunities and information that help you promote and achieve your goals. And for some of you, your group membership will help you find the people that you will eventually want to invite to join your fan club.

Some people are most comfortable jumping right in and joining a group; others like to do some research beforehand. Some people like groups that rely on a predictable structure and schedule; others prefer groups that are flexible and spontaneous. Regardless of your preferences and your interests, there is a group out there for you!

13

Making a Positive Impression

Once upon a time, all the people you know today met you for the first time and developed a first impression of you. Was it a positive one?

There's always the odd or funny story about people who started off on the wrong foot and ended up becoming best friends, business partners, or spouses. But for the most part, the people you are friends with today, and who are interested in being in a relationship with you, formed a positive impression of you when you first met. That positive impression is what interested the person in spending more time with you, getting to know you, and letting you get to know him or her as well. Positive first impressions tend to open doors to relationships and opportunities, whereas negative first impressions tend to close doors and opportunities.

Some of the impression you create on others is out of your control. People who meet you will bring to the encounter their own set of biases and viewpoints that will affect how they interpret your behaviors and assess your words, translating them into some kind of impression of you.

Even so, there's still a lot you can do to help present a positive impression of yourself. For example, you can dress in ways that are appropriate for a given situation. You can make eye contact and use body language that will invite a person to trust you and get to know you. You can also use listening skills that will reassure a person that you are interested in making a personal connection with him or her or, in the professional domain, that you are engaged and competent. Finally, you can pay attention to the requirements of a given environment and present yourself in alignment with those requirements to show that you're capable of succeeding in a certain role or situation.

Through your appearance, your body language, your words, and your behaviors, you can create a positive impression that will help you succeed in achieving your goals and in developing fulfilling relationships.

As you have seen so far, your belongings—your friends, the people you work with, and the communities you belong to, for example—have a significant impact on your sense of fulfillment and your ability to succeed in life. This chapter will focus on all the things you can do to present a good impression of yourself to your belongings—because by making a positive impression on others, you will increase the chances that others will respond positively to you. For example, people will only be interested in becoming a fan of yours if they see you in a positive light. Also, you will get the most out of your group memberships if you have made a positive impression on the people in those groups. When people like you or respect you (which is what occurs after you make a positive impression), they will usually be willing to invest in a relationship with you and/or to provide you with opportunities to do what you've presented yourself to do (for example, be the group's Webmaster, secretary, treasurer, social coordinator, etc.). The bottom line is…making positive impressions on people is essential to developing healthy belongings, and developing and maintaining healthy belongings is essential to having a meaningful and fulfilling life.

What Is an Impression?

The impression you make on someone is the image that a person develops of who you are as a person when they first meet you—your traits, your values, your strengths, and your weaknesses in a snapshot. Making a *positive* impression is about acting in a way that helps others develop a respect and/or a liking for you. In an organizational setting, making a positive impression is about providing others with a sense that you can contribute in a situation. In a personal setting, making a positive impression is about giving people a sense that you are a positive person to be around, whether that comes in the form of you seeming pleasant, likable, fun, witty, or smart.

The *impression* you make on someone is the image that a person develops of who you are as a person when they first meet you—your traits, your values, your strengths, and your weaknesses in a snapshot.

As soon as people meet you, they will develop a first impression of you, based on how you act, speak, and present yourself, as well as based on the way that the person views the world. Since you can't tinker with other people's biases and frames of reference (the way they view the world), we are going to focus in this chapter on all the parts of making an impression that are in your control:

- your appearance
- your body language
- your verbal communication
- your beliefs
- your behaviors.

Your *appearance* refers to how you dress and how you are groomed (for example, cleanliness; hairstyle; for men, a shaven face). *Body language* points to how you hold your body and includes things like your posture, eye contact, the way you hold your arms, and the direction you face while your standing. *Verbal communication* refers to the content and quality of the words you express to others. Your *beliefs*, as we discussed in Part I, are those thoughts, feelings, or ideas that you hold to be true about yourself and the world...regardless of whether they're actually true. Finally, your *behaviors* (as discussed in Part I) refer to the way you act and conduct yourself in the world.

Table 13.1 presents the components that make up a first impression and gives examples of how you can make a positive impression versus a negative impression in each of these areas. To learn what kinds of appearance, communication, beliefs, and behaviors tend to make positive versus negative impressions, take some time read this table.

Table 13.1: Components of an Impression: Examples of Positive vs. Negative Impressions

Impression Area	Positive Impressions	Negative Impressions
Appearance	Your clothes are clean, neat, and appropriate for the situation (a suit at a corporate job interview; shorts and a t-shirt at a summer barbecue).	Your clothes are dirty, wrinkled, or inappropriate for the situation (shorts and a t-shirt at a corporate job interview; a suit at a summer barbecue).
Body language	Your handshake is firm.	Your handshake is weak.
	You stand with your arms comfortably at your sides.	You stand with your arms crossed against your chest.
	Your posture is upright, not slumped.	Your shoulders are slumped.
	You make eye contact while talking and listening	You look down at the floor or away from a person while talking or listening.
	You smile.	You frown or maintain a straight face.
Verbal communication	You speak clearly and at a reasonable tempo and volume.	You speak faster, slower, louder, or quieter than typical social norms.
	You use language that is right for the situation (proper grammar and technical jargon at a job interview).	You use language that is inappropriate for the situation (slang or poor grammar at a job interview).

Impression Area	Positive Impressions	Negative Impressions
	You offer positive feedback to others when you see something you like or appreciate.	You offer negative criticism to others without constructive feedback.
	You communicate concerns openly when they arise.	You keep your concerns bottled up inside and let your frustration negatively affect your behaviors.
Beliefs	You believe that people are important.	You see people as unimportant.
	You believe that you are capable.	You believe that you are incapable.
	You believe that you have something to contribute and to gain.	You believe that you don't have anything to contribute or gain.
Behaviors	You are punctual, meet your responsibilities, and follow through on your promises.	You are late, fail to meet your responsibilities, and don't follow through on your promises.
	You act in-sync with how you speak.	You don't act in-sync with how you speak.
	You show sincere interest in your work and/or the present relationship.	You show apathy toward your work and/or the present relationship.

So you can see that, although each of us is unique, there are some common things—no matter who you are and no matter what you're personality type and preferences—that you can do to create a positive impression on other people.

You can dress neatly and appropriately. You can use body language that communicates openness, trustworthiness, and confidence, and you can speak in ways that communicate social sensitivity and competence. You can believe positive and helpful things about yourself, your situation, and the people around you and can express these beliefs through your behaviors. Finally, you can behave in ways that convey you are reliable and invested in your work and relationships. Table 13.1 covers the universal elements of appearance, body language, verbal communication, and behavior that work together to make a positive impression on someone.*

If you find that other people are consistently not interested in maintaining relationships with you or that people in your environment—work, social, or otherwise—are unwilling to give you opportunities to take on new responsibilities and new roles, you may have made a less than positive impression on these people.

Universal within the Western culture.

The Importance of First Impressions

As the old adage goes, "You never get a second chance to make a first impression." In other words, the first impression you make on someone often sticks, so it's important to make it a good one. As a result, you want to come into a situation ready to make a good impression so you can start the relationship off on the right foot.

The impression you make on others is like a gate that either opens or closes opportunities for you. If you make a positive impression on someone, a gate of opportunity will open for you: for example, you might be given an opportunity to build a friendship, to develop a romantic relationship, to take on a new role at work, or to change careers. If you make a negative impression on someone, a gate of opportunity may close for you. For example, someone may lose interest in developing a relationship with you, your superiors may pass you over for promotion, or a potential employer may not offer you a job that you've applied for.

Interestingly, if the first impression you make on someone is good, he or she will tend to see your positive traits at future meetings. On the other hand, if your first impression on someone is negative, he or she will tend to focus on your negative traits. Psychological research has shown this phenomenon to be true, and it's one of the reasons why positive first impressions are so important.

Imagine you are hiring a babysitter to watch your children and one candidate shows up on time for the interview, while the other candidate shows up 20 minutes late. Then, during the interview, both candidates ask for a little more pay than you'd hoped to offer. When the on-time sitter makes her pay request, you might think, "She's probably worth it. She seems reliable." But when the late sitter makes her pay request, you might attribute this to some negative trait on her part—a take-what-you-can attitude or an unrealistic understanding of the pay scale for babysitters. Why do you view each candidate differently? Because you've formed a good first impression of the on-time applicant and a negative first impression of the late applicant, and first impressions tend to have staying power.

As you can see from the previous babysitter example, the first impression you make on someone will set the tone for…

- how someone interacts with you going forward
- which of your traits a person notices
- how a person interprets your communication and your behavior.

The first impression you make on someone has a powerful influence on how your interactions and relationship with that person will unfold.

Impressions Can Change

If you make a negative first impression on someone, you may have a chance to recover from it, but it's harder to reopen that gate of opportunity once a person has developed a less than sterling image of you. A 2004 study by one researcher confirmed that first impressions are challenging to overcome and that it takes hard work and consistent behaviors to reverse them.**

Happily, if you've made a bad impression, it's still possible to improve the image someone has of you—by adjusting your dress, body language, communication, beliefs, and behaviors, as needed. However, it will take some awareness, hard work, and commitment to the process. You'll also need to study the environment you will be presenting yourself in and you'll have to learn how to present yourself more positively within that environment. That is, in addition to the universal things you can do to make a positive impression (for example, dress appropriately and communicate effectively), there will be some situation-specific things you can do to make a positive impression on people. You need to learn the rules of the game at your company, in a new group of friends, or at a club you've just joined so you can present yourself in-sync with those rules. This is a great way to make a positive impression.

Do you remember the client I mentioned in chapter 9 who wanted to get promoted to police sergeant so he could become a leader in his organization? As it turns out, this client was having difficulty passing the oral interview part of the promotion exam. During our work together, we discovered that my client needed to make some situation-specific adjustments to improve the impression he was making on those in a position to promote him. For those of you not familiar with the oral interview process, it consists of a panel of experts who have usually never met the candidates. In other words, the oral interview process is an opportunity to make simultaneous first impressions.

In the case of my client, he had an excellent performance record and high scores on the written part of the exam. But when he went into the room for the oral interview, he had trouble making a positive impression on the raters. He dressed appropriately, but where he dropped the ball was in his beliefs, which led to ineffective communications. In the beliefs arena, my client had two things working against his probability of success: (a) he didn't always believe that he would make a capable corporal and (b) he believed that the panel members wanted him to act more like a police recruit than a seasoned veteran. These two beliefs caused him to be hesitant in his communication (which created the impression that he lacked confidence) and to be stiff and formal in his approach (which created an impression of extreme rigidity). The interviewers were looking for someone who was confident, relaxed, and approachable, but my client was creating the opposite impression.

One of the methods that I use for all of my clients who are trying to improve their impressions is to videotape them. I used the videotaping method with this client as well and showed him what he looked like when he was simulating an interview, compared with what he looked like after a few minutes when he forgot the camera was on and he was confident, smiling, and more relaxed. We spent a few weeks working on giving him the skills to match his behaviors to his intentions (to promote an impression of confidence and flexibility), and the next time my client took the promotion test, he placed number one on the oral interview part. He had learned how to make a good first impression.

** Lustig, C. et al. (2004, November). Psychological Science as cited in The University Record Online, University of Michigan. http://www.umich. edu/~urecord/0405/Oct25_04/36.shtml. Retrieved September 24, 2007.

What Kind of an Impression Are You Making?

There's only one way to know for sure what kind of an impression you've made on someone and that is to ask for the person's feedback. Getting feedback from others, though hard to hear at times, can be a great way to learn what you can do differently in the future to make a positive impression.

If you've been turned down for a job, call the interviewer and ask for feedback on what the interviewer recommends you do differently when interviewing for jobs in the future. If someone ends a romantic relationship with you, ask the person if there was anything you could have done differently to have made the relationship better. In matters of love, reasons for breaking up aren't always logical (nor are they always true, as people try to avoid hurting other people's feelings), but you still might be able to gain insight that will make you a better partner for someone in the future.

Even in your successful relationships, you can ask for feedback on how you can be more supportive, more helpful, and more effective in your role. The information you gain will not only allow you to sharpen the kind of impression you make on others in the future but will enable you to make your current relationships—at home and at work—even better than they already are.

> *A caution when asking for feedback*: Before you ask someone for feedback, be sure that you are prepared to act on what the person may tell you. Do not make the mistake of asking a person for feedback and then disregarding his or her recommendations to you. This is a sure-fire way of leaving a negative impression with someone.

If you are unable to gain feedback on the kind of impression you are making on others or if you need additional tools, here are some signs you can look for to indicate whether you have made a positive or negative impression on someone.

Table 13.2: Signs That You've Made a Positive vs. a Negative Impression

Positive Signs	Negative Signs
In Your Personal Life	
The person shows interest in developing a relationship with you by exchanging contact information, making plans with you, and following through on those plans.	The person avoids making plans with you or consistently cancels plans once they've been made.

Positive Signs	Negative Signs
The person shows excitement and enthusiasm around you and genuine interest in your life and what's going on for you.	The person shows apathy around you and lacks energy or interest in your life and what's going on for you.
The person initiates contact with you to talk on the phone or to make plans to spend time together.	You find yourself having to call the person all the time to talk or to make plans to spend time together.
Time with the other person seems to flow naturally. The person seems unfiltered and comfortable in talking with you.	Time with the other person seems to feel forced. The person seems to carefully choose his or her words when talking to you.
You and the other person seem to lose track of time when talking on the phone or spending time together.	The other person is constantly checking his or her watch or asking about what time it is when you are together.

In Your Work Life

After a first job interview, you get called back for a second interview or you are offered the job.	After a first job interview, you are not called back for additional interviews or offered the job.
Your superiors give you new projects, responsibilities, or roles over time.	Your superiors are unwilling to offer you new projects, responsibilities, or roles over time.
Your supervisor asks you about your future plans and aspirations.	Your supervisor doesn't ask you any questions.
Your supervisor asks for your opinion or seeks your input on matters.	Your supervisor doesn't ask for your opinion or seek your input on matters.

In truth, there is no set formula for figuring out if you've made a positive or a negative impression, but the signs in Table 13.2 might be indicators of the impression you tend to make on people if you find a *consistent pattern* of these indicators across multiple relationships in your life.

For example, if your boss is unwilling to give you new responsibilities, it might simply be because she has trouble delegating or giving up control. But if you notice that all of the bosses you've had are unwilling to give you new responsibilities, this might relate to the kind of impression you are making on them.

In the personal realm, if you have a friend who always cancels plans with you, then it's possible that your friend is too self-involved to be a good friend right now. On the other hand, if you notice that all the people you meet resist making plans and developing friendships with you, you may be making a less than positive impression on them.

How to Make a Good Impression

Some people have a better knack for making a good impression than others, but everyone can learn skills to improve the impressions they make. Here are the three steps I recommend that you follow to make a good impression on new people that you meet.

Step 1: Mind Your Appearance

If you are conscientious enough to be reading this book, you are probably the kind of person who knows when to take a shower and brush your hair. But how to dress, in a society where the boundaries between work and home, the professional world and the casual social world, are becoming more and more blurred, may not always be clear even to the best of us. This section is meant to be a reminder that even in a world that is becoming less and less formal, where punctuation drops out of emails and grammar is for the birds, a neat, clean appearance goes a long way to make a good impression. This is particularly true in the work world, but it can also be true in social relationships, friendships, and communities.

Imagine you decide to join a book club. When you first get there, you see a couple people who are sitting in the book circle, on opposite ends of the room. At one end of the room is a man with a long, untrimmed beard; the man is wearing a t-shirt with a few holes in it. His jeans are ripped and he has dirt under his fingernails. At the other end of the room is a man wearing a stylish pair of glasses, who appears well-groomed and is wearing a white button-down shirt and khaki pants. Who do you choose to sit next to? Most people will choose to sit next to the clean-cut person. Yes, some people will be drawn to someone who is a little different (the man with the beard), but most people will be drawn to the person with the clean, neat appearance (the man with glasses), perhaps because of survival instincts. It's not to say that people won't become friends with someone who's a little different, just that it generally makes your job of making friends easier if you maintain a clean and put-together appearance.

No, you don't have to be a beauty queen or prom king to get people to like or respect you, but you do generally need to present a well-maintained or polished appearance to gain interest or respect in the personal or the work world. At an instinctual level, when we see someone who is well-groomed and dressed in the current style of clothing, we give them a certain amount of respect. Accurate or not, we interpret a put-together appearance as a sign of competence. So an easy way to score some points and get off on the right foot when you meet someone new is to show up showered, dressed in fresh-looking clothes that are coordinated and in line with current fashion, and wearing a neat or well-styled hair cut. You don't have to sport a Rolex or wear Gucci, but you do need to look as if you are living in the 21st century.

If fashion isn't your area of expertise, ask a friend to help you shop or get the sales clerk to help you pick out some coordinated outfits. If you don't have a lot of money to spend on clothes, focus on buying a few key pieces of classic clothing that won't go out of style and that you can wear at important times, or learn to shop at discount stores that offer name brand products at discount prices.

The last thing to consider when putting yourself together is the situation you're dressing for. Every environment calls for a different kind of dress and appearance. Jeans are fine for going to the movies, but aren't acceptable at many workplaces. A suit looks great during the day if you work on Wall Street, but if you show up at a friend's party on a Saturday night in the same suit, people might assume you're uptight or stuffy. If you're unsure how to dress for an occasion, it's always a good idea to ask. If you're going to a party, ask the host how he or she plans to dress or how he or she would like the guests to dress.

For a job interview, ask the HR person about the dress code for the office. Later, when you show up at the interview in the right clothes, you will immediately be communicating a positive piece of information to the interviewer...that you have the ability to fit in to that workplace. In other words, in the first thirty seconds of meeting the interviewer, you will be creating a positive impression. Now the interviewer will be conditioned to look for other positive traits in you as the interview unfolds.

As an overview, when it comes to making a positive impression, here are the reasons why appearance matters. How you groom, dress, and put yourself together can...

- convey respect or disrespect for the person you're interacting with
- show awareness of the rules of the game (social, cultural, or organizational)
- exhibit self-possession and discipline
- indicate your position or potential position in an organization (for example, sales manager vs. sales associate)
- indicate whether or not you should be taken seriously
- tell others what you think or how you feel about yourself.

Most of you already know the importance of physical appearance in making a good impression, so I won't spend any more time on this point. The main take-away I want to

342

leave you with is that if you'd like a little lift when it comes to making positive impressions, spend some time thinking about the right way to dress for a particular situation and show up with a fresh and clean appearance that matches that situation. Wearing appropriate clothes is an easy way to convey competence to other people.

Step 2: Find Out the Rules

The second way that you can make a positive impression is to take some time before you meet someone new or before you join a new community to learn about the person's preferences or the community's norms. If you're going on a blind date, talk to the person on the phone beforehand to learn something about him or her. If you're going to interview for a job, do your homework ahead of time to discover the nature of the workplace you'll be entering. Each social or organizational community has different definitions of acceptable and discouraged conduct.

When getting ready to join a new community, don't be afraid to ask questions and find out things like the following: Are there topics that I should bring up or avoid talking about? Is humor appreciated in this group or environment, or is it better to keep things serious? Should I be on time or is it better to arrive a little late? (For example, even though a party invitation says that 8 PM is the start time, does the host tend to run late?) The more research you can do before your first meeting, the easier it will be to make a positive impression. But if you can't do any research before your first meeting, get to the meeting a little early and watch and listen. Look for the ways things are done in that particular community and be prepared to adjust your communications and behaviors accordingly.

Step 3: Act to Win

Once you discover the rules of a community or culture, then do what you need to do to create the most favorable impression that you can for that particular situation. It may feel strange at first to adjust your behavior to make a positive impression—like you're being inauthentic or untrue to yourself—but if you want to be successful in life, you will often find yourself changing to meet the expectations of the communities that you have become a part of. Yes, you want to remain true to your personality, but you also want to have meaningful connections to others. Sometimes, this means adopting the norms of the group. By choosing communities that are in-sync with your preferences and your life plan, the changes you make will relate more to social or cultural etiquette than your personality; if you do end up needing to flex beyond your preferences, the adjustments will be worthwhile to you because they will allow you to achieve your life plan.

For example, I have a preference for introversion, but if I want to be in management, I am going to have to adopt and use extroverted behaviors during the interview process to get a management job. After I get the job, I am going to have to continue to use extroverted behaviors to be effective. To make a positive impression on my employer and the people I manage, I will need to flex beyond my preferences. This adjustment will be worthwhile to me because it will allow me to achieve part of my life vision, which is to mentor others and help them become leaders themselves.

Although there will be times that you will need to learn to adopt the behaviors of a preference type other than your own, sometimes the opposite will be true: to make a good impression, you will need to give yourself permission to be your natural self, rather than trying to present a different image to the world. That was the case for my client the police officer, who struggled to pass his oral interview and get promoted. It turns out that my client had the natural traits he needed to impress his superiors and pass his oral interview, but he kept suppressing them because he didn't realize they would be of value to the role he was seeking. He was naturally friendly and caring but erroneously believed that the interviewers were looking for someone more formal and stoic. Once my client learned to embrace these traits and convey them in the workplace, he was able to pass the interview and get promoted.

If you are struggling in a particular area to make a good impression (for example, appearance or verbal communication), look at Exercise 13.1 for ideas on how to improve specific areas of making a good impression and follow whichever recommendations apply to you.

Exercise 13.1: Techniques for Improving the Impression You Make on Others

Instructions: Ask for feedback from others or observe how others respond to you to determine which area(s) of making a positive impression that you want to improve. You can also review the information in Tables 13.1 and 13.2 to help you in the process of determining areas for improvement. Once you've determined which areas you'd like to improve, locate that area in the following section and consider some of the suggested exercises and tips.

Appearance
- Ask a fashionable friend to go shopping with you, or find a helpful sales clerk and ask for assistance while shopping.
- If you can afford it, spend a little more to get a good haircut and ask the hair dresser to teach you how to recreate the style at home.
- Set aside time to iron your clothes each morning or each week or pay to have your clothes dry-cleaned or professionally laundered.
- Keep your wardrobe current by buying a few new items each season and/or buy clothes that are neutral and classic (and thus less likely to go out of style).

Body Language
- Videotape yourself interacting with someone and see if any of your body language looks unusual, awkward, or off-putting; practice making adjustments to eliminate this body language.
- Practice your handshake with friends and family and ask them for feedback—is it too weak or limp? Is it too firm?
- Practice making eye contact while you talk and listen to others.
- Keep your arms uncrossed and in a comfortable position

while you talk to others; if you feel nervous, wear something with pockets so you can slip your hands inside.

- Practice using good posture; do core-strengthening exercises like those in Pilates to help improve your posture.
- Remind yourself to smile, even when no one is around. Soon smiling will become habitual and a regular part of your demeanor.

Verbal Communication

- Videotape yourself in normal conversation with others and see if you are talking at a good speed and a reasonable volume; if not, work on making adjustments.
- Ask others for feedback on how you talk: Is it too fast? A little slow? Too loud? Too quiet?
- Next time you find yourself wanting to complain about something, skip the complaining or see if you can form the comment in terms of a positive change that can be made.
- Make it a practice to say one nice thing to each person you see every time you see them.

Beliefs

- Replace negative thoughts about yourself or others with positive thoughts.
- Take classes to improve the skills you feel need improving.
- Set aside time to reflect on the good things in your life.
- Don't forget to enjoy the simple but positive things in life.

Behaviors

- Listen to what others have to say, ask questions, and offer to be helpful or supportive.
- Show up on time (to be more timely, set all your clocks ahead by 15 minutes, or tell yourself you need to get somewhere 15 minutes earlier than you really need to).
- Follow through on your commitments by scheduling on your planner when you plan to do each task you've promised you'll do for someone.

In summary, there are lots of different ways you can begin improving the impressions you make on others. Whether you put more effort into the way you dress, you learn to speak a little softer or a little louder, or you practice being a better listener, you can refine the image you convey to the world and increase the chances that other people will form a positive impression of you.

Your Preferences and Making a Positive Impression

Because of the behaviors associated with the different preferences, it will be easier for those with certain preference types—extroverts, judgers, sensing judgers, and intuitive thinkers—to adjust their behaviors to make positive impressions than those with the following preference types—introverts, perceivers, sensing perceivers, and intuitive feelers. I mention this only to better prepare you for the change process—not to discourage anyone from trying to make adjustments to their behaviors. Remember, anyone can do anything, regardless of preference. Here's what you can expect, if you are in the second group of preference types, if you find you need to adjust your behaviors to make a more positive impression.

Introverts (I's)

As an introvert, you will probably experience an intense desire to keep your thoughts and feelings to yourself, which will make it hard for others to give you feedback, because so much of you remains hidden. To make a positive impression on others, you will need to gradually get comfortable with verbalizing your thoughts and sharing your feelings (both positive and negative) with your community members. The less mysterious you are, the more of a positive impression you will make.

As an introvert, you may also tend to wait for people to adjust to you, instead of taking the first step to adjust to them. But by learning to adjust to the norms of a community, you will show community members that you are able to fit in and contribute to the group.

Finally, as an introvert, you may prefer to observe activities, rather than to initiate them, but to make a good impression on others, you will need to begin initiating action on behalf of the community of which you are a member. For example, the next time that you go to a social function where there are people that you don't know, instead of waiting for someone to introduce you, introduce yourself. And once you get comfortable with that, start introducing new people to the group. These actions will communicate that you are confident, friendly, and concerned about people connecting with each other. It will feel awkward at first, but if you keep practicing it, you will soon become very good at this skill.

Perceivers (P's)

As a perceiver, you will likely experience a screaming need for freedom and naturally resist any conformity to someone else's way of doing things or the group culture. If you want to make a positive impression on others and if you want to be a contributing and receiving member of a community, however, you will need to steadily begin to exchange your need for freedom with the community's need for structure. This means adopting certain behaviors to conform to the community so you can make a good impression on community members and function effectively as part of the group. For example, if the group has a dress code, even an informal one, you will need to start conforming to it. Also, you will need to be on time if the group values punctuality.

Sensing Perceivers (SP's)

As a sensing perceiver, you will most likely think about or feel an urgent need to break the rules of the community or organization and express your own, unique personality and identity. It's okay to think or feel this need; however, you will want to learn how to put the needs of the community ahead of your own personal needs in certain situations to make a positive impression and, more important, to be an effective, contributing member of the community. For example, if the group is involved in planning for a future social event, like an outing or party, instead of not participating or telling everyone that planning is a waste of time, suggest one or two things that the plan should have. This will let people know that you are interested in the group's next event being a successful one.

Intuitive Feelers (NF's)

As an intuitive feeler, you may feel that "acting" out certain behaviors to make a positive impression is not genuine. To overcome this feeling of inauthenticity, remind yourself that sometimes acting is necessary to promote harmony and build relationships. For example, you may have had a sharp disagreement with one of the group members recently that has yet to be resolved. Instead of visibly carrying a grudge and absenting yourself from any activities where the member will be, make it a point to participate with enthusiasm. Focus on the benefit that the larger group will gain from your enthusiastic participation and don't dwell on the personal hurt that you may be experiencing.

Conclusion

You don't need to leave the impression you make on others up to fate, luck, or chance. Instead, you can consciously work to make a positive impression on others in how you appear, how you communicate, what you believe, and how you interact. To be successful in creating a positive impression, make sure that your body language communicates openness, confidence, and competence. Pay attention to how you speak and be prepared to adjust your language to the situation. Believe good things about yourself and others, and make it a priority to dress professionally or appropriately.

It's important to make a positive first impression because this impression will be the one that people remember you by. If the impression you make is positive, then it will be easier for you to develop the kinds of relationships that will help you feel fulfilled as well as achieve your goals. If the impression you make is negative, then you may end up closing the door to important opportunities. You might also be attractive to the wrong kinds of people. So make it a priority to create a positive first impression, and you will be paving the way for your progress toward achieving your goals. It's such a small thing, but it can have such a large impact. Make that impact and you'll be well on your way to achieving your life plan.

14

Pursuing Your Passion

Have you ever met someone who loves what he or she does for a living? Someone who radiates energy when he talks about what he does for a living? Someone who gets excited about going to work to get started on her day? When you meet someone who loves what he or she does, it's usually a surprise. Many of us equate work with drudgery: work is an obligation, a huge stressor, or a bore. It's too challenging or not challenging enough. Whatever the reason, many of us don't enjoy our work.

So when we meet someone who loves what he or she does, it catches us off guard. We think, "Someone who loves his job??? Is that really possible???? Maybe it's possible for him, but not for me." We tend to think that only a few "lucky" people get to have jobs they like, and we tend to chalk up our own job dissatisfaction to being just the way life is. Instead of seeing the possibilities for our own careers, we often see the limitations. We get so grounded by the reality of our circumstances—focusing on the fact that we have to pay the bills or provide for our loved ones or that we don't have training for other careers or that the fields we are *really* interested are very competitive—that we lose sight of the fact that all of these challenges can be overcome.

You will be amazed at your ability to become one of those people who love what they do, if you set your mind to it. Finding work that you love all goes back to having intentions and a good plan. If you are clear on what you want to do for a career and you create a plan to accomplish it, with some hard work, you'll be on your way. This chapter will focus on helping you uncover where your particular passion lies, so you can spend more of your time doing what you love, whether it be in a paid profession or outside of your employment hours. It's wonderful to have a job that you love, but if necessity makes it so that you can't change careers right now or if you simply don't want to change careers, you can still find ways to spend more of your time doing what you love.

Doing work that you love may be one of the goals in your life plan. If so, this chapter will help you achieve that goal. If this is not yet one of your goals, you may end up adding it to your life plan after you are done reading this chapter. Doing work that you love has two major benefits: first, it will add more enjoyment to your life. Second, it will help you be more successful at achieving your other goals. For example, doing work that you love will enable you to keep your energy stores filled, so you can use that energy to work toward all of your other goals (work or non-work-related). In addition, doing work that you love often exposes you to a community of like-minded people. Working with people who love the same things you do can provide you with the extra support and encouragement you need to pursue your life vision. If the idea of doing work that you love appeals to you, this chapter will help you get started on your journey.

The Nature of Your Work

There are two kinds of work out there—paid and unpaid. Paid work is any work you do that provides you with financial compensation—work as a bus driver, administrative assistant, nurse, accountant, information technology specialist, scientist, consultant, doctor, or lawyer, for example. Your paid work is a strategy for living in the world (to pay the bills, put food on the table, support yourself and your family, and save for retirement). If you get a paycheck, then that's your paid work or—as most of us know it, your *job*.

Unpaid work is work that you choose to do in your free time and that does not provide any financial compensation. You might engage in unpaid work to keep your house running, your family taken care of, and your life (for example, doing cooking, laundry, home repair, car repair, cleaning, or yard work), or you might do unpaid work because it brings you pleasure, as is the case for hobbies (for example, photography, painting, writing, gardening, fishing, hunting, or playing basketball).

There is one kind of work, called your *avocation*, which

can be paid or unpaid. *Your avocation is life work that you are passionate about.* It is work that brings you pleasure to engage in and that feels like it fulfills some aspect of your life's purpose. Sometimes, a job and an avocation are one and the same, but not always. (We'll talk in-depth about your avocation in the second half of this chapter.)

When you put your paid work together with your unpaid work, most of your hours in a day are accounted for (sleep makes up much of the rest). So, if you are feeling unfulfilled or unsatisfied in your life, examining your paid and unpaid work to see whether either of these areas are lacking in enjoyment or satisfaction for you can provide you with valuable clues for adjusting your work for more fulfillment. Let's start this process now by creating a snapshot of the work that you do— paid and unpaid—so you can have an accurate work picture to assess. You can create this snapshot by completing Exercise 14.1.

Exercise 14.1: Creating a Snapshot of the Work That You Do

Instructions: The goal of this exercise is simply to bring into your awareness the different kinds of work you do throughout the day, week, month, and year so you can later assess whether this is the way you'd really like to be spending your time.

1. List each of the paid jobs that you do in one of the circles in Figure 14.1 (one job per circle), for example, engineer and military reservist.

Figure 14.1: Job Circles - 1

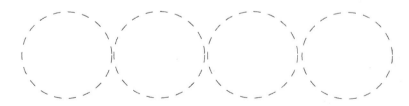

2. List the *unpaid* work that you do on a routine basis in each of the circles in Figure 14.2 (one "job" per circle). Think about your

chores and errands as well as the activities you engage in that take effort but bring you pleasure. Unpaid work generally falls into the categories of domestic chores, personal errands, volunteer work, and hobbies. (Examples of unpaid work: grocery shopping, yard work, office softball team, hospital volunteering.) You may need to add more unpaid job circles on a separate sheet of paper.

Figure 14.2: Job Circles - 2

3. Now that you've written your different kinds of work on paper—paid and unpaid—take some time to reflect on the work that fills your days. A little later, we'll get into the details of whether your work is satisfying to you, but for now, just try to get a general sense of the work that you do. There are probably no big surprises regarding your paid work, but what do you notice about your unpaid work?

- Do you have a lot of unpaid work or a little? _____
- Is most of your unpaid work obligatory or does a good portion of it bring you pleasure? How do you feel about this fact? _____
- Are there unpaid activities that have been taking up a lot of your time that you haven't consciously acknowledged before? _____
- What can you learn by examining all the ways you spend

354

your time in work outside of your regular paid job? Are there any patterns, issues, or dissatisfactions that need addressing? _____

_____

You should now have a better awareness of all the work you do in your life. The next section will help you pinpoint which of these jobs bring you satisfaction versus dissatisfaction.

Once you have a complete picture of the work that you do—once you've laid it out on paper—you can move to the next step of assessing whether your work hours satisfy you and whether they move you closer to the goals you've set for your life.

Does Your Work Satisfy You?

How you spend your time is essential to your fulfillment in life. If you spend your time doing things that you enjoy, value, and feel are important or meaningful, you will likely feel fulfilled at the end of each day. On the other hand, if you spend your time doing things that you dislike, hold in low regard, and feel are insignificant or unimportant, you will probably feel unfulfilled at the end of each day. You might also feel sad, angry, disappointed, unmotivated, or bored.

For example, if you are a strong believer in protecting the natural environment, but you work in a job that forces you to participate in negative environmental practices, you will probably feel very dissatisfied with your work as well as unfulfilled as a person. You might feel guilty, angry, sad, hypocritical, or trapped. Your job might pay your bills, but it will require that you perform work that goes against your values. As long as you remain in that job, you will likely feel unfulfilled or dissatisfied in your life, or some portion of your life. On the other hand, if you work for a company that follows beneficial environmental practices, you will feel better about your job, and if it meshes with your preferences as well, you will likely feel fulfilled by it.

One of the common reasons that clients hire me as their

coach is because they are dissatisfied with the work that they do and they'd like support in the process of figuring out how to change their careers. Other times my clients don't realize that their careers are holding them back from living completely fulfilling lives, but over time, our conversations reveal that this is actually the case. So, if you are feeling restless about your own career—if you are feeling bored, stressed, frustrated, irritated, fatigued, or unmotivated by your job—you are not alone. Many people are working in jobs that don't fulfill them. The good news is that we all have the power to shift to work that we enjoy or to learn to increase our enjoyment from the work that we already do.

Let's spend some time assessing whether your work—paid and unpaid—satisfies you. The reason we will be looking at both kinds of work is because these two things together take up most of your time. If you enjoy your unpaid work but not your paid work, you may still be unsatisfied with your life. Similarly, if you feel engaged and interested in your paid work but are unhappy with the unpaid work in your life, you will feel at least some dissatisfaction in your life.

To get a clear picture of which areas of work in your life you may want to adjust to improve your life satisfaction, take some time to complete Exercise 14.2.

Exercise 14.2: Assessing Your Work Satisfaction

Instructions: This exercise will help you assess why it is that you are dissatisfied with a particular type of work in your life. Once you understand the reasons for your dissatisfaction, you will be able to make targeted adjustments or alter aspects of your current job to enjoy that work more. You will need a set of colored pens, pencils, or markers for this exercise.

1. To begin, take the work snapshot you created in Exercise 14.1 and write down each of the jobs (paid and unpaid) that are in your circles in Table 14.1.

Table 14.1: Job Summary Exercise

Job	Satisfaction Rating	Low Rating

2. For each job you have listed, choose a number on the following scale that indicates your degree of satisfaction with this particular work. Write that number in the column marked "Satisfaction Rating."

When it comes to this work, I am…

1 - Completely satisfied
2 - Very satisfied
3 - Somewhat satisfied
4 - Neutral ("This work doesn't fulfill me, but I don't mind doing it.")
5 - Somewhat dissatisfied
6 - Very dissatisfied
7 - Completely dissatisfied

3. If you have rated any jobs with a 3, 5, 6, or 7, put a checkmark in the column marked low rating. If you think you might want to adjust any of the jobs you marked with a 4 (neutral) rating, add a checkmark for these jobs as well.

4. For each job that has a checkmark in the "Low Rating" column, ask yourself the following questions about that job (the questions are categorized by the different identity and personality elements).

Behaviors
- Do I enjoy some or all of the tasks that I am responsible for at this particular job?
- Am I dissatisfied with my compensation, commute, or work environment for this job?

Belongings

- Do I respect or feel valued by the person or people who manage me? ...and by the clients whom I serve?
- Do I respect or feel valued by the person or people who are my peers or who I manage?
- Do I enjoy being in the company of the people with whom I work?

Beliefs

- Are the values expressed by the work I do in conflict with my own values?
- Do the people I work with value or respect the beliefs and values that I possess?

Personality

- Does my job require that I flex beyond my preferences? Am I unwilling or unsure of how to do that?
- Do the people I work with know, value, or appreciate my preferences?
- Do the people I work with have preferences that are different than mine? Am I unwilling or unsure of how to get along with them?

Now that you've completed the exercise, take some time to reflect on your answers. Do any patterns emerge? If the same issues are leading to dissatisfaction in each of your jobs, consider what factors might be leading to this pattern. Chances are, if you find a pattern across all your different kinds of work, there are adjustments you can make within yourself to address these repetitive issue. If there are no patterns, you can zero in on the specific work you don't enjoy and make adjustments to it. The next section of the chapter will provide you with support in making these adjustments.

Many of us feel irrevocably tied to work we do that we don't enjoy. We feel like we have no choice but to keep doing things that bother us or don't fulfill us. In most cases, however, we *do* have options and choices; we simply need the necessary tools to make adjustments to our lives so that we can spend our time doing things that bring us fulfillment and that won't bring us down.

Making Adjustments and Changes

If you discovered in Exercise 14.2 that you have work in your life that is unsatisfying to you, don't worry. There are adjustments you can make to begin to enjoy your work more or to change that work altogether.

Making Adjustments Within

Let's say that you discover a pattern of not feeling valued by the people you work with, regardless of whether it's at your paid job, your volunteer work, or within your family or a personal relationship. This pattern is probably a sign that there is something within your perspective or interaction with people that is allowing this pattern to persist. For example, it's possible that you have a *misperception* of how people value you, such that you believe people don't value you when in fact they do. If you have been undervalued in the past by a family member, you may be projecting this experience onto others when it isn't truly the case. This is just one example of how your perspective or interaction with others may be allowing a pattern of being undervalued to persist.

Alternately, you may tend to gravitate toward people who don't show you respect, such that your perception of being undervalued is accurate, but you are still responsible to some degree for allowing this behavior to persist. Specifically, you are making subconscious choices to have relationships with people who don't treat you with respect or care. As a result, the power is within you to develop new relationships, with people who do show you respect and care. If you notice that patterns persist in your life, consider working with a life coach or therapist to learn to understand and undo these patterns. It's often hard to get an objective perspective on what's going on when it comes to our unconstructive patterns of viewing and interacting with the world, and a trained professional with a neutral perspective will be in a good position to help you understand what's going on and to create new patterns of positive perception and interaction.

359

If patterns of dissatisfaction don't emerge across all the kinds of work that you do, then you can get specific about looking at what it is about a particular job that you don't like and then you can focus on how to make adjustments to address that specific dissatisfaction. For example, let's say that you discover while doing Exercise 14.2 that you don't feel valued by the volunteer coordinator at the hospital where you visit with patients each week. Once you realize that this is your reason for dissatisfaction with this volunteer work, you can go ahead and address it.

First, you can communicate with the volunteer coordinator about your concerns, to see whether you can elicit from her a better sense of how she views your contribution to the hospital. An effective way to communicate your concerns will be to use "I" statements (for example, "I want to make sure that I am meeting your expectations for my performance") rather than "you" statements (for example, "**you** don't value my work") and then to make specific requests for how the coordinator can do something differently in the future to help address your concern (for example, "Is it possible for us to meet together on a regular basis to review my performance?"). Using "I" statements will help you communicate your concerns effectively, without putting the volunteer coordinator on the defensive.

If the coordinator agrees to do a performance review, you may discover that she does value your work, but that she has not said anything previously because she hasn't had a formal outlet for expressing this to you. As a result, you may start liking your volunteer work better. If the coordinator ends up being unable to make changes to help you feel more valued as a volunteer (set up a performance review and share constructive feedback), then you have the option of moving on and finding a new volunteer position at a different hospital. When you gather information about other volunteer opportunities, you can spend time talking with each volunteer coordinator to assess how good they are at providing performance feedback (for example, "It's important for me to do well in my job. Can you tell me how you measure your volunteers' performance and communicate how they are doing to them?") As this example shows, now that you know what's important to you in your work (paid or unpaid), you can work to bring it into your life.

If you've ranked a particular job with a dissatisfaction level of a 6 or a 7, there are probably multiple areas that will need addressing for you to bring your satisfaction level up to a 1 or a 2. You will want to go through each of the reasons you've marked in Exercise 14.2 for your dissatisfaction and contemplate how you can address each of them in order to become more satisfied with that particular area of work. Sometimes, you can make a few adjustments to a job to get more satisfaction out of it, and sometimes you will need to move on and find a new job altogether. Here's an example of each.

Maria hated doing laundry. It was just one of those chores that she couldn't stand doing. Every time Maria did laundry, it put her in a bad mood. And since she didn't like doing laundry, Maria wouldn't do it very often. Maria's family's dirty clothes would pile up. Then her husband would get upset with her because he'd run out of underwear and her kids didn't have clean clothes for school. Was there anything Maria could do to take the job of laundry off her plate? Maybe Maria could figure something out. She could see if her husband would be willing to swap out one of his chores with her and do laundry instead. If her budget allowed, Maria could consider sending her laundry out for cleaning by someone else. Alternately, Maria might be able to get her kids involved in doing their own laundry, or, if she had a regular babysitter for the kids, she might be able to have the babysitter take care of the children's laundry. With some creativity and solution-oriented thinking, Maria could probably eliminate from her life a job she really didn't like doing.

Maria's neighbor Mike didn't like doing laundry either, but

he didn't really hate the actual chore so much as that he disliked the fact that he always seemed to end up doing it late on Sunday nights when he really wanted to be on the couch relaxing in front of the TV or with a book. In Mike's case, he didn't need to find someone else to do his laundry, he just needed to adjust his schedule and get in the routine of doing laundry first thing on Saturday mornings. Once Mike took the time to consciously acknowledge that it bothered him to do laundry on Sunday nights, he was able to contemplate a solution. He made a commitment to start doing his laundry first thing when he woke up on Saturdays and found that doing laundry stopped being such an irritation for him. Most Sunday nights when he was ready to relax, his laundry was taken care of and he could sit down with a book or at the TV.

The previous examples show that it *is* possible to make adjustments in your life to take work off of your schedule or to make that work less bothersome. In Mike's case, he adjusted the time and day that he did laundry each week, and doing laundry no longer bothered him. In Maria's case, she hadn't made any changes yet, but she had some good options as to how she could stop doing laundry altogether.

Exercise 14.3 will help you generate ideas on how to address areas of dissatisfaction with a particular kind of work in your life.

Exercise 14.3: Generating Solutions to Bring More Satisfaction Into Your Paid and Unpaid Work

Instructions: For each job that you've given a low rating for satisfaction level (in Exercise 14.2), complete the following statements. If needed, complete this exercise on a separate sheet of paper so you can add space for additional reasons for dissatisfaction or possible solutions to those reasons.

Reasons for dissatisfaction (use the questions from step 4 of Exercise 14.2 to help you complete this section):
1.
2.

3.

Possible solutions to address Reason 1:
a.
b.
c.

Possible solutions to address Reason 2:
a.
b.
c.

Possible solutions to address Reason 3:
a.
b.
c.

After you've completed this exercise (and it may take some time to come up with all of your solutions), take out your calendar and make appointments with yourself to try one or more of your proposed solutions. For example, using the laundry example from earlier, if you decide you want to try to outsource your weekly laundry, make an appointment on your calendar to do some phonebook or Internet research on laundry services in your area and to call these service providers for prices. Then take some time to decide which laundry service you would like to use and make a mental commitment to use this service the following week. (*Note: Since it's hard to make a lot of changes at once, I recommend that you prioritize which areas of work in your life you want to focus on making more satisfying first, and add appointments to your calendar to deal with other areas at a later time.*)

What happens if the people you need to support you in altering your work so it becomes more enjoyable seem unsupportive? If your belongings are unsupportive of the changes that you need to make, first, make sure they understand why something is important to you by communicating clearly and directly with them about how this life change will make you a happier person and a more pleasant person to be around. Next, if a person impedes you from making a life change (for example, your spouse refuses to take on laundry as a chore, let your children do laundry, or even use family money for a laundry service), see if you can find a way to make the change without the help of these particular people (for example, have the babysitter do the laundry or get a small job you enjoy to pay for extras like laundry service). You may also decide that this battle isn't worth fighting and that you can learn to deal with the work you don't enjoy, or you may decide to end a relationship if you find that someone is consistently unsupportive.

Finally, depending on the kind of work frustrations you are trying to address, some solutions to your reasons for being dissatisfied with a job will be straightforward; others will be more complex or harder to come by. It might be tempting to assume that some challenges can't be overcome, but since doing so won't help you move forward, I recommend that you be as open-minded and creative as possible when you come up with potential solutions. So don't restrict yourself; instead, see what solutions can be generated and worry a little later about trying to make them work. Consider getting input and ideas from others as well. Their fresh perspectives may help you come up with ideas you'd never thought of before.

Do Your Preferences Align With Your Work?

Another aspect of finding satisfaction and fulfillment in your work involves spending your time doing activities and work that mesh with your preferences. For example, if you are an extrovert, you will want to look for work, hobbies, and volunteer opportunities that allow you to spend time with other people (for example, sales, management, event planning). If you are an introvert, you will want to choose work that has a solitary and independent component to it (for example, research, analysis, project planning).

If any one of the following statements resonate with you as the reason(s) you are unsatisfied with a job (paid or unpaid), then you may be in a work role, career field, or company that does not mesh well with your preferences.

- I don't enjoy some or all of the tasks that I am responsible for at this particular job.
- My job requires that I flex beyond my preferences and I am unwilling or unsure of how to do that.
- The people I work with don't value or appreciate my preferences.

The first two statements are indicators that, at least to some degree, your work does not require you to draw on some or all of your preferences. The reverse way of saying this is that your job requires you to engage in tasks and skills that belong to a different preference type. The third bullet point indicates that regardless of whether your job requires you to draw on your preferences, you work in a social environment that does not support you in using those preferences.

Although your work does not need to align perfectly with your preferences to bring you satisfaction, it does need to have some degree of compatibility with your preference combination for you to enjoy and feel satisfied by what you do. If it doesn't, you might end up feeling like a square peg trying to fit into a round hole—and that's not very comfortable or enjoyable. Instead of feeling fulfilled, you will feel dissatisfied in some way—bored, stressed, uncomfortable, disoriented, or disappointed, for example—because you will be using your weaker skills most of the time rather than your stronger skills and because you will be doing work that is less appealing to you than if it were aligned with your preferences.

There are many benefits to doing work that aligns with your preferences. In particular, if you have a job or do work that is in alignment with your preferences...

- you will probably be more successful at your job
- you will have to expend less energy to be more successful at that job
- you may also get more day-to-day satisfaction out of your job
- you will have more energy to spend on other

important aspects of your life
- your work will probably feel less like a job and more like a natural extension of your life.

If your paid work doesn't match your preferences, you have two good choices. Consider finding new paid work that does match your preferences or bring some unpaid activities (hobbies, social groups, volunteer work, etc.) into your life that align with your preferences (as well as your interests) so you feel fulfilled and energized outside of your paid work. This will ultimately help you enjoy and perform better at your job because you'll feel energized by the outside activities that align with your preferences and will be able to bring this energy back to your job. To discover which careers are best aligned with your energizing and decision-making preferences, I recommend that you buy a book titled *Do What You Are* by Paul Tieger and Linda Barron-Tieger. This is an excellent resource that I use with my clients to help them discover work that aligns well with their preferences and increases their job satisfaction.

As you think about your work and your preferences, what conclusions are you able to draw? As you reflect on the work and activities in your life, do you feel that they fit well with your preference type or that they instead work against your preference type? If you're having trouble determining the answers to these questions, write down each of the typical tasks that make up the jobs you noted in the circles in Exercise 14.1 and run through each task to see how it meshes with the behaviors, beliefs, and belongings for your preferences (see preference chapters, 3–7, for a review). Doing so should help you get a better sense of how each job aligns with your particular preference combination.

Here is an example of how someone's preferences may not sync up with the work that they do.

Lisa is an intuitive (N) communications specialist. She spends most of her day writing the content that goes into employee benefits brochures. The rest of her day is devoted to proofreading the content that other people wrote. What's wrong with this picture? As an N, Lisa spends most of her day writing about employee benefits, which is a very practical and concrete topic. This means that she doesn't get much opportunity to use her intuition and insights. For the rest of her day, she is involved in proofreading, which requires sensory behavior. Once again, she does not get to express her preference for intuition or use the related skills in her job. This doesn't mean that Lisa can't be a communications specialist. She can still have a writing career, but she would be better off writing for a different industry. For example, working for an academic institution or a science fiction/ fantasy magazine would likely provide Lisa with material that would stimulate her intuitive preference. The academic institution would provide Lisa with an opportunity to work with people who are discovering and developing new theories, while the science fiction/fantasy magazine would allow her to use her imagination to create, populate, and interact in worlds that don't exist.

If after reviewing the information from the preference chapters in Part I, you realize that you're in a job that isn't sufficiently compatible with your preferences or you realize that your life is filled with activities that don't align with your preferences, consider what the reason might be so you can address it. The following list includes the most common reasons that you might find yourself doing work that doesn't sync up with your preferences:

- lack of knowledge about what kind of jobs will match your preferences
- fear that you don't have the talent or skills to do work aligned with your preferences
- fear that the work aligned with your preferences won't provide enough financial compensation
- fear that others will judge you negatively if you do work that aligns with your preferences
- desire to please others (for example, you love painting but your mother told you that artists

never make any money; everyone in your family is a doctor, so you feel like you have to be a doctor too)

- desire for the financial compensation that comes with a particular job even though it doesn't match your preferences
- flexibility (you've learned a skill set outside of your preferences and become quite good at doing it, such that you are able to enjoy your work even though it's not in-sync with you preferences).

If you are doing work that satisfies you, then it doesn't matter whether that work syncs up with your preferences. The last bullet point is an example of one case in which a person might be in a job that doesn't match his or her preferences but is still happy with that job. Often, though, if you are doing work that doesn't sync up with your preferences, or the majority of your preferences, then you will not be satisfied by that work. If you find yourself falling into this category, spend some time with Exercise 14.3, brainstorming on how you can address your complaints about a particular job. You can also review the "Developing an In-Sync Identity" sections in the preference chapters from Part I (chapters 3–7) or read Tieger and Barron-Tieger's *Do What You Are* to provide you with ideas for other kinds of work you might enjoy. Whether you make adjustments to your current job or decide to train for or seek new work altogether, it is within your reach to engage in work that satisfies and fulfills you.

Pursuing Your Avocation

Now that you know how to bring more satisfaction to the different kinds of work that you do in your life—an important skill—we are going to focus on dreaming even bigger—helping you discover your avocation.

Your avocation is the work you are passionate about doing. When you are engaging in your avocation, it feels like the right place for you to be. One's avocation is often what people call their "life's work" or even their "life's purpose."

Not everyone applies that degree of significance to their avocation, but avocations do at least tend to bring meaning to your life as well as enjoyment.

There are as many avocations out there as there are people. Some people's avocation is to inspire others through music; others' is to inspire through visual art. Some people's avocation is to tell people's stories (as in the case of some journalists and writers); other people's avocation is to heal people's hearts and minds (as in the case of some spiritual leaders, mental health professionals, and certain kinds of volunteers). Some people's avocation is to demonstrate the brilliance of the human body through athletic feats (as in the case of professional sports players, Olympic athletes, and marathon runners); other people's avocation is to use the brilliance of the human mind to promote advances in science and medicine (as in the case of scientists, researchers, and doctors). Some people's avocation is to tend gardens and landscapes that make their neighborhoods more beautiful places to be.

As you can see from the previous examples, when we engage in our avocations, not only do we benefit, but other people tend to benefit too—from the art, healing, medical breakthroughs, beautiful scenery, and so on that are generated as others engage in their lives' work. Even when we engage in what might seem like a purely self-focused avocation, like flying remote-controlled airplanes on weekends or tying flies for fishing, others will usually benefit because we will be happier people and will transmit that happiness to those around us through our positive presence. Thus, when we develop lifestyles that allow us to engage in our avocations, we become stronger contributors to the community.

> Your *avocation* is the work (paid or unpaid) that you are passionate about doing. When you are engaging in your avocation, it brings you fulfillment and may even be described as your "life's work."

A person's paid job and avocation can be one and the same,

but not always. For example, if a journalist gets paid to tell people's stories and that journalist is passionate about doing this kind of reporting, then the journalist has a paid avocation. On the other hand, a different journalist might get paid to report on people's stories and be very good at it but might not feel passionate about the work. Instead, this journalist loves to write poetry and to read it at open-mike nights at local coffee shops. In this case, the journalist's avocation is not his paid work—telling people's stories—it is writing poetry, which he does as a hobby. As you can see from these two examples, your paid work can double as your avocation, but this won't necessarily be the case.

Most of us think that in an ideal world, we'd get paid to do what we're passionate about—we'd get paid to engage in our avocations. Interestingly, though, I've known people who lost their passion for something (photography, repairing cars, playing sports) once they got paid for doing it. In other words, there is no one-size-fits-all answer here. For some people, having a paid avocation is a top priority, whereas others find that they prefer to protect their avocations from the strains and stresses that come with paid work. It may take some time to discover which path is right for you—paid avocation or unpaid—but with some trial and error, you will likely be able to figure out which approach works best for you.

What Is Your Avocation?

Perhaps you already know what your avocation is. As you've been reading this chapter, has a particular kind of work, hobby, or activity been coming up in your mind over and over as being the thing that gives you the most pleasure in life, the activity that adds a lot of meaning to your existence, or the work that enables you to fulfill what you feel is your life purpose? If so, this activity may represent your avocation.

It's also possible that you are engaging in your avocation in your life right now but you have never called it by such a name. Maybe you've never registered on a conscious level how fulfilling this work, hobby, or activity is to you. If this is the case, you can bring even more joy and fulfillment into

370

your life by recognizing that this activity is your avocation, making it more of a priority in your life, and even putting more resources toward developing it (time, training, supplies).

A third possibility is that you have yet to discover what your avocation is. There is an activity, hobby, or kind of work out there that will fulfill you as an avocation, but you need to do some self-reflection and some experimentation to figure out what that avocation is. Exercise 14.4 will help you begin identifying what your avocation may be.

Exercise 14.4: Identifying Your Avocation

Instructions: This exercise is designed to help you gain insight into the activities and hobbies you enjoy doing, create a plan to explore a given activity further, and then experiment to see if this activity provides you the kind of fulfillment that makes it your avocation.

1. Answer the following questions:

What are your interests (for example, reading, woodworking, photography, cooking, horseback riding, biking)?

_____

_____

What do you enjoy doing outside of work?

_____

_____

What are you good at doing? (not always part of an avocation, but sometimes it is)

_____

_____

What do other people tell you that you are good at? (not always part of an avocation, but sometimes it is)

_____

_____

How did you enjoy spending your time when you were a child (before you had the pressure to earn an income)?

_____

_____

If you won the lottery and no longer had to work to pay the bills, what would you do with your life?

_____

_____

If you want additional ideas for an avocation, turn to Appendix B and note here any activities or hobbies from the list that excite you, even if you've never done these activities before.

_____

_____

2. Take some time to look over your answers to Question 1. Circle any of the items that excite you and seem like they could represent your avocation.

3. Compare each circled activity with the behaviors, beliefs, and belongings that support your preference type (see the "Developing an In-Sync Identity" section of the preferences chapters, 3–7) to see how well this activity appears to mesh with your preferences.

4. Now prioritize these activities, assigning a 1 to the activity that most excites you and jumping up a number (for example, 2, 3, 4) for each subsequent activity.

5. Starting with your number one activity, create a bulleted list of the things you can do to start pursuing this activity or line of work as an avocation (for example, buy supplies, take classes, join a group, etc.). If step 3 has revealed that the compatibility of this activity with your preferences appears to be low, feel free to pursue it anyway if you still feel excited about the activity, just be aware that you may need to stretch out of your preference comfort zone to be successful at this activity.

6. Pull out your calendar and schedule time to do each of the items on your bulleted list. Also add an appointment to your calendar to check in and see how you are enjoying the activity a few weeks or a

couple of months after you've begun engaging in it. If you discover that it is an avocation for you, continue developing it (making more time for the activity, traveling to new places to learn more about the activity, spending time with more experienced people who can teach you more about the activity, etc.)

7. If you discover that the activity is not your avocation, ask yourself whether you should put this activity aside altogether or whether combining it with something else will turn it into an avocation for you (for example, instead of playing sports, coaching sports; instead of writing for a newspaper, writing for a nonprofit organization; instead of teaching elementary school children, teaching college students). If the former is the case, go back to the previous step 4, focus on the activity you labeled with the next highest level of priority, and create a plan for exploring it. If the latter, experiment with combining the original activity with a new element.

As captured in Exercise 14.4, there are three basic steps to pursuing your avocation. *First, learn about an activity that you think could be your avocation* and maybe even immerse yourself in that activity. For example...

- do some research to learn more about the activity
- take a class
- hang around with people with similar interests
- talk to people who are doing the thing you are interested in.

Second, make time to engage in the activity. Rearrange your schedule if needed, add appointments to your calendar, and follow through on the appointments and commitments.

Third, if you find that an activity is not fulfilling you at the level of an avocation, go back to the drawing board and explore a different activity to see if it engages and excites you more than the first activity did. Be willing to look around, explore, and experiment until you discover your avocation.

When some people discover their avocations, it's as if fireworks go off. They feel so comfortable doing this work—they are so excited by it and so fulfilled by it—that they want to jump up and down and tell the world. There is no doubt in their minds that they have discovered their avocations. In contrast, for other people, the rewards of their avocations are more subtle. No fireworks go off, but they feel contentment and joy when they engage in the work of their avocations. Without their avocations, their lives feel like they're missing something; with their avocations, everything in their lives seems brighter and more pleasant—because the energy and fulfillment generated by their avocations trickles into all areas of their lives.

As you begin to experiment with an activity to see if it brings you the fulfillment of an avocation, see if you can have fun with the process. If you are impatient about discovering your avocation, it can be frustrating...so try instead to have an adventurous outlook on the process and be willing to take some time to experiment. Even if you don't find your avocation right away—which many people don't—you will probably learn a lot in the process and meet some great people along the way.

Challenges in Pursuing Your Avocation

As with any new venture, challenges may arise when you begin seeking your avocation. Here are some of the challenges to look out for and some ideas on how to work through them.

Time. If you tend to say, "I'm too busy with my daily responsibilities or current paid work to pursue an avocation," you are facing the challenge of not having enough time or the *perception* of not having enough time. It might be true that you are too busy right now to pursue your avocation—but that doesn't mean you can't change your lifestyle or your schedule to make time for your avocation. Our lives get filled up with the things that we give priority to; as a result, if you put a priority on engaging in your avocation, you will probably be able to *make* time for it. You may have to give something up to get the extra time (for example, some TV time, your morning coffee stop, money to pay a house cleaner or yard service so you have more time), but in the end, the benefits and enjoyment of engaging in your avocation will make the trade-off worthwhile.

Another way to deal with the challenge of time is to start small. If you feel like you can't make time for your avocation, start engaging in it for 15 minutes a day or one hour a week and see where this manageable routine leads you. You may enjoy this time so much that you find a way to build a little more time into your routine each day or week, or you may find that even this small amount of time each day or week is enough to satisfy to you.

Experience. If you tend to think, "I don't have the skills to pursue my passion," don't worry, that's okay…we all have to learn the skills to be successful at something at some point in our lives. You don't need to know everything now; you just need to have a willingness to learn—through research, classes, or meeting others with a similar interest…whatever works for you and is right for a given activity. There are many classes out there and many books on many topics, and most people are surprisingly willing to share information and teach you the skills they know. By teaching and sharing their avocations, most people find that the experience becomes even more enjoyable and meaningful for themselves.

Lack of insight. If you tend to think, "I have no idea what else I could be doing" when you look at your current work and consider an avocation, you probably simply need more knowledge and support in discovering your avocation. Lots of people are in this position. How many people have you heard say something like, "I'm still trying to figure out what I want to be when I grow up?" You've probably heard lots of people say this. You can use the tools in this chapter (see Exercise 14.4) to figure out what your avocation is, as well as read books like *Do What You Are* (Tieger and Barron-Tieger) and *What Color Is My Parachute?* (Richard Nelson Bolles), which can help you on the journey. Career counselors, who focus on paid work, and life coaches, who can focus on paid or unpaid work, can also offer assistance.

Fear. If you tend to ask, "What if I start something new and I fail?" fear may be stopping you from engaging in your avocation. If you're worried about failure, ask yourself, "What's the worst possible thing that can happen? Can I handle it?" Usually, the answer is yes, which can be reassuring as well as help you to keep things in perspective. So what if you try something and you don't meet your expectations for success? Will your life go on? Will you have learned something new? Can you try again or can you try something different? Usually the answer is yes to these questions as well. So don't let fear hold you back. It's okay to be nervous about something, but that doesn't mean you have to stop moving forward. Be willing to fail. It's only through trial and error that we can discover what we enjoy and what we're good at.

Resistance from an unintentionally masked personality. If you find yourself thinking any of the following thoughts—"My family doesn't value my avocation, so it's not worthwhile," "It's a waste of time to engage in my avocation," or "It's selfish to engage in my avocation"—you may have trouble pursuing your avocation because you are experiencing resistance from your (masked) personality. In the case of these types of thoughts, you are probably subscribing to unsupportive beliefs or belongings that encourage you to be different than you are. In other words, you are allowing your personality to be masked rather than embracing your true self. If this is the case for you, I recommend that you return to Part I, which focuses on learning to live in-sync with your true self and/or consider working with a life coach or therapist.

I had a client who struggled with this last challenge of resistance from his masked personality. Although my client

376

was very successful in the corporate world as a project manager (he was a sensing judger), this was not his avocation. He did his avocation—carpentry and woodworking—on the weekends. At first my client discounted his avocation because it wasn't an income-producing pursuit—he judged it to be a waste of time.

Interestingly enough, when a coworker said that he would pay my client to make a jewelry box for his wife, this gave my client the motivation he needed to start claiming his hobby as a genuine avocation. Eventually, he took his wares to the County Fair in San Diego and got very positive feedback from customers and shared this with me in a session.

During our next coaching session, though, my client said that he'd never be a good woodworker. "What happened to change your mind?" I asked. "Last week you told me about all of the positive comments you got on your work." My client explained that his father saw his work over the weekend and pointed out all the problems with it. This had a powerful effect on my client, making him lose faith in his avocation. Although my client (his true self) enjoyed woodworking, my client's father (belongings) was telling him that he wasn't any good at it.

Happily, as we processed my client's interaction with his father, I was able to help him realize that on the one hand he had his father's negative opinion of his abilities and on the other hand he had several people, including paying customers and recognized craftsmen, who thought he was pretty talented. My client was able to see that the positive opinions of his carpentry work outweighed the negative opinions of his father, and he was able to develop a new belief about himself: he was a talented and skilled woodworker. Armed with this supportive belief, my client resumed his woodworking avocation. Eventually, his part-time avocation became his full-time occupation as the demand for his quality products increased.

As you can see with the example of my woodworking client, challenges may interfere with the process of fully

377

engaging in your avocation and getting the most out of it, but these challenges don't have to derail you altogether. Instead, try to be on the lookout for these challenges and when they occur, work to deal with them—with the support of other people (fans, helping professionals).

Conclusion

Doing work that you love—whether it's paid or unpaid—can have a tremendous positive influence on your life. It can energize you, inspire you, fulfill you, and uplift you. Whether you keep your avocation simple—doing a hobby by yourself for a few hours each week—or you turn your avocation into a career—say, opening a store where you sell your handmade pottery or running a childcare center for children with autism—engaging in an avocation can bring meaning, purpose, and joy to your life.

When pursuing your avocation, be willing to explore and experiment; start small; and, as you get comfortable with your avocation, consider deepening it by exploring new aspects of it and dedicating more time to it (for example, if you're a gardener, teach others how to garden, start a community garden, or write a newspaper article on gardening). The rewards that you experience from your avocation might make you want to sing an aria from a mountaintop—or just spend the afternoon creatively shaping a block of wood.

15

Honoring Your Beginnings

I began this book by focusing your attention on reclaiming your true self—teaching you how to unmask and discover your personality—so you can return to who you really are and achieve your life goals as a result of reconnecting with your true self.

As we discussed early on, you develop your identity (that is, your belongings, beliefs, and behaviors) as a result of your early life experiences—those experiences that you encounter while interacting with your family, your environment, and your culture. As such, you may need to take some time away from the people—often, your family—who were involved in the development of your identity while you work on strengthening your connection to your true self.

We discussed the idea of stepping back from family, particularly those family members you might describe as challenging, in chapter 11. If this advice resonated with you, you may have chosen to set more boundaries with family members, opting not to discuss certain topics of your life with them, spending less time with them, or spending time with them in new places (in a public place, at your own home, wherever is most comfortable and supportive for you).

Alternately, you may have made more subtle changes, like not worrying so much about how your parents are judging you or giving yourself permission not to respond to provocative comments from siblings. In some way or other, you may have been taking a break from your family or putting a distance between yourself and your family. While you may choose to keep these changes in place permanently (because they have liberated you to pursue a life that is meaningful and fulfilling to you), you may still simultaneously benefit from a process of reengaging with your family.

This chapter will provide you with the guidance you need to successfully reengage with your family so you can gain from the gifts they have to offer you while staying true to your personality and your life vision. (Note that many of the techniques in this chapter can also be used to reengage with old friends if this is something you hope to do.)

Forging Adult Relationships With Your Family

Depending on your particular upbringing and the kind of relationships you had with family members during your childhood—great, mediocre, poor; stable, inconsistent, or unstable; completely supportive, somewhat supportive, or completely unsupportive—you will probably feel varying degrees of need to separate yourself from your family as well as to reengage with your family. This is a very personal process and one that will take some experimentation and time. What is common for all of us, though, is that part of the healthy maturation process for human beings involves some separation from our families—what psychologists call *individuation*—and then a reengagement with our families from an adult place.

Individuation From Your Family

In an ideal world, the separation process will take place bit by bit over the course of your upbringing until you reach your early adult years (your 20s), at which point in time you will become financially, physically, and emotionally separate from your family. This is not to say you won't rely on your family for occasional support but that you will have grown into a healthy adult who can take care of yourself and direct your own life.

In truth, the point at which you individuate from your family can happen in any decade of your life. It's not about chronological age, but personal readiness and awareness. Individuation happens for some people naturally, especially if their parents had the skills and know-how to foster that kind of healthy growth and independence in them; other people need to proactively pursue individuation because their parents have not shown them the way.

380

> *Separation* or *individuation* from your family is a natural part of the developmental cycle, which will lead you to become an independently functioning adult in terms of the emotional and physical realms. If you don't experience a natural separation from your family, you will benefit from learning to separate from your family and can then reenage with your family from an adult place.

Regardless of whether you naturally developed an independence from your family or you need to consciously pursue individuation, you will discover some useful points in this chapter on how to get the most out of your family relationships. Whether you are planning to reengage relationships with very challenging family members or you simply want to do better at staying in touch with your true self while around your family, this chapter has some useful advice for you.

Reengagement With Your Family

At some point after you separate or individuate from your family—whether that time is measured in months or years—you will likely find benefits from eventually reengaging with your family. What does it mean to reengage with your family? Well, this is a personal process that will look different for each person, but the basic idea here is that you will be making a mental commitment to be fully present in your family relationships and to interact with your family members from a place of your true self. Instead of taking a mental break from your family—symbolically putting them on hold while you work on yourself—you will be consciously integrating your family into the process of improving your own life.

Another way of describing reengaging with your family is to say that you will be developing new adult relationships with your family members. Instead of enacting old patterns from your childhood, you will be committing to acting in new ways that are mature, communicative, and reflective of your true self. Your family may or may not notice the difference; your family may or may not respond positively

381

to your changes. Regardless, you will be working to interact with your family as an adult and from the authentic place of your true self. This may lead to more positive relationships with your family. At minimum, it will help you manage your family relationships so that they do not impede you from achieving your life goals.

A Lifelong Process

Although this chapter presents separation from and reengagement with your family as two separate processes, in reality, the two processes can also happen at the same time. For example, on one hand, you may be setting boundaries with your family (separation), while on the other hand you are simultaneously learning to communicate with your parents in a proactive rather than a reactive way (reengagement). In such cases, you will be separating from your family in some ways while reengaging with your family in others.

So this chapter presents separation and reengagement as a linear process with a beginning and an end—where separation occurs at the beginning of the process and reengagement occurs at the end of the process. In truth, though, the process of separation from and reengagement with your family will likely be continual, like the ebbs and flows of an ocean tide that will take place throughout your life. There may be no single beginning or ending to the separation–reengagement process but rather a series of cycles of moving away from your family and moving toward your family, depending on where you and your family members each are in your own personal cycles of growth.

In this chapter, for simplicity's sake, the separation and reengagement processes are treated as if they are linear, distinct stages, but try to remember that, in reality, these processes can occur at any time, even overlapping with each other at times.

Benefits of Family Relationships

Although it can be challenging to learn how to stay true to your personality when interacting with family, learning how to do so can be a great opportunity for you to get even better at staying in-sync with your true self (your personality). That is, if you can learn how to stay true to your personality when with your family—those who helped you develop your identity in the first place—then you will become really good at staying true to your personality in other areas of your life. It's like running a marathon. If you gain the skills and confidence to run 26.5 miles, you will undoubtedly have the skills and confidence that you need to run shorter distances throughout the year.

All of the obstacles and frustrations that family relationships can confront us with also provide us with opportunities to learn more about ourselves. Whatever personal issues we face on our own will likely be magnified and enlarged when we are with family since the family setting may be the origin for such conflicts. So spending time with family is a good opportunity to assess how we are doing at strengthening our ability to behave, believe, and belong in-sync with our true selves. If we ask why certain issues with our families trigger us to feel certain emotions or to abandon our true selves, then we can gain insight into the areas of our personalities that we still need to reflect on, pay attention to, and strengthen. Here's an example of someone who used her challenges with her family to learn more about herself.

> Every time Leslie went home for the holidays, she and her older brother would inevitably end up arguing with each other over some issue. One year it was about the war in Afghanistan; the next year it was about what was the funniest sitcom on television right now. This year, Leslie decided that she didn't want to get into an argument with her older brother, so she talked to her coach about it. Her coach asked her to reflect upon what was going on inside Leslie's head and heart when she and her brother interacted. The more Leslie thought about it, the more she realized that she had always felt like she was in her brother's shadow, and arguing with him was her way of establishing her individuality. Her coached applauded her insight and asked Leslie if she felt like this was a healthy way of establishing

her individuality. Leslie smiled and said probably not.

Armed with this new insight, Leslie went home for the holidays. At dinner that night with the family, she announced, "I want to tell everyone that I feel really lucky to be a part of this family." She then turned to her big brother and said, "I'm sorry for always arguing with you all the time. I realized a while ago that I am only doing that because I respect you and want you to respect me too. But arguing is the wrong way to go about that, so I apologize." Her brother looked at her for a long while without saying anything and then told her, "Leslie, not only do I love you because you're my sister, but you're one of the smartest people that I know. I have always been intimidated by your intelligence. I'm sorry too for arguing back instead of just accepting the fact that you are smarter than me in a lot of areas." As it turns out, by processing her reactions to a specific, recurring area of family conflict, Leslie was able to learn something valuable about herself and strengthen her family relationships at the same time.

Each family is different. Given this reality, some families are easier than others to forge healthy and strong relationships with. In the best case scenario, here are the benefits you can hope to receive by building a healthy relationship with your family.

- Your family will offer you love and caring.
- Your family will offer you support in a difficult time.
- Your family will help you reenergize.
- Your family will offer you the benefits of their strengths and skills.

At minimum, you can expect the following benefits of reengaging with your family.

- Going back home can remind you of the strengths you developed because of your

family background (regardless of whether that background was positive or negative).
- Going back home brings up core issues in you that need healing and provides you with an opportunity to understand and improve yourself.

Some family relationships are so toxic that it is more supportive to your true self to minimize these relationships rather than reengage them. Toxic family relationships can involve family members who are verbally or physically abusive to you, who have problems with addiction, or who have psychological disorders that lead them to be dysfunctional in relationships. It can be very hard to learn how to manage toxic family relationships, as most of us strive to be loved by our families and want to stay connected to them no matter the cost. Similarly, we want to help and support our loved ones as they struggle with challenges like addiction or mental disorders.

Learning how to manage a toxic family relationship will be a very personal process in which you will need to figure out what kind of boundaries work best to avoid your family members having a negative effect on your own life. The common formula for successfully managing any kind of toxic family relationship, though, will be to set strong boundaries and to retain these boundaries: to restrict how much you see or talk to a family member and what topics you will discuss. These boundaries may change over time, depending on how the other person grows and changes. For example, if a family member with an addiction recovers, you may choose to engage in a more connected relationship with the person as you discover that he or she no longer has a negative effect on your life.

Reclaiming Your Background

Before you actively reengage your family, I recommend that you do some internal work of your own to come to terms with the aspects of your family that frustrate, disappoint, or trouble you. Once you have worked through these issues, you will be in a better position to shape family relationships that fulfill you and align well with your true self. The ultimate goal of this internal work is to do what I call *reclaim your family background*: that is, look at your past from an adult perspective and integrate your past experiences into your current existence—whether your upbringing was good or bad, wonderful or painful, or somewhere in between.

You already know what your family history is because you lived it, but now it's time to look at your childhood experiences from the eyes of an adult who is living life in-sync with his or her true self. Now that you know your true self and you recognize the behaviors, belongings, and beliefs that support it, you have the knowledge you need to recognize the way your upbringing both supported and challenged you. You also have the skills you need to process those experiences, make sense of them, celebrate them, grieve them, learn from them, and move on from them…whatever needs to be done so that these experiences are accessible to you and don't lead you to mask your personality.

Even if you had a great upbringing, chances are, there will still be some aspects of your childhood experience that are worth bringing into consciousness to consider and understand. For example, if you were a middle child, you may have learned to get attention by entertaining your family with stories and jokes because if you didn't, it was easy to get lost in the shuffle of the things going on with your older and younger siblings. Now, as an adult, you may unconsciously carry that pattern forward…feeling like you have to entertain others to be listened to or even to earn their love. This dynamic may have been created regardless of how loving your family was during your childhood. It's not an inherently negative pattern, but it can be helpful for you to be aware of this pattern so you can be more conscious and selective about how and when you use your sense of humor to entertain people. In other words, you can decide whether this is how you want to continue to interact with people, and if so, when and how and why.

When it comes to reclaiming your background, you will be doing two things: (a) acknowledging all the gifts and/or strengths your childhood has given to you and (b) coming to peace with the challenging or disappointing parts of your past as well. The first task will help you appreciate the value of your past and the family relationships that made up your past. The second task will allow you to become an "integrated" person, rather than to be fragmented or cut off from parts of yourself or your past. Here is an example of what it might look like to be fragmented or cut off from a part of yourself.

If you lost a parent at a young age but never fully processed your grief because you were too young to understand what was going on or because you simply didn't have anyone to help you deal with the loss, that grief would remain part of you but you wouldn't have access to that grief. This reality wouldn't mean that your grief didn't exist, just that your grief would be buried somewhere unknown inside of you. As a result, your grief would unconsciously affect the way you lived your life, rather than you being able to make conscious decisions in relation to the pain you carried (for example, you might avoid developing friendships with people who have two parents because you unconsciously feel envious of these people).

By reclaiming your grief—by acknowledging it, feeling it, processing it, and working through it—you will no longer be beholden to it. You might always carry sadness related to your loss, but that sadness wouldn't manage your life. You would learn, instead, to manage it. By learning to accept your past (not as something that defines you but as something that you experienced), you will be able to make more conscious decisions and make less decisions from an unconscious place.

Making conscious decisions will help you stay on a path to achieving your life vision because you will be in control of your decisions and can make choices that align with the intentions of your life plan. In contrast, making unconscious decisions will make it harder to stay on the path to achieving your life vision because you will not be aware of your decisions and thus can't make sure that they sync up with the intentions of your life plan. For example, if a life goal was to bring more friendships into your life, but you didn't realize that you resisted making friends with people who had two parents (looking back at the earlier example), you would most likely have trouble adjusting your behaviors to make new friends. However, once you became aware of your unconscious intentions to avoid making friends with certain kinds of people, you'd have the freedom to make adjustments to your limiting behaviors. You can't change what you don't know, but you can change what you do know.

To begin working on reclaiming your background, you can complete Exercise 15.1. As you can imagine, coming to terms with the gifts and liabilities of your childhood can take days, weeks, and even years, so you may choose to complete this exercise more than once and at different points in time, as you move to new levels of the reclaiming experience.

Also note that Exercise 15.1 is intended to be only part of the process of your reclaiming your background, and you will likely need to supplement this process in other ways. For example, if you find the challenges and disappointments of your childhood particularly painful, I strongly recommend that you work with a helping professional while you process these memories and experiences. Regular appointments with a trained professional will provide you with the kind of consistent support you will need when working through difficult memories and experiences. No matter what your situation is, writing in a journal and talking to those close to you can also be helpful in processing the experiences of your upbringing and integrating them into your current identity.

Exercise 15.1: Reclaiming the Strengths and Challenges of Your Upbringing

Instructions: This exercise is designed to help you embrace the strengths of your childhood and deal with any disappointments from your childhood. You will need additional sheets of paper and some 3x5 index cards to complete this exercise. I also encourage you to do this exercise with a professional helper, like a life coach or therapist, to provide you with support in the process.

1. Let's start with the positive things that your childhood taught you. List all of the gifts and personal traits (for example, a good sense of humor, curiosity, worthwhile education, athletic ability, generous nature) you are thankful to have gained from your family or childhood experiences. You may have gained these things from your family, the people you knew, and/or the experiences you had during this time frame. In addition, you may have gained these positive traits from either positive or negative experiences. (For example, if you had a parent with multiple sclerosis and this burdened you with a lot of responsibility for your siblings and your parent, this may have been a challenging experience, but you may have nonetheless gained positive traits from this experience, such as empathy and good leadership.)

a._____
b._____
c._____
d._____
e._____
f._____

2. For each of the traits or gifts listed in step 1, write down why you are thankful for this item. What are you grateful to have in your life today as a result of the gifts or traits gained from your childhood?

a._____
b._____
c._____
d._____
e._____
f._____

3. Reflect on the challenging aspects of your childhood and, using a separate sheet of paper, write down the major frustrations, disappointments, and difficulties that occurred for you during your childhood. (For example, "It was very disappointing to me that my

father was never around.")

4a. When you think about the frustrations, disappointments, and difficulties that occurred during your upbringing, what thoughts come to mind? (For example, "I wasn't a good enough kid for my dad to want to spend time with me.") Write each thought on an index card.

4b. How are these thoughts affecting your current behaviors, beliefs, and belongings (the three Bs)? (For example, belief: "I feel like most people don't want to spend time with me"; belongings: "I tend to make friends with people who are unreliable"; behavior: "I tend to put up with bad treatment to maintain a relationship.")

_____

_____

_____

_____

4c. If any of your three Bs are being affected negatively, what would you like to do to break the cycle of negativity? Brainstorm on some ideas and write them down.

_____

_____

_____

_____

4d. Also, for any thoughts that are limiting, write down on the corresponding index card a responsive thought to counter that negativity. (For example, "I am a pleasant person to spend time with because I am considerate and have a good sense of humor.") Carry the index card with you in a purse or a briefcase for the next month, pay attention to times that that limiting thought arises, and when it does, read the counter-thought to help you turn that limiting thought into a thought that can move you forward.

5. When you think about the frustrations, disappointments and difficulties that occurred during your upbringing, what **emotions** do you feel?

_____

_____

_____

6. For each emotion that you feel, write a one-page journal entry or schedule a conversation to have with a trusted friend or a helping professional to discuss and process that emotion.

By processing the thoughts and emotions you carry in relation to your past, you will learn to manage these thoughts and emotions rather than allowing them to manage you. Also, by learning to understand and accept the reality of your past, you will free yourself up to move past the negative aspects of that past and will gain an appreciation for the gifts your past has given you. You will also be in a good position to reapproach the challenging relationships from your past, because you will be centered in the truth of who you are and where you have been. Being in charge of the thoughts and emotions related to your family background will allow you to be proactive in these relationships rather than reactive.

Reengaging With Your Family

After you do the internal work of reclaiming your background, you will be ready to actively reengage with your family. Of course, as we saw earlier, the process of separating from your family, reclaiming your family background, and reengaging with your family may not be a linear one with distinct stages. Instead, these stages may overlap, with you setting boundaries (separating), processing your past (reclaiming), and trying to act in-sync with your true self when around your family (reengaging) at the same time or in close proximity to each other.

In a practical sense, here are some hints on how you will know when the time is right to dedicate energy to reengaging with your family members. One way to know is that you simply feel like it. After taking a mental break from your family and working to improve your own life, you may gain the desire to spend more energy on strengthening your family relationships. If so, this could be a great time to work on interacting with your family from a place of the true self.

Alternately, life circumstances might throw you together

391

with your family for an extended period of time (like when you're looking after a sick loved one or you have a newborn and a parent comes to help). Though you might not have chosen this time to focus on reengaging your family relationships, life circumstances have brought you together with your family, so you may end up using this time to forge an adult relationship with your family. There is no one right answer to when the time will be right to reengage with your family, but the preceding situations represent two possible times. In addition, here are some other signs that it might be a useful time to actively reengage challenging family relationships.

- You have done the internal work of looking at your upbringing from the eyes of your adult self—processing your disappointments and celebrating your strengths.
- You have a solid fan club that you can turn to when you need to process issues that have arisen within challenging relationships.
- You have done some honest processing about your interactions within challenging relationships and have learned new skills to help you avoid overreacting to your old triggers.
- You are regularly acting in-sync with your true self, within both your personal and professional life.
- You are at a point in your life where you are making progress toward your life plan.

Once you realize that you are ready to reengage with your family, how do you go about doing so? How do you come back and honor your family in a way that also informs them of who you are and what you're about? I recommend that you follow these five basic steps:

1. manage your expectations
2. draw boundaries

3. forgive your family
4. cultivate gratitude
5. remember your fan club.

Reengaging with your family may mean you choose to spend more time with them than you have in the recent past. It may mean that you choose to communicate more honestly with your family than you ever have before. Or it might mean that you share with your family more of your private thoughts and feelings. Regardless of the ways you choose to reengage with your family, following the preceding five basic steps can help the process go more smoothly than it otherwise might.

Manage Expectations

First, I recommend that you manage your expectations of the reengagement process so that these expectations support you rather than lead to frustration or disappointment. Table 15.1 contains a list of realistic versus unrealistic expectations. For success during the reengagement process, I recommend that you set expectations in alignment with the left column of the table (the column representing realistic expectations).

Table 15.1: Realistic Expectations for the Reengagement Process

Realistic Expectations	Unrealistic Expectations
When I try to communicate honestly and diplomatically with my family, I can expect to feel proud of myself for having the courage to try something new.	When I try to communicate honestly and diplomatically with my family, I can expect my family to appreciate what I am sharing and to communicate honestly and diplomatically with me in return.
When I set boundaries with my family, I can expect to gain the space I need to support my true self and pursue my life vision.	When I set boundaries with my family, I can expect them to enthusiastically embrace and respect those boundaries.

393

Realistic Expectations	Unrealistic Expectations
When I interact with my family in new ways that are supportive of my true self, I can expect to feel proud of myself for making such a big change after years of a different behavior pattern.	When I interact with my family in new ways that are supportive of my true self, I can expect my family members to change their behavior to be more supportive of my true self.

While the circumstances in the right column of Table 15.1 might come true and you will probably *hope* that they come true, you probably don't want to set these as your *expectations*, since you really don't know how your family is going to react to the changes that you will be making as you forge a new kind of relationship with them and you can't control their behaviors. Instead, I recommend focusing on the positive benefits you can expect to experience yourself by making these big changes. That way, even if your family members resist the changes you are making, you will have some positive benefits to focus on and to motivate you when challenges arise as you try to shape an adult relationship with your family.

Note that sometimes when interacting with family, you are going to lose sight of your true self, and your identity will unexpectedly mask your personality. This is another realistic expectation to add to the list. No matter how much work you've done to strengthen your true self, staying true to your personality can be very hard to do within the family setting. As a result, there will probably be times when you slip into old habits of unintentionally masking your personality or when you allow yourself to lose faith in your life vision because of time you've spent with your family.

Instead of getting down on yourself for falling out-of-sync, though, I recommend that you simply observe what's happening, process your thoughts and feelings with nonfamily fan club members, do what you can to understand the situation, and move on. That is, pick yourself up and get back in-sync. A few hours, a few days, or even a few weeks of behaving, believing, or belonging out-of-sync with your true self is usually not enough time to throw you significantly off course from your life vision; and eventually, over time, you will get better at letting your true self remain in control in those difficult situations.

Draw Boundaries

Second, when trying to reengage with your family, I recommend that you continue to draw boundaries with your family, something you may have started doing after reading chapter 11 on building your fan club. If you are going to successfully reengage with your family—that is, open up dialogue and interact from a place of your true self—you will want boundaries in place to help keep that reengagement in the constructive zone. For example, you may want to share your honest feelings with your mother about the new career you plan to pursue (reengagement) but you may also need to be ready to ask her to refrain from criticizing that career field in response to your news (boundary-setting). In this way, you can work toward having an honest and authentic relationship with your mother without having to suffer attacks on your true self.

Boundaries are the parameters you set for the interactions you will have with your family members. These are the lines that you are asking your family to respect, like a low fence between the two of you that allows you to have an authentic relationship and simultaneously support your true self. Here are the areas around which you might set boundaries with your family:

- how much time you choose to spend with your family during a get-together
- how often you see your family
- the places that you are willing to interact with your family
- the topics of conversation you are willing to have with your family
- the kind of favors you're willing to do for your family (family is often about supporting each

other, but if your family has unfair or unrealistic expectations of you, this may be an important boundary for you to set).

Although your family might be resistant to respecting your boundaries, in the end, these boundaries are meant to help you have happier, healthier interactions together. If your family questions the boundaries you set with them, try to focus them on your positive intentions for setting these boundaries (for example, "We can avoid arguments if we don't talk about X," "I have learned that I need some of my own time to unwind and recharge during holidays," "You are an important part of my life, but I also have other important people in my life who I need to spend time with").

Forgive Your Family

Inevitably, your family is going to frustrate or disappoint you at some point in time, and perhaps they will do so multiple times. This phenomenon just happens, even with people who love you and who are well meaning. As a result, the third step to follow when reengaging with your family is to be willing to forgive your family for the frustrations and disappointments you experience in their presence.

I'm thinking, in particular, about the smaller disappointments and frustrations: the questioning comments about how you spend your money, live your life, or raise your kids. I'm talking about the insensitive comments that pop out of your family members' mouths because they know you so well and they think that they can say anything to you. Yes, these comments are frustrating, and sometimes painful, but remember, your family loves you and they are doing the best they can. In most cases, your family doesn't mean to hurt your feelings.

So my recommendation is, try not to sweat the small stuff. Acknowledge to yourself that something bothers you, but try not to hold grudges or let these incidents ruin your relationships with your family.

If your family does something that hurts you in a way

that you can't let go of, if you feel that a family member has intentionally hurt you, or if you don't feel you can have a healthy relationship without addressing a family member's behavior or comments, then you can address it with the person. Here is what I recommend you should do. First, discuss the incident with a member of your fan club or a helping professional. This person will help you validate the severity of the injury and also counterbalance some of the hurt you are experiencing with positive support and encouragement.

Next, after some time has gone by and if you feel the family member will be receptive, set up some time to communicate your experience with the family member. Use "I" statements, (for example, "I was really hurt by the words you used to describe me last week") instead of "you" statements (for example, "You hurt me last week"). Be willing to forgive if your family member apologizes. If he or she doesn't, consider how you want to proceed and be willing possibly to adjust your boundaries to spend less time with your family member. Remember, you can't control how someone in your family responds to your communications, but you can at least be authentic about communicating how you are feeling and you can control how much time you spend with someone.

If you struggle with forgiveness, try to remember that forgiveness isn't about excusing bad behavior but instead is about making a choice to let your anger and resentment go so you are free to live the life you want for yourself. Most people who talk about forgiveness for a deep transgression say that they did not forgive for the sake of the other person but for themselves. If you harbor anger and resentment, it will tend to fester and disrupt your ability to move forward in life. If you learn to let it go—to forgive or "give it up"—you will be free to move on with your life and your life plan.

Cultivate Gratitude

The fourth step in successfully reengaging with your family involves cultivating gratitude for the gifts your family has given you and continues to give you. Remembering the things you are thankful for in relation to your family will help you weather challenges in those relationships. For example, it's easier to overlook your father's irritating way of asking you when you're going to get a promotion when you feel thankful for the fact that he taught you to have a strong work ethic or that he paid for your education. It's easier to make light of your mother's interest in your dating life when you are in touch with how much she loves you and how much love she has shown you during the course of your life.

One way to cultivate gratitude is to write down all the things you are thankful for regarding each of your family members. Another way is to take a moment each time a family member irritates you and ask yourself to think of one thing you are thankful for from this person. That's not the typical response when someone irritates you, but it can be amazingly useful. The more gratitude you cultivate toward your family, the easier it will be for you to take more lightly challenging aspects of their behavior.

Remember Your Fan Club

Finally, when reengaging with your family, don't forget to draw on your fan club for support. Whether you stop to call a good friend halfway through the Thanksgiving holiday to get a little lift to carry you through family time or you simply remind yourself of all the people in the world who support you and your life vision when one of your family members challenges it, your fan club will be an invaluable tool for you as you reengage with your family. After family visits, you may also want to process, regroup, and recharge by spending time with someone in your fan club—on the phone, over email, or in person.

What's Your Role in Family Dynamics?

When looking at family relationships, it's important to remember your contribution to the relationship dynamic, especially when it comes to areas of conflict. Remember that most people are doing the best that they can with the information and skills that they have, including you. Let your family know that you appreciate them accepting you (good, bad, and ugly) and share with them some of the things that *you* will be doing differently to make things better for the family. (If you need to apologize for some past behaviors, do so; but try not to get bent out of shape if your family members don't follow suit. More than likely, they are not yet at that place. That's okay. You do the right thing and be happy with that.) Also, try not to be overly concerned with explaining everything, but focus instead on doing things differently. If the occasion arises when you need to explain something, do it, but otherwise, just enjoy the experience of being yourself around your family.

Conclusion

When you are ready to reengage with your family, it will most likely be a trial and error process. It will take time and a lot of patience; there will be some frustrations and disappointments. The truth is, no matter how much you want to improve relationships for the better and interact with your family as an adult rather than a child—and no matter how much your family members want to do the same—change in family relationships takes time and can be hard. We're talking, after all, about trying to change patterns that have been in place for years and years. Happily, the process of reengaging with your family is often worth the effort, but it helps to have realistic expectations of the pace of change.

Although it can be time-consuming and energy-consuming to reclaim your background and to reengage with your family, there are many benefits of doing so. Reclaiming your background will build your self-confidence because you are, in a sense, learning to accept and come to terms with all the parts of yourself and all of your life experiences. Also, when you are able to accept your own flaws and those of your family, you tend to be more accepting of others in general, which has the added benefit of improving the quality of your belongings. Finally, learning to process the challenges of your upbringing will give you the gift of being able to support others who have had to overcome similar backgrounds and challenges.

By reclaiming your family background and reengaging with your family, you will be strengthening your ability to live your life from the place of your true self. And when your true self is in charge, your life vision will be easier to achieve.

16

Giving Back

In your life, have you ever taught someone something or leant a helping hand or given something of yours to someone else because you knew it would make the person smile? Have you ever inconvenienced yourself so you could do someone a favor? Have you ever cancelled plans so you could spend time with someone who was in need of a friend? If so, you have already given back.

I have intentionally determined to end this book with some words about giving back because I believe that giving back is one of the most important aspects of living a meaningful and fulfilling life. I happen to believe that it's all of our responsibility to contribute to the communities we live in (all boats rise together!), but I also sincerely believe that your life will be richer if you give back. By helping others, you will help yourself.

Giving back is about taking the positive energy and blessings you've received in your own life and reinvesting them in the community—in your friends, family, acquaintances, coworkers, and even strangers. Giving back is often about engaging in Type III relationships. If you recall from chapter 8, Type III giving relationships are those in which you are the predominant giver, for example, when you are a parent, a teacher, a mentor, or a volunteer. Type III relationships are a wonderful means of giving back to the community because they are structured for giving back. When you enter the relationship, there is another person or other people just waiting to receive your support.

This is not to say that you can't give back in Type I receiving or Type II mutual relationships. If you recall, Type I relationships are those in which you predominantly receive from others, and Type II relationships are those in which you and another person contribute equally to the relationship. You can give back in Type I receiving and Type II mutual relationships as well. For example, you might write a sincere letter of thank you to a teacher at the end of a course, which your teacher will probably receive enthusiastically and feel rewarded by. Similarly, in a Type II mutual relationship, when a friend is feeling down, you can listen and offer your support.

Although you can give back in any type of relationship, this chapter will focus specifically on how you can give back to the community through Type III giving relationships since these relationships are designed wholly for giving back. I have found that engaging in Type III relationships can be a wonderful way to renew your energy, strengthen your sense of purpose in life, and grow as a person. Truly, when you help others, you help yourself.

Two Very Different Seas

When I teach the importance of giving back to clients or students, I start by showing them three pictures. The first is an aerial view of a region in the Middle East that shows two lakes joined by a river. Then I show my students a close-up of the first lake, the Sea of Galilee. In this picture, they see deep blue water surrounded by lush green trees and growing fields. I then show a close-up of the second lake, the Dead Sea. In this picture, my students see dark, almost black water surrounded by a dry and empty desert.

What is the difference between these two lakes? The difference between them is that the Sea of Galilee is thriving because it takes in water and gives out water. It has a healthy balance of giving and receiving. The Dead Sea is salty and dead because it only takes in water from the Jordan River and nothing flows out of it. The Dead Sea has no outlets. Unlike the Sea of Galilee, which is populated with fish and other marine life, the Dead Sea cannot support most forms of aquatic life because of its high salt content.

The states of the Sea of Galilee and the Dead Sea are not unlike the states you will find your own life in, depending on whether you engage in Type III giving relationships or have mainly Type I receiving relationships. If you have some relationships in your life in which you give back to others, you will find that your own life will grow and flourish, like the Sea of Galilee with its abundant fish and plant life. On the other hand, if you resist giving back to others or engaging in Type III giving relationships, you will find that your own life may stagnate. Where there could be meaning and fulfillment, there will instead be emptiness, frustration, or sadness.

Happily, you always have the possibility of growth and change. Even if you don't have any Type III giving relationships in your life now, or if you tend to draw in energy from others rather than to send it outward, you can always make adjustments to your life to reverse this dynamic. In a short span of time, you can release your energy outward so that more can ultimately flow back to you and help you live a fulfilling, vibrant life.

> Giving to others can be a wonderful way to renew your energy, strengthen your sense of purpose in life, and grow as a person.

Benefits of Type III Giving Relationships

In case you're still wondering what the benefits of a Type III giving relationship are, let's take some time to explore this question. Let's start with an example of a Type III giving relationship in my own life that taught me so much. When I was stationed as a young Marine at the Twentynine Palms Marine Corps Air Ground Combat Center, I volunteered to work in a home for abused kids. A friend of mine was a resident counselor at the home and she recruited me because she knew the kids would benefit from having more male role models.

Although my role as a counselor was Type III giving, ironically, I *received* a lot in return. First, my work with the children at the home reminded me that no matter how bad you think your life is, there are people whose lives are much worse. Working with children who had suffered so much gave me a valuable perspective on the many blessings in my own life. Second, I got to see first-hand the power of human

403

kindness. All I did was show up for a few hours each week to talk to and hang out with these kids, but those hours were transformative. For these children to discover that a man could treat them kindly, after they had suffered abuse from the other men in their lives, was both healing and mind-expanding. Through our healthy interactions, these children were gaining a new sense of how their lives could be. They were discovering that they were lovable and that it was possible for them to be loved. And I was learning that I could help people just by giving them a few minutes of my time and attention every week.

What you gain from Type III giving relationships will probably vary depending on the exact nature of that relationship, but here are some common benefits you can expect to receive by giving back. Type III relationships are valuable because they can…

- offer you perspective about the blessings in your own life
- renew your energy supply
- give you a sense of purpose in life
- help you see your value and worth reflected in another person's eyes
- discover an avocation that you were not previously aware that you enjoyed
- teach you about yourself. (Where do you struggle with giving and why? What kind of giving brings you joy?)

Type III giving relationships are wonderful because they offer us a chance to connect with what's best in ourselves: our capacity to offer love and support to other human beings. When we connect to this capacity, it often inspires us to be even better people. We feel energized and inspired because it feels good to give, and we can then funnel that positive energy back into our own pursuits, including our life visions.

A Thousand Ways to Give Back

Many of us feel too busy to take the time to give back; or we think that volunteering or giving back will be all about drudgery...work, sacrifice, and no fun. In truth, if you find the right outlet for your giving, it will be something that you look forward to doing and that you feel great about each time you finish. Happily, there are countless ways to give back to others and to engage in Type III relationships, so the chances of discovering a fulfilling Type III relationship for you are good.

The Three Ts

I like to express the most common ways you can give back as the three T's: time, talent, and treasure.

Time (physical presence). Offering your time is about being physically present for someone or a group of people in an active way. This means that you are paying attention and interacting with the person that you are spending time with. It means giving the person or people your complete attention while you are with them. An example of giving your time in a Type III relationship would be to serve as a companion and mentor to someone in the Big Brother or Sister program.

Talent (creative energy). Offering your talent is about sharing your creative energy in a way that benefits someone else. It involves using your unique skills during the giving process. If you were a lawyer, an example of giving of your talent in a Type III relationship would be to offer *pro bono* legal assistance to clients who can't afford to pay for legal service.

Treasure (material possessions). Offering your treasure is about placing your material possessions in the hands of others. This can take the form of money, old appliances, clothes, and even cars. This is the usual form of giving back that people engage in because it involves the least time commitment.

Match to Your Preferences

Another way to make giving fun or rewarding is to give back in ways that are aligned with your preferences. Staying in-sync with your preferences when getting involved in a Type III relationship will help you remain committed and get more satisfaction and energy out of the giving-back process.

Table 16.1: Giving Back in Ways That Match up With Your Preferences

Preference Type	How to Give Back	Examples
Intuitive thinker (NT)	Contribute knowledge that will help mankind move forward	• Work at a research institute • Teach English to community residents • Write an article or book on a new theory you have developed
Intuitive feeler (NF)	Build relationships that will help make individual people better	• Work at a crisis center • Mentor a child who is struggling academically • Visit nursing home patients
Sensing judger (SJ)	Join organizations that will make society stronger and safer	• Work at a social service agency • Serve on your local school board • Join a neighborhood crime watch
Sensing perceiver (SP)	Share talents and experiences that make a meaningful impact on the world around you	• Work at a museum • Teach someone how to play the piano • Paint a wall mural

You can see from Table 16.1 that there are a lot of different ways to give back. With some exploration, you will be able to find the kind of Type III giving relationship that works for you (see Appendix C for more ideas on volunteer opportunities). If you don't know where to begin, start by looking at work for someone junior to you to mentor. If not at work, then find an organization and volunteer there. Start out small. Read a story to kids, serve a meal, make phone calls for a telethon. Do some research on the opportunities out there and find one that excites you. Give that particular Type III role a try for a couple of months. If it feels right, keep on investing your time in it and enjoy the benefits of giving back. If it doesn't feel right, try something new until you find a Type III giving relationship that works for you. When you do, you may not ever want to go back to a life without this kind of giving relationship. Most of my clients discover many rewards once they begin adding Type III giving relationships to their lives.

Is There Such a Thing as Unhealthy Giving?

Giving, in almost all cases, is a good thing—but there are two situations in which giving can become problematic. First, giving can be problematic if you give to manipulate other people. Second, giving can be problematic if you give so much that you end up neglecting yourself.

The first form of problematic giving is what I call *martyrdom*—when you present yourself as a giver because you feel it will gain you the attention, love, or support of others. Martyrs tend to talk a lot about their giving because they want to remind others of how much they've given, sacrificed, or done for people in the hopes that people will feel indebted to give back. Unfortunately, this kind of giving tends to be ineffective. Instead of winning love, care, and affection from others, it tends to incite guilt, anger, or irritation in others. Instead of bringing people closer to you, it pushes them further away.

Next time you do something helpful for someone else, pay attention to how you make this gift to the other person. Is it free from expectation of what you will receive in return, or are there strings attached? If the person doesn't respond in a certain way, do you feel angry or resentful? If you expect something in return for your giving, you might be falling into the trap of martyrdom. If this is the case, try to step back and let go of your expectations of the other person. Instead of wanting or expecting something in return for the gift, try to give it freely. Tell yourself that you will do something nice for someone and not expect anything in return. If you have trouble doing this, take some time off from giving, and spend some time taking care of yourself. Once you start giving yourself the things you need, you will need and expect less from others. You will then be in a better place to offer authentic giving.

The second form of unhealthy giving is *overextending yourself*. This happens when you try to take care of others (or the world around you) at the expense of taking care of yourself. Your care for others is authentic and sincere, but it is so great that it causes you to neglect yourself. It's also possible that you believe that others are worthy of care, while you believe that you aren't worthy of care. Whatever the reason for overextending yourself, this is not a healthy, sustainable type of giving. Signs that you need to bring more balance to your giving relationships and your own self-care include...

- frequent illness
- fatigue
- more time being spent in supporting others' goals than in pursuing your own
- a sense of your life being frozen in time (no movement toward your important life goals)
- resentment or apathy toward the people you are giving to.

If these signs sound familiar, it may be time to pull back a little from your Type III giving relationships. If there are some giving roles that provide you with more energy than others, stick with the nourishing ones and cut back on the draining ones. Or just reduce the amount of time you spend giving to each relationship. You can also consciously schedule time for yourself, whether that be time to exercise, read, socialize with friends, or take a nap. You will likely discover that as you begin to take care of yourself, you will actually get better at taking care of others. You will have the energy needed to be a better mentor, friend, wife, husband, parent, and so on. Equally important, you will have the energy you need to pursue the goals that are important to you in your own life.

Conclusion

Most of us have this idea that the world outside of us— our communities—will go on running without us. We see the community as some automated system that runs on a self-generating electric engine. The truth is, though, *we* are the electricity that keeps the community going.

It's often average citizens who call in tips to the police that help to catch criminals or get the fire department to a burning home in time to save the family inside. Ordinary people are manning our hospitals, growing our crops, mentoring our children, and keeping our streets clean. The community needs *us* to keep on ticking.

So give back to the community. Shape the community to be what you want it to be for you, your friends, your family, and your grandchildren. If you know of an issue that needs to be championed, start a letter-writing campaign or run for office. If you want to see more beauty in your neighborhood or your city, spend the day picking up trash, paint a wall mural, or start a community action group. Find a way, small or big, to channel your positive energy into the world around you. If you do, you will probably discover that others will be inspired to do the same. Bit by bit, together, you and others can make the community the kind of place you want to live. And in giving back to your community, you will find that your own life becomes richer...because, as you will discover over time, *we are all connected.*

Conclusion
Acting on Your Insight

If you have learned from this book how to lead a life in-sync with your true self, then the world will be a better place not just for you, but for everyone else in the world, myself included. As we learned in chapter 8, "Rain does not fall on one roof alone" and neither does sunshine. Just imagine the positive changes that would take place all around us if everyone started doing what they were born to do...if accountants who really loved children began teaching elementary school, if patent lawyers who loved science put the brilliance of their minds to medical research, and if salespeople who were gifted at singing started making music. Our schools would improve, medicine would advance, and our lives would be brighter. What gifts do you have to contribute to the world? Teaching? Performing? Writing? Explaining? How will moving your own life forward make other people's lives better as well? Whatever your life code and interests, you have special gifts that when used will not only enrich your life but the lives of those around you.

While I hope that this book has been enjoyable to read, I hope that it has been much more than entertaining—I hope that it has been life-changing. If you practice using each of the tools offered in this book—that is, if you *act* on the insight gained by this book instead of just reading the book—you will truly find yourself moving forward in life. You can move forward by completing the exercises in this book, taking time to reflect on your life and observe the world around you, and making adjustments to the way you live your life and interact with others. You can move forward by turning to your fan club for support, joining groups, and calling on mentors, life coaches, and even therapists if needed. If you act on the insight you've gained by reading this book, your life will change for the better.

Before you close this book and begin acting on your insight, though, let's review the key lessons you can rely on to help you move forward. And remember, you can always

411

return to this book from time to time, reading the conclusion as a review or specific chapters that apply to your current life situation, to help you keep moving forward.

Lead a Life That Is In-Sync With Your Preferences

Let's start with a review of your preferences, your personality, and your identity. As you learned in chapter 1, your personality (also known as your true self) is made up of the preferences you've had since you were born. In this book, we focused on five major preference pairs: extroversion/introversion, sensing/intuiting, thinking/feeling, judging/perceiving, and direct/indirect communication. Depending on your life code, you will have one preference from each of these pairs. Your identity, on the other hand, is made up of the elements of you that develop over time in response to the external world and your journey through that world—your belongings, beliefs, and behaviors. To move forward in life, your personality and your identity need to be in-sync with each other. Your belongings, beliefs, and behaviors need to support your true self.

If you find that your personality and your identity clash, your identity is probably unintentionally masking your personality. Unintentional personality masking is a state that occurs when your behaviors, beliefs, and belongings are in opposition to your personality and you are unaware of it. Somewhere along the way, because of the belongings from your past or the society in which you were raised, you developed beliefs that your personality was "not okay" and so you learned to mask, or behave in opposition to, your personality. To move forward in life, you often need to unmask your personality—that is, adjust your identity (behaviors, beliefs, and belongings) so that it better supports your personality.

If you've taken the personality assessment (MajorsPTI) from my coaching Web site (www.lifechangingcoaching.com/movingforward) or spent a lot of time reading the preference chapters (3–7) in this book and reflecting on them, you probably have a solid understanding of which personality preferences make up your particular life code. Hopefully, you have also gained (and retained) a good understanding of the behaviors, beliefs, and belongings (the identity) that support your particular personality preferences. Feel free to return to the preference chapters from time to time, particularly the "Developing an In-Sync Identity" sections, to refresh your memory on the belongings, beliefs, and behaviors that best support your particular life code.

Knowing your preferences will also allow you to become familiar with your weaknesses or blind spots. Once you know your blind spots, you will have the knowledge you need to overcome them—to behave outside of your preferences for a finite period of time to achieve a specific goal. This skill will help you achieve life goals that require behaviors that are different than those normally associated with your preferences. For example, a goal of mine is to teach others, an extroverted activity. Since I am an introvert, I need to adopt extroverted behaviors for periods of time during my week so I can fulfill my life goal of teaching. To counterbalance the energy that I expend when teaching, I am careful to build quiet time into my week to reenergize.

In summary, understanding your personality preferences will enable you to design a life that supports those preferences. It will also give you insight into your weaknesses so that they don't hold you back from achieving your life vision.

All Boats Rise Together: Valuing Your Belongings

After reading this book, I hope you have also become convinced of the importance of belongings in your life. Through my own life experiences and by watching my clients grow, I have discovered that our belongings are essential to obtaining satisfaction in life and achieving our hopes and dreams. Like my client from chapter 11 who was able to improve his relationship with his daughter by sharing new ideas with his uncle (a positive influence) rather than talking to the pessimistic workout buddy, you can gain the support you need to achieve your life plan by turning to fans for support and minimizing the time you spend with toxic influences. Like my client from chapter 8 who volunteered at a teen call center and developed Type I receiving, Type II mutual, and Type III giving relationships and emerged from a dark period in his life, you can elevate your own mood by reaching out to other people, joining groups, and engaging in volunteer opportunities.

You *Can* Overcome Challenges and Attain Meaning and Fulfillment

Another goal of this book has been to show you that challenges in your life *can* be overcome and that it *is* possible to fulfill your life vision. Although it's easy to believe that life's obstacles are insurmountable and that it's unrealistic to achieve your goals—especially when you are feeling tired, overwhelmed, or lost—this belief isn't accurate. A more accurate belief is that life's obstacles can be *overcome* and that you are capable of accomplishing what's most important to you. I have watched many of my clients add meaning and fulfillment to their lives, and the same is possible for you. With the right social support and tools, you can work through most challenges to design and eventually start living a life of purpose and progress.

Be Creative and Open-Minded

First, you can overcome life's obstacles by being open-minded and creative about how to address challenges. Instead of assuming you can't accomplish something, assume that you can. Give yourself permission to think outside of the box—to generate every possible solution you can think of—and then work backwards from those solutions to see how you can make one or more of them work.

For example, if you've always dreamed of working as a nurse, but you don't believe you have the time to study for a nursing degree, consider every option related to this dream. Are there flexible nursing programs that can work with your schedule: night, weekend, or online degree programs? If not, can you change to a flex schedule at work or switch jobs to open up your daytime hours? Alternatively, can you volunteer

414

in a hospital for now and plan to pursue your degree in a few years when your life pace slows down or your children are older? Instead of taking no for an answer when addressing life challenges and pursuing your life vision, try to be persistent and creative. Think about different ways you can fulfill your life vision and overcome obstacles, even if the ultimate result comes in a different form than you originally anticipated.

Draw on Your Belongings

Second, you can overcome life's challenges and achieve your life vision by drawing on the support of others. Other people can help you reenergize as well as gain valuable perspective on how to work through challenges and attain your goals. Other people also have valuable knowledge that will make you smarter and better able to realize your dreams. Lastly, taking time to give back to others will ground you when you're feeling lost and might also help you keep your own problems in perspective. When you see other people's troubles, your own troubles often seem more manageable.

The wonderful reality is...with some creativity and sufficient social connection, you can overcome life's challenges and create a meaningful and fulfilling life.

Crossing the Finish Line

As we discussed in chapter 10, achieving your life vision is a marathon journey. You won't just need short bursts of speed to bring your life vision into existence; you will need steadfastness and commitment. That steadfastness and commitment can come from having things like courage, patience, discipline, and deliberacy.

Remember, you don't have to be unafraid to pursue your goals; you just need to be willing to keep moving forward in spite of your fear. It also helps to have patience when pursuing your life vision, because the journey of attaining your life vision will take time and hard work. Patience will help you get through those times that you have trouble seeing the finish line because it is so far in the distance.

Discipline—the ability to do something regularly, even if it's hard, oftentimes in the absence of external support—will also help you make it to the finish line of your life vision. If you are having trouble being disciplined, maybe your commitment to a goal is flagging. Going back to a goal and making sure that you are sincerely interested in achieving that goal (and, in many cases, that it matches your personality preferences) can help you work through the discipline challenge. Perhaps adjusting your goal to something you are more interested in will help you increase your commitment and level of discipline.

Finally, it's important to be deliberate (intentional) if you want to be successful at achieving your goals. If your intentions are out-of-sync with your actions, you may sabotage those actions in such a way that you are unable to actually reach your goals. For example, if you interview for a job as a financial analyst (your behavior) but you really dream of being a writer (your intention), you may underperform at the analyst interview. Instead of setting yourself up for failure and frustration, take some time to make sure your intentions are aligned with the life plan you have created for yourself. In this way, when you undertake the steps of your life plan, you will know your efforts (your behavior) are moving you closer to the life that you dream of (your intentions) rather than the life that your unintentionally masked personality steers you toward.

When you achieve one goal, it often opens up your interest in achieving another goal. If you foster courage, patience, discipline, and deliberacy, you will be able to attain many goals across your lifetime. You will have the satisfaction of experiencing many things and completing many marathons.

Conclusion

In this book, I've tried to persuade you in two ways: first, that you have natural-born preferences; second, that community is the ingredient that sources and provides a context for all of the changes you might make to your attitudes and behavior. Drink these two insights in deeply and the time will come when you will feel the urge to act. At the same time, however, you may feel the urge to do nothing. This is because we fear change. We fear the unknown. It's normal to feel this way, but the simple fact is that insight alone is not enough. *You must act.* So bide your time, muster your courage, and take the plunge. Live the life you've always dreamed of and share it with people who support you. Enjoy rich relationships and the meaning and fulfillment that come from a life well lived, a life reflective of your true self.

Appendix A
Groups and Organizations

Athletic Groups
Baseball teams
Basketball teams
Bicycle clubs
Frisbee teams
Hockey leagues (broom, ice)
Runners clubs
Softball teams
Surf clubs
Swim clubs
Tennis clubs
Volleyball teams
Weightlifting teams

Career Groups
Chambers of commerce
Networking associations
Professional associations

Civic Groups
Community watch associations
Homeowner association boards
Neighborhood clean-up teams
Parent–teacher organizations
Service organizations

Educational Groups
Adult academic classes
Adult recreational classes
Alumni associations

Hobby Groups
Boating clubs
Book clubs
Camping clubs
Card-playing groups
Classic cars clubs
Collectors groups
Comic book clubs
Dance ensembles

Farming associations
Fishing groups
Flying clubs
Gardening clubs
Historical reenactment groups
Knitting circles
Model clubs
Quilting groups
Scrapbook clubs
Tournament scrabble

Social Groups
Gourmet clubs
Motorcycle clubs
Movie clubs
Music clubs
Residential mixers
Speed dating
Theatre groups
Walking groups

Religious Groups
For a list of many of the religious
groups in existence, you can visit
http://en.wikipedia.org/wiki/
Major_religious_groups

Volunteer Groups
Charity-based thrift shops
Community landscaping groups
Crisis and help centers
Environmental groups
Hospitals and hospices
Library story hour
Senior centers
Soup kitchens and homeless shelters
Teaching English

Appendix B
Activities and Hobbies

Arts and Crafts
Acting
Candle- and soap-making
Costume design
Dancing
Directing
Drawing
Graphic design
Jewelry-making
Mosaic-making
Origami
Painting
Photography
Playing an instrument
Pottery
Producing
Sculpting
Sewing, cross-stitch,
needlepoint
Singing
Sound and light effects
Woodworking
Writing

Athletics
Aerobics
Baseball
Basketball
Frisbee
Golf
Martial Arts
Pilates
Racquetball
Rock climbing
Skiing
Softball
Surfing
Swimming
Tennis
Volleyball

Collecting
Antiques
Autographs
Coins
Comic Books
Crystals, gems, rocks
Die-cast toys
Dolls
Memorabilia
Miniatures
Postcards
Quotes
Sports cards
Stamps
Teddy bears

Games
Backgammon
Bridge
Chess
Computer gaming
Crossword puzzles
Fantasy sports
Poker
Sudoku
Tournament scrabble

Outdoors

Astronomy
Birding
Boating
Camping
Canoeing
Cycling
Fishing
Hiking
Horseback riding
Hot air ballooning
Hunting
Kayaking
Kite-flying
Parachuting
Spelunking
White-water rafting

Other

Aquariums
Baking
Blogging
Car racing
Cooking
Dog breeding
Gardening
Genealogy
Ham radio operation
Home-brewing beer
Home decorating
Home renovation
Home repair
Jigsaw puzzles
Juggling

Landscaping
Magic
Military history
Model building (planes, rockets, trains, etc.)
Motorcycle riding and racing
Rebuilding cars
Robot design
Wine-making
Yoga

Appendix C
Volunteer Opportunities

Please note: This list is provided for information purposes only. Inclusion on this list does not signify endorsement of the group by the author or publisher.

Name	Website	Phone
Action Without Borders	http://www.idealist.org	212-843-3973

Action Without Borders is a global network of individuals and organizations working to build a world where all people can live free and dignified lives in a healthy environment.

America's Promise Alliance	http://www.americaspromise.org	703-684-4500

To mobilize people from every sector of American life to build the character and competence of our nation's youth.

American Red Cross	http://www.redcross.org/	202-303-4498

Providing the opportunity to participate in activities benefiting the local and international communities.

Big Brothers Big Sisters International	http://www.bbbsi.org	215-717-5130

Big Brothers Big Sisters International is a global alliance of country-specific national associations of Big Brothers Big Sisters volunteer mentoring programs working to improve the lives of children and youth around the world.

Boys & Girls Clubs of America	http://www.bgca.org/	404-487-5700

Boys & Girls Clubs provide safe places for kids to learn and grow—all while having fun.

Corps Network	http://www.nascc.org	202-737-6272

Giving young men and women the chance to change their communities, their own lives, and those of their families.

Name	Website	Phone
Habitat for Humanity International	http://www.habitat.org	229-924-6935
Habitat's goal is to eliminate poverty housing.		
Make-A-Wish Foundation	http://www.wish.org	602-279-9474
The Make-A-Wish Foundation® grants the wishes of children with life-threatening illnesses to enrich the human experience with hope, strength, and joy.		
USA Freedom Corps	http://freedomcorps.gov/	877-872-2677
Building a culture of service, citizenship, and responsibility in America.		

Glossary

behaviors — the way we act and conduct ourselves in the world; the things we *do*; one of the three layers of our identity

beliefs — those thoughts, feelings, or ideas that we hold to be true about ourselves and the world around us…regardless of whether they're actually true; one of the three layers of our identity

belongings — the relationships that we form with other people and the communities to which we belong; one of the three layers of our identity

decision drive — the impulse you feel to either make a decision quickly or to draw it out; involved in step 3 of the decision-making process—making a final decision—and represented by the judging versus perceiving preference

detailed (or sensory) information — information that can be gathered by using one of the five senses (seeing, hearing, smelling, tasting, and touching); this kind of information can be measured and described

direct communicator (D) — someone with a communications preference for expressing things in clear and specific language

effective energy management — renewing your energy supply on a regular basis so you have the power to fulfill life responsibilities, tackle life's challenges, and successfully advance your life goals

extrovert (E) — a person with a reenergizing preference for extroversion; someone who recharges by interacting with others

<u>feeler (F)</u> — a person with an information-evaluation preference for feeling; someone who evaluates information using value-based and personal concerns

<u>helping professional</u> — a professional (such as a life coach, counselor, social worker, psychologist, or psychiatrist) trained to help you achieve your life goals, address life challenges, or deal with mental health issues

<u>identity</u> — the elements of you that develop over time in response to the external world and your journey through that world—your belongings, beliefs, and behaviors

<u>identity confusion</u> — a state that occurs when your identity is out-of-sync with your personality and you aren't consciously aware of the dissonance

<u>indirect communicator (R)</u>—someone with a preference for communicating using passive language that implies a request is being made rather than stating that request directly

<u>information evaluating</u> — the process of gathering information to help you make a decision; step 2 of the decision-making process, represented by the thinking versus feeling preference

<u>information gathering</u> — the process of gathering information to help you make a decision; step 1 of the decision-making process, represented by the sensing versus intuiting preference

<u>instinctual (or intuitive) information</u> — information that is perceived through one's intuition or "gut," rather than through the five senses; this kind of information is perceivable, but not quantifiable

<u>in-sync, in-sync identity</u> — a state of living in which your identity is aligned with your core preferences or personality

intentional personality masking — involves deliberately adopting behaviors, beliefs, or belongings that are different than the ones typically associated with your preference to achieve an intended result; intentional personality masking requires you to be aware of your personality preferences

introvert (I) — a person with a reenergizing preference for introversion; someone who recharges in solitude

intuiter (N) — a person with an information-gathering preference for intuiting; someone who gathers intuitive (intangible and conceptual) information

intuitive (or instinctual) information — information that is perceived through one's intuition or "gut," rather than through the five senses; this kind of information is perceivable, but not quantifiable

judger (J) — a person with a decision-drive preference for judging; someone who prefers to make decisions rather than leave decisions open

life coach — a trained professional who can help you address life challenges or achieve life goals through regular meetings and possibly homework assignments; unlike therapists, who focus on treating mental health problems and underlying psychological reasons for "problem" behaviors and life challenges, life coaches typically use solution-oriented approaches to helping you solve problems

life plan, life vision — a picture of what you'd like to achieve in your life, supported by a detailed plan of how to turn that picture into a reality

MajorsPTI — a personality assessment that helps you discover your personality preferences

Myers Briggs Type Inventory (MBTI) — a personality assessment that helps you discover your personality preferences

out-of-sync, out-of-sync identity — a state of living in which your identity is not aligned with your core preferences or personality

perceiver (P) — a person with a decision-drive preference for perceiving; someone who prefers to keep his or her options open rather than to make a decision

personality preferences, preferences — your natural inclinations for "being" in the world; they refer to the instinctual ways that you function best as a person

personality, true self — the traits, natural inclinations, and temperaments you've had since you were born; your personality is primarily made up of five preferences (1. extroversion or introversion, 2. sensing or intuiting, 3. thinking or feeling, 4. judging or perceiving, 5. direct communication or indirect communication)

personhood, whole person — the sum of your personality and identity

preferences, personality preferences — your natural inclinations for "being" in the world; they refer to the instinctual ways that you function best as a person

point goal — a smaller goal or step or task you need to complete to achieve your larger process goal; point goals need to be concrete and tangible

process goal — a large goal for your life that is part of your life vision and that is achieved by engaging in a series of point goals; process goals can be general and abstract sensor (S) — a person with an information-gathering preference for sensing; someone who gathers sensory (tangible and concrete) information

sensory (or detailed) information — information that can be gathered by using one of the five senses (seeing, hearing, smelling, tasting, and touching); this kind of information can be measured and described

therapist — a trained and/or licensed psychologist, counselor, or social worker who can help you address mental health issues (for example, depression or anxiety) through weekly meetings that involve talking and sometimes the completion of homework assignments; therapists can also help you deal with normal life challenges and work to achieve your goals (for example, dieting or smoking cessation); many therapists will help you focus on understanding and addressing the underlying psychological or familial issues related to a problem, although solution-oriented therapists and cognitive-behavioral therapists will help you focus on changing your behaviors and/or thoughts to address your challenges and goals (psychiatrists, who typically specialize in prescribing medicine to address mental health issues, occasionally also provide talk therapy services)

thinker (T) —a person with an information-evaluation preference for thinking; someone who evaluates information using logic-based and impersonal concerns

three Bs or three identity Bs — the three outer layers of your whole person that consist of your behaviors (what you do), your beliefs (what you think or how you feel), and your belongings (your relationships)

true self, personality — the traits, natural inclinations, and temperaments you've had since you were born; your personality is primarily made up of five preferences (1.

extroversion or introversion, 2. sensing or intuiting, 3. thinking or feeling, 4. judging or perceiving, 5. direct communication or indirect communication)

<u>unintentional personality masking</u> — a state that occurs when your behaviors, beliefs, and belongings (your identity) are in opposition to your personality and you are unaware of it; typically occurs as a result of social conditioning

<u>whole person, personhood</u> — the sum of your personality and identity

Index

adjusting friendships and romantic relationships 200

adjusting your group memberships 317

adjusting your relationships 193

allies 280

avocation 370

behaviors 8, 9, 10, 28, 30, 52, 54, 86, 87, 106, 107, 127, 128, 152, 153, 425

beliefs 8, 9, 10, 26, 27, 30, 31, 53, 54, 87, 106, 107, 128, 129, 152, 153, 425

belongings 8, 53, 54, 87, 88, 107, 128, 129, 152, 153, 425

Berens, Linda 147

boundaries 395

building your fan club 281

building your life vision 234

challenging family members 289

challenging friends and acquaintances 286

challenging relationships 285

circles of support 304

clarity of preference 32

clingers 280

courage 257

dealing with challenging family relationships 294

decision drive 73, 119, 425

decision-making process 71

deliberacy 263

determining your

communcations preference 147

decision-drive preference 122

information-evaluating preference 99

information-gathering preference 79

reenergizing preference 45

different domains of life fulfillment 219

direct communicator 11, 142, 425

behaviors 152

beliefs 152

belongings 152

what direct communicators need 152

discipline 261

ending challenging friendships 290

entourage 280

extrovert 11, 45, 425

behaviors 52

beliefs 53

belongings 53

what extroverts need 52

family 279

fan club 276

building 281

fans

types of 278

feeler 11, 97, 99, 426

behaviors 107

beliefs 107

belongings 107

what feelers need 107

finding new groups 319

first impressions 334

five foundations iii

five personality preferences 11

friends 278

getting along with the opposite

communications type 155

decision-drive type 131

information-evaluating type 109

information-gathering type 89

reenergizing type 59

getting connected to the community 303

giving back 401

groups

adjusting your memberships 317

finding new 319

handling challenging relationships 290

healthy type III relationships 187

healthy type II relationships 178

healthy type I relationships 172

how to end a challenging relationship 292

how to find time to reenergize 56

how to handle multifaceted relationships 201

how your identity elements interact 26

identity 3, 4, 8

identity mask 21

impression 330

indirect communicator 11, 142, 426

  behaviors 153

  beliefs 153

  belongings 153

  what indirect communicators need 153

information-gathering preference 76

in-sync 1, 5

intentional personality masking 35

introvert 11, 45, 427

  behaviors 54

  beliefs 54

  belongings 54

  what introverts need 54

intuiter 11, 71, 75, 427

  behaviors 87

  beliefs 87

  belongings 88

  what intuiters need 87

intuitive information 75

job satisfaction 355

judger 11, 120, 121, 427

  behaviors 127

  beliefs 128

  belongings 128

  what judgers need 127

life code 13

life plan 211

life vision 211

building 234

limiting type III relationships 189

limiting type II relationships 185

limiting type I relationships 173

MajorsPTI 412, 427

making a good impression 340

managing your energy effectively 44

mask 3, 5, 6, 21

MBTI 12, 33, 35, 428

out-of-sync 5

overcoming blocks against joining groups 323

patience 259

perceiver 11, 120, 121, 428

  behaviors 128

  beliefs 129

  belongings 129

  what perceivers need 128

personality 1, 3, 4, 6

personality preferences 11, 14, 15, 16, 17

pursuing your avocation 368

redefining family 299

reengaging with your family 381, 391

reformulating material dreams 227, 229

reintroducing yourself 299

relationships 403

  adjusting 193

  adjusting friendships and romantic 200

  challenging 285

  dealing with challenging family 294

  handling challenging 290

  healthy type I 172

  healthy type II 178

  healthy type III 187

  how to end a challenging 292

  how to handle multifaceted 201

  limiting type I 173

  limiting type II 185

  limiting type III 189

three types of 168
type I 172
type II 178
type III 187, 403
ringers 281
sensor 11, 71, 74, 429
   behaviors 86
   beliefs 87
   belongings 87
   what sensors need 86
sensory information 74
thinker 11, 97, 98, 429
   behaviors 106
   beliefs 106
   belongings 107
   what thinkers need 106
three Bs 8, 12, 13, 26, 31, 106, 127, 152, 390, 429
three types of relationships 168
toxic people 318
true self 3
type III relationships 187
type II relationships 178
type I relationships 172
unintentional personality masking 22, 23, 24, 31, 36, 124, 430
what direct communicators need 152
what extroverts need 52
what feelers need 107
what indirect communicators need 153
what introverts need 54
what intuiters need 87
what judgers need 127
what perceivers need 128
what sensors need 86
what's really going on with
   direct communicators 157
   extroverts 61
   feelers 111
   indirect communicators 158
   introverts 63

intuiters 91
judgers 134
perceivers 133
sensors 90
thinkers 112
what thinkers need 106
when to receive and when to give back 170
whole person 3

About the Author

Paul Edward is an award-winning author, leader, Marine and speaker and is one of the world's foremost experts in the field of personal and organizational development.

Paul Edward is a certified life coach, organizational and coaching psychologist, university lecturer, and a former United States Marine officer, who has combined his experience to become a leading force in the ever-growing field of human and organizational behavior. In this field, Paul has made ground-breaking contributions to our understanding of how people and organizations solve problems, increase connection, and make sustained progress. His principles have been tested and proven in organizations ranging in size from massive state prison systems to single families.

Paul was also the Executive Editor of *A Roadmap for Effective Offender Programming in California*, a ground-breaking research report on state prison reform and *Safety First: A Stronger, Safer You*. Paul's written work has appeared in the San Diego Union Tribune, the US Naval Institute's *Proceedings* magazine, and the San Diego *Navy Compass* newspaper. Paul's daily blog, *Small Steps with Coach Paul*, has an international readership, including subscribers in China, Argentina, Germany, and Russia.

Paul has taught leadership, business management, human relations and emergency management classes at more than 40 different educational and business institutions across America. His course on managing terrorist incidents is one of the highest rated courses in the California State University system of schools. He is a recognized expert in psychological type and teaches personality psychology principles to psychologists, therapists, coaches, and other mental health and helping professionals around the world.

Paul has served on government-appointed veterans boards at the county and state level. He has testified before state legislatures, and he and his research have been cited by California's Governor and Speaker of the California State Assembly.

Paul is a former Marine officer and combat-decorated veteran of the 1990 Persian Gulf War. After more than 20 years in corporate leadership positions, Paul started his own company in 2006 and since then has devoted himself full-time to coaching, consulting, teaching, writing, speaking, and research. He lives in Southern California with his wife of almost 20 years, Pamela, and their two sons, Austin and Christopher.

You can contact Paul at *info@movingforwardbook.com*.

Please visit Paul's website at **www.LifeChangingCoaching.com** for more information and resources.